HUMANITY & SIN

The Creation, Fall, and REDEMPTION of Humanity

ROBERT A. PYNE

CHARLES R. SWINDOLL, GENERAL EDITOR

WORD PUBLISHING

NASHVILLE

A Thomas Nelson Company

HUMANITY AND SIN
Swindoll Leadership Library

Published by Word Publishing, a unit of Thomas Nelson, Inc.,
P. O. Box 141000, Nashville, Tennessee 37214. All rights reserved. No portion
of this book may be reproduced, stored in a retrieval system, or transmitted in any
form or by any means—electronic, mechanical, photocopy, recording, or any other—
except for brief quotations in printed reviews, without
the prior permission of the publisher.

Unless otherwise indicated, Scripture quotations used in this book are from
the New American Standard Version (NASB). Copyright © 1960, 1962, 1963,
9971, 1973, 1975, and 1977 by the Lockman Foundation, and are used by permission.

Scripture quotations identified NIV are from the *Holy Bible: New International Version,*
copyright © 1978 by the New York International Bible Society.
Used by permission of Zondervan Bible Publishers.

Scripture quotations identified KJV are from the *King James Version of the Bible.*
Scripture quotations identified NRSV are from The *New Revised Standard Version,*
copyright © 1976 by the Division of Christian Education of the National Council of the
Churches of Christ in the U.S.A. Used by permission.

Published in association with Dallas Theological Seminary (DTS):
General Editor: Charles R. Swindoll
Managing Editor: Roy B. Zuck
The theological opinions expressed by the author are not necessarily the official
position of Dallas Theological Seminary.

Library of Congress Cataloging in Publication Data:

Pyne, Robert A.
Humanity and Sin : the creation, fall, and redemption of humanity /
Robert A. Pyne : Charles R. Swindoll, general editor.
p. cm.— (Swindoll leadership library)
Includes indexes.

ISBN 0-8499-1372-1

1. Man (Christian theology). I. Swindoll, Charles R.
II. Title.   III. Series.

BT701.2.P95   1999   98-15089
233'.1–dc21   CIP

Printed in the United States of America
99 00 01 02 03 04 05 06 BVG 9 8 7 6 5 4 3 2 1

Contents

Foreword

WHO AM I? Why am I here? Where am I going? Probing questions like these have haunted philosophers and poets throughout the ages. Volumes have been written by authors seeking to understand not only our origin and our essential nature but also our final destiny. Yet in spite of all this well-intentioned effort, humanity has never fully answered these vital questions on its own. When will we ever learn that the finite cannot comprehend the infinite?

However, God does provide answers within His Word. Over five decades ago Lewis Sperry Chafer highlighted the wide expanse between mere human insight into these questions and the profound answers found in the Word of God. "Anthropology—the science of man—is approached from two widely different angles, namely, that of human philosophy and that of the Bible. The former is extra-Biblical and avoids every feature of Scripture revelation. The latter is intra-Biblical and confines itself to the Word of God and such corroborating human experience as may give confirming witness to the truth disclosed. . . . Extra-Biblical anthropology assigns no place for God in matters of man's origin, career, or destiny, while intra-Biblical anthropology, being an induction of divine revelation, asserts far-reaching truths in all these fields" (*Systematic Theology* [1948; reprint, 8 vols. in 4, Grand Rapids: Kregel, 1993], 2:125).

When I was a young man working as an apprentice in a machine shop, I learned an invaluable principle. Before you try to fix anything that is broken, you must first understand how it was meant to function. Otherwise you may make the problem worse. The same is true in our relationships with others and in our own lives. Before we rush out to "fix" the problems that are apparent, we should first know how God designed us to operate.

Bob Pyne's book serves as a "reference manual" for understanding the nature of the human race. With keen theological precision Pyne has assembled the key teachings of the Bible on our origins, our essential nature, our sinful condition, and our eternal destiny. Here is a thought-provoking work, straight from the Scriptures, which attempts to answer with integrity and skill some of life's most puzzling questions.

Don't rush through these chapters. Read slowly . . . write your own observations in the margins . . . and take the time to look up the Scripture references. Ask God to give you His insight into our essential nature. Then pause and let the wonder in. Give praise to our Lord with the words of the psalmist: "I praise you because I am fearfully and wonderfully made; your works are wonderful, I know that full well" (Ps. 139:14, NIV).

—CHARLES R. SWINDOLL
General Editor

Acknowledgments

My FAMILY AND I will always remember 1997 as "the year of the book," but the efforts and encouragement of many good friends consistently eased the burden and made it possible for this project to be completed.

Several doctoral students (Gerardo Alfaro, Kevin Bauder, Tim Chong, Steve Giese, and Larry Terlizzese) provided excellent advice on the outline, and three interns (Rick Baker, Don Laing, and Larry Terlizzese) provided cheerful legwork, research, and feedback on the early drafts. David Rankin, Burge Troxel, and the late David Edwards went out of their way to provide computer help, and the Foundations Class at Northwest Bible Church, Dallas, supported me in prayer throughout the project.

Along with the students in my anthropology classes, many friends read portions of the manuscript and offered suggestions and encouragement: Gary Barnes, Jeff Bingham, Darrell Bock, Ray Bohlin, Lanier Burns, Glenn Lucas, David Moore, Stephen Spencer, Kari Stainback, Donna Weber, and Scott and Robin Williams. My friend and student Karen Giesen graciously spent many hours with the manuscript, patiently correcting my mistakes as editor and writing coach. Roy B. Zuck and Stanley Toussaint were diligent and helpful in their suggestions, demonstrating kindness even when they disagreed in some areas with their former student. I have been blessed with wonderful counsel on this project, but I haven't always followed the suggestions of my readers, so please don't hold them responsible for mistakes that remain.

I would like to extend special thanks to Charles Swindoll and Roy Zuck for including me in this series; to my wonderfully supportive department chairman, Lanier Burns, whose lectures on anthropology raised my interest in the subject and supplied concepts (and probably phrases!) that have become my own; to Scott and Robin for dear friendship and a ready office on the back porch; and to my parents and mother-in-law for their diligent prayer and unfailing support.

I also thank Steve, Danny, Ben, and Becky for being proud of Dad, for bringing the daily refreshment of ball games in the front yard, and for happily providing so many good stories. Kids, you are my joy and delight! The highlight of every day is coming home to your hugs and laughter.

Finally, I thank my sweet wife, Julie—my best friend, most gracious critic, and most consistent encourager. She read each page of the book as it was being produced, serving every day as my "target audience." She cheerfully surrendered many Saturdays and evenings we would normally have enjoyed as a family, always reminding me that for everything there is a season. Her suggestions have been invaluable and her devotion irreplaceable. It should be apparent from the pages that follow that I believe in depravity, but Julie's example does make me wonder if there might be exceptions.

I lovingly dedicate this volume to Julie, Steve, Danny, Ben, and Becky.

i

The Biblical Doctrine of Creation

WE AMERICANS have an odd set of expectations for our leaders. We want them to stand head and shoulders above us, like Saul among the Israelites, inspiring us as modern-day heroes. Paradoxically we also want them to be ordinary people—next-door neighbors who don't try to act like royalty. We want them to be special but not magisterial, gifted but not without peer. We want them to set the course while following our directions. Every election year finds politicians torn between these competing expectations, unsure whether to present themselves as Apollo or Everyman, but fully aware that they are more accountable to us than we are to them.

Philosophers and historians have explained this anomaly in various ways, but at its root is a fairly simple principle. We like to be inspired to do great things, but we do not like to be told what things to do. We would rather lead than follow, and we would rather be served than serve. Freedom and submission seem incompatible.

As one might expect, this independent spirit is also expressed in the way we think about God. It is increasingly difficult even for Christians in our culture to accept the notions of divine sovereignty and transcendence, because God's power seems to compromise our freedom. This attitude can be traced all the way to Eve's encounter with the serpent, so it certainly is not uniquely American. At the same time we typify a modern culture that has in many ways exalted human freedom while attempting to understand and explain reality apart from God. People used to rebel against God by turning to other gods. Since the rise of modern science it has been more common to reject deities altogether. As a result, we think we are accountable only to ourselves.

All this would have been foreign to those living in the ancient Near East. They were undoubtedly just as self-centered as we are, but their culture was entirely different. They generally respected the authority of kings, whose decisions were not encumbered by checks and balances, and the people reverenced their gods, whom the kings were often believed to represent. These deities were thought to be active in nature, as powerful forces beyond human control or comprehension dominated the features of daily life. Nature and theology had not yet been assigned separate spheres, and this world was the domain of the gods.

THE COSMOLOGY OF THE ANCIENT NEAR EAST

Those who live in preindustrial societies do not usually take life for granted. Their survival generally depends on cycles of nature that are somewhat predictable but not always reliable. Regular seasons, appropriate rainfall, expected harvests, and healthy flocks allow communities to thrive, and any interruption in that pattern can be devastating.

People have always attempted to reduce the odds of disaster by gaining control over nature. Modern farmers manage it with pesticides, greenhouses, and irrigation, but the more animistic or polytheistic peoples of the ancient world addressed the problem through sacrifices and other religious rituals. Having identified the elements of creation with various deities, they often regarded nature's cycles as evidence of ongoing battles between the gods. For example, the drying up of plants in autumn meant the death of the fertility god, while springtime brought its resurrection. By trying to appease particular gods with festivals and sacrifices at appropriate times, the people hoped to gain their blessing and maintain the cycle in the form of regular and fruitful harvests.

The people who raised their families in or near the land of Canaan understood the origins of their world in much the same way. It was made by the gods who inhabit it, perhaps in the context of an epic battle. For example, in *Enûma elish,* the Babylonian creation epic, the heavens and the earth are created from the body of a defeated goddess, Tiamat.

> The lord [Marduk] trod on the legs of Tiamat,
> with his unsparing mace he crushed her skull,
> (and) when he had severed the arteries of her blood,
> the north wind bore it to unknown fields.
> When his fathers saw this, they were joyful and rejoiced,
> they brought him gifts of homage.
> Then the lord rested and contemplated her corpse,
> intent on dividing the form and doing skillful works,
> he split it like a dried fish,
> set up one half and made it the firmament,
> drew a skin over it, posted guards
> and instructed them not to let its water escape.[1]

This same myth goes on to state that the first persons were made from the shed blood of Kingu, one of Tiamat's helpers, so that the gods themselves would no longer have to labor. Many of Israel's neighbors held similar views, reflecting the hardships of life in their belief that people were created to toil on behalf of the gods. Their literature describes people being formed from the blood of lesser gods to dig ditches, tend livestock, and support their deities with offerings of food. If the communities continued their labors and continued to appease their gods, they would fulfill the purpose for which they were created, and they would survive in the land.

THE DISTINCTIVE COSMOLOGY OF GENESIS

When the Israelites arrived on the scene, they brought with them the revelation of God, newly recorded in the Pentateuch. The historical narratives of Genesis reflect a much older series of (primarily oral) traditions, but they were placed in their present form for the benefit of the new nation as they prepared to enter the land. The written history of God's promises gave the Israelites a clear sense of their own calling and destiny, and the Law described God's expectations in considerable detail. In every way, God's revelation helped equip them to survive as a distinctively monotheistic people in a predominantly polytheistic region.

For those who worshiped the sun, moon, planets, and stars, creation myths explained not only the origin of the universe but also the origin of the gods themselves. By contrast, Genesis speaks of one God who has no peer, and His work of creation took place not through a life-threatening battle or a magical incantation, but through the simplicity of His spoken word. That which the nations worshiped, God had made, and He faced no opposition.

From the time of the patriarchs to the Babylonian exile, the people of Israel were regularly tempted to worship pagan deities. The Genesis creation account demonstrates the absurdity of that temptation. There is no need to fear the gods of other nations, nor is there any benefit to be derived from their worship, for the God of Israel rules over all. "For all the gods of the peoples are idols, but the LORD made the heavens" (Ps. 96:5). Everything that exists must be under His control, for He is the incomparable Creator.

Today we are tempted toward a different sort of idolatry. Some have attempted to revive the worship of pagan deities, but usually only in the name of self-empowerment. They appeal to gods or (more often) goddesses out of egocentrism, not fear of the unknown, and in this they demonstrate the same naturalistic impulse so common to the rest of our culture. We do not think of our world as the domain of the gods, for through science the universe has been demystified. The heavens are filled with communications satellites, not spirits, and the sun is just another star. We don't worship the creation; we study it, and all too often we explain it away.

Ironically our culture needs the same corrective word given so long ago to Israel and her neighbors. "In the beginning God created the heavens and the earth" (Gen. 1:1). What we see around us did not arise from unaided natural causes any more than it arose from a bloody battle between the gods. It was created by the spoken word of the sovereign, eternal God. It may not appeal to our democratic sensibilities, but Genesis describes a God who reigns with unchallenged authority over every aspect of creation. In the language of the psalmist, "The LORD is a great God, and a great King above all gods, in whose hand are the depths of the earth; the peaks of the mountains are His also. The sea is His, for it was He who made it; and His hands formed the dry land" (Ps. 95:3–5). The implication for today, as for the ancients, should be clear: "Come let us worship and bow down; let us kneel before the LORD our Maker. For He is our God, and we are the people of His pasture, and the sheep of His hand" (95:6–7).

THE PLACE OF HUMANITY IN GOD'S CREATION

Israel's neighbors told their stories about the origin of the gods and the universe in order to address an immediate concern—the role of people in a world where survival was always in doubt. We have difficulty relating to that kind of world because we live in a day in which life is generally taken for granted. When we do worry about health and safety, we tend to hope for naturalistic solutions—a correct diagnosis, a skillful surgeon, the right prescription, or an "alarm system" that will bring the "cavalry" from over the hill. Some say there are few atheists in foxholes or hospital waiting rooms, and it may be true that most people in those situations take at least a moment to pray, but the modern world prefers to trust in technology rather than divine intervention. If the doctors (or the bombs) are smart enough, we will live to fight another day. Technology has given us control over life and death, or so we would like to think, and in that sense it makes us feel powerful.

At the same time, modern technology has a way of making us feel very small. In February 1990, Voyager I was far beyond the orbit of Pluto, moving away from us at a speed of forty thousand miles an hour. NASA scientists directed it to turn and take a final picture of the earth from that distance, and in the resulting photograph our planet appears as a tiny blue speck. That prompted astronomer Carl Sagan to write:

> Look at the earth in this picture—a pale, blue dot. That's here. That's home. That's us. And on that dot everyone you love, everyone you know, everyone you ever heard of, every human being who ever was, lived out

their lives. Every act of human heroism or betrayal, the sum total of human joy and suffering, thousands of confident religions, ideologies, and economic doctrines, every hunter and forager, every creator and destroyer of civilization, every king and peasant, mother and father, hopeful child, inventor and explorer, moral teacher and corrupt politician, every saint and sinner in the history of our species lived there—on a mote of dust suspended in a sunbeam.

The Earth is a very small stage in a vast cosmic arena. What is the glory and triumph of the greatest conquerors and builders of empires? They were the momentary masters of a fraction of a blue dot. Our posturings, our imagined self-importance, the delusion that we have some privileged position in the universe, are challenged by this point of pale light. Our planet is a lonely speck in the vast and enveloping cosmic dark.[2]

Anyone who contemplates the immensity of the universe cannot help feeling small. Had Abraham accepted God's challenge and attempted to count the stars, he would probably have numbered them in the low thousands. Centuries later, with the help of one of Galileo's telescopes, he might have seen as many as 100,000 stars, but even that would have been a low estimate of their number. Scientists estimate there are approximately 100 billion stars in our Milky Way galaxy. Assuming that Abraham found a way to identify all those, he would still have a long way to go, because our galaxy is one of thirty or more clustered into what is called the Local Group. The Local Group joins many larger clusters, each consisting of thousands of galaxies, in a vast supercluster that spans 100 to 200 million light-years. And then there are more superclusters beyond ours. Compared to all that, we are very small indeed. At the same time, being small does not necessarily mean we are insignificant.

David, too, felt small when he gazed at the night sky. But his conclusion was quite different from Carl Sagan's. In what has been called a devotional commentary on the Genesis creation account, David expressed wonder that the Creator of such a vast universe is concerned about us. He wrote, "O LORD, our Lord, how majestic is Thy name in all the earth, who hast displayed Thy splendor above the heavens! . . . When I consider Thy heavens, the work of Thy fingers, the moon and the stars, which Thou hast ordained; what is man, that Thou dost take thought of him? And the son of man, that Thou dost care for him? Yet Thou hast made him a little lower than God, and dost crown him with glory and majesty! Thou dost make him to rule over the works of Thy hands; Thou hast put all things under his feet, all sheep and oxen, and also the beasts of the field, the birds of the heavens, and the fish of the sea, whatever passes through the paths of the seas" (Ps. 8:1, 3–8).

David saw that though we might not look like anything special, particularly when we compare ourselves to the universe as a whole, we have been placed in a unique position by our Creator. People have been created not to labor as servants of the gods, but to rule over creation as God's vice-regents.

The psalmist's description of humanity's authority depends on the Genesis creation account, where God said, "Let Us make man in Our image, according to Our likeness; and let them rule over the fish of the sea and over the birds of the sky, and over the cattle and over all the earth, and over every creeping thing that creeps on the earth" (Gen. 1:26). Genesis does not describe what people were to do with this authority except to say that they were to "be fruitful and multiply, and fill the earth, and subdue it," while ruling over the rest of God's creatures (1:28). Though it was demonstrated in Adam's cultivation of the garden (2:15) and his naming of the animals (2:19–20), little more is said of humanity's supremacy over creation.

Some believe this principle has given people free rein to abuse the environment, but anyone using Genesis 1 to justify environmental neglect would be demonstrating poor understanding of the text and poor stewardship of creation. Genesis 1 teaches that people rule under the authority of God, not independently of Him. God is the absolute and unquestioned Sovereign, who spoke the universe into existence, and whatever authority we have is merely delegated to us as His creatures. To rule under God's command, one must represent Him appropriately before the rest of creation. That requires obeying His commands (2:16–17) and respecting the things He regards as good (1:31). Abusing the creation does not fulfill humanity's vice-regency; it betrays it.

A CLASH BETWEEN WORLD-VIEWS

The exalted place given to humanity in Genesis 1 presents a sharp contrast to the popular world-views of both ancient and modern cultures. In the ancient Near East, where gods were thought to control the agricultural cycles, people were created to be their laborers. In the modern world, from which all gods have been banished, people feel insignificant in the immense cosmos. Genesis brings a corrective to each perspective. To highlight the distinctive character of the biblical revelation, consider the contrasts between the polytheistic world-view of Israel's neighbors, the naturalistic (or atheistic) world-view common to so many of our modern neighbors, and the theistic world-view described in Genesis.

According to the polytheistic perspective of many ancient communities, the universe was created in the aftermath of a bloody battle between the gods. Most modern persons would reject that notion, arguing instead that the universe resulted from a chance combination of natural causes, probably best explained by the big-bang theory. Genesis is consistent with the big-bang theory in that both describe the beginning of the cosmos in a singular moment, but it denies that this occurred by chance or through purely natural causes. Creation is the orderly act of the sovereign God, who reigns alone and is unhindered in His work.

The polytheists who lived in and around Israel regarded people as servants of the gods. Life was hard and labor was difficult, but that was simply the way the world was made. Modern naturalists recognize that life has been hard, but they often expect it to get easier as new discoveries help people control the future. From that perspective we are not servants of the gods, but masters of our fate. The biblical text, by describing people as God's own vice-regents, treats us as servant/masters. We are servants of God, but masters over the rest of creation. In that sense Genesis views people as more exalted than the polytheists imagined, but less alone (and more accountable) than the modern atheists believe.

The polytheists thought people served under what might be described as divine anarchy. The gods continued to do battle, and the outcome was always uncertain. Today's naturalists, on the other hand, believe people rule under cosmic anarchy. With no god in the heavens, we compete against only the elements as we exercise dominion over our little corner of the universe. But in Genesis, people both serve and rule under a divine theocracy. God is in charge, but we exercise authority as His representatives.

These different world-views also yield different perspectives on the dignity of humanity. In the polytheistic model, people had little dignity for they lived at the whim of unpredictable and finite gods. According to naturalism, human beings have a self-defined dignity, for no authority exists beyond human communities and value can only be socially determined. However, according to Genesis 1, people have inherent dignity because they have been made in the image of God. We will discuss that concept in detail in chapter 4, but it essentially means that the value of human life depends on the God who made us, not on the assessment of others.

A BRIEF DEFENSE OF BIBLICAL CREATION

With such sharp differences between the biblical revelation and the common perspectives of both ancient and modern cultures, how might the biblical viewpoint be defended? We don't have the space here to offer a full defense of the biblical world-view, but a few comments may be helpful. Against Israel's polytheistic neighbors God demonstrated His strength in the Exodus, in the conquest of Canaan, and in occasional confrontations between His prophets and idolaters (1 Kings 18; 2 Kings 19). The biblical revelation frequently compared the living God to the false gods of the nations, but the proof of His uniqueness inevitably hinged on His actions. Psalm 135, for example, recites the Lord's past record in the Exodus and the conquest (vv. 8–12), then looks forward to His future acts of judgment and deliverance as definitive displays of His incomparability (vv. 14–18). Similar arguments may be found in the Prophets. When the Lord restores His people and judges the oppressing nations, all will know that He alone is the living God (Isa. 44:6–28; 45:14–17; Ezek. 36:33–38).

Until the day comes when God reveals His powerful presence so conclusively that every knee will bow in recognition of His authority (Phil. 2:10–11), we continue to appeal to what He has already done. Paul said in Romans 1:20 that God's "invisible attributes, His eternal power and divine nature" have always been evident through creation. As a result, people should always have known better than to deny the existence of God. Even in what seems to be His silence, "He did not leave Himself without witness, in that He did good and gave you rains from heaven and fruitful seasons, satisfying your hearts with food and gladness" (Acts 14:17).

Looking at the "witness" God has provided in creation, theologians have for centuries used two major arguments in seeking to prove the existence of God. The arguments follow the same basic pattern, arguing that what we see around us must have come from a sufficient cause. While they do not constitute formal proofs, these arguments do show that theism is reasonable and worthy of consideration. This remains true in spite of modern scientific advances. In fact, recent scientific discoveries have probably made these arguments stronger, not weaker.

The Cosmological Argument

The *cosmological* argument maintains that the existence of the cosmos, the creation itself, implies the existence of a Creator. Central to this argument is the following proposition: If anything now exists, something must be eternal. Otherwise, something not eternal must have emerged from nothing. If something exists right now, it must have come from something else, come from nothing, or always existed. If it came from something else, then that something else must itself have come from nothing, always existed, or come from still something else. Ultimately, either something has always existed, or at some point something came into being from nothing.

Someone may contend that it is possible that nothing now exists, but that is both absurd and self-defeating. Someone must personally exist in order to make the statement that nothing exists, and it is undeniable that we ourselves exist. To restate the argument: Since I exist, either something is eternal or something came from nothing.

In light of recent discoveries concerning the big bang, few scientists would suggest that the universe is eternal. In a bestselling book theoretical physicist Stephen Hawking argued that there was no need for a beginning, but he resorted to some questionable mathematical devices to arrive at that conclusion.[3] Most cosmologists agree that the universe began in a singular event in which space and time exploded into existence. The laws of contemporary physics prevent us from understanding exactly what happened at that moment, but some have suggested that the current expansion of the universe is part of an ongoing cycle. They believe it has been expanding and contracting forever, keeping time for eternity like a self-winding watch. However, even if such a cycle did take place in the past, it has apparently come to an end. Since the density of matter in the universe is far too small to halt its present expansion, apparently it will not be contracting again. That means we live in a cosmos that is winding down, not one that is eternal.

Since the best scientific evidence suggests that the universe had a beginning and will have an end, we can again restate the focus of the cosmological argument. Either something eternal exists which has given rise to this finite universe, or at some point something came from nothing. (Daniel Dennett said that it came "out of next to nothing,"[4] but that kind of fudging will not suffice.) Some have suggested that the universe did in fact come from nothing, and they have based that possibility on the use of "virtual particles" in quantum physics. Heisenberg's uncertainty principle states that one can determine the precise position of a subatomic particle or its precise velocity, but never both. Since such particles move instantaneously and unpredictably, they exist in one place "really" and in another "virtually." A "virtual particle" is a place in which a real particle may at some time show up. Advocates of "vacuum genesis" have suggested that "the entire universe originated as a single, extraordinarily massive virtual particle, one that sprang unbidden from a vacuum billions of years ago."[5] However, since virtual particles exist only as potential locations of real particles, there would be no virtual particles if there were no real ones. If real particles *did* exist, we are back to the original question. Have they always existed, did they come from nothing, or did they come into existence by means of something (or someone) eternal? Having essentially eliminated the first two options, we are left with the third. Something must be eternal, but it is not the universe, and it must be sufficient to cause (and even maintain) the existence of the universe. Theists understand this to be God.

The Teleological Argument

Scientists and others have often observed that the universe seems ordered in its structure rather than random. The *teleological* argument (from the Greek *telos*, "end" or "goal") states that there must be an adequate cause for this apparently purposeful design. One of the most well-known examples of this argument comes from William Paley's analogy of the "Watchmaker." If we were walking on a beach and found a watch in the sand, we would not assume that it washed up on the shore after being formed through the natural processes of the sea. We would assume that it had been lost by its owner and that somewhere there was a watchmaker who had designed it and built it for the purpose of telling time.

David Hume noted that the teleological argument does not necessarily point to a single, eternal God, since it is always possible that lesser deities performed some of the creative duties. That may be so, but the argument still calls for an explanation that cannot be provided through naturalism. This remains so even after Charles Darwin, whose theory of natural selection has been described as "the blind watchmaker" because it seems to give rise to order without purpose.[6] As we will see in the next chapter, there are some examples of apparent design that evolutionists cannot adequately explain, leading to a contemporary revival of the teleological argument in biology. Moreover, it looks as though the universe has been "fine-tuned" to support life as we know it, and that suggests the prior existence of some purposeful agent.

The presence of this "fine-tuning" is known as the anthropic principle, and it appears to be more than coincidental. Turning the "knobs" of the universe just slightly would make human existence impossible.[7] For example, the four fundamental forces of physics (the strong and weak nuclear forces, gravity, and electromagnetism), are perfectly balanced to yield the elements necessary for life. If the strong nuclear force constant were any larger, there would be no hydrogen in the universe. Without hydrogen the building blocks for life would be unstable and there would be no water. If that same constant were any smaller, there would be no elements other than hydrogen in the universe. If the electromagnetic force constant were either larger or smaller, chemical bonding would be insufficient. If the gravitational force constant were larger, the stars would be too hot and would burn quickly and unevenly. If it were smaller, they would be too cool for nuclear fusion and would not produce the heavier elements necessary for life as we know it.

In the same way, if the universe expanded just a little bit faster, matter would be moving apart too rapidly to form galaxies. If the expansion rate were just a little slower, it would likely have collapsed on itself before the stars were even formed. Likewise, if the ratio between the mass of protons and the mass of electrons were different, we would not have chemicals, let alone life. With regard to this and other constants, Hawking observed, "The remarkable fact is that the values of these numbers seem to have been very finely adjusted to make possible the development of life."[8]

Other writers have developed this argument in much greater detail and with many more examples of the apparent order in the universe, but these should be sufficient to demonstrate the point.[9] All the knobs have been set precisely, and touching them would make the existence of the cosmos impossible. This does not, of course, prove the existence of God, but it does present circumstances in which belief in an intelligent Designer is certainly reasonable. The universe may exist by a very lucky accident, but affirming that with any confidence would have to be an act of faith.

IMPLICATIONS OF DIVINE CREATION

If the universe exists by the will of a sovereign God, that fact has important implications. Most notably, all of creation is accountable to Him as Creator, and He alone deserves our worship.

Allegiance to False Gods Is Forbidden

If the Lord alone is God, then those who worship other deities rob Him of His due praise (Isa. 42:8). When Aaron said of the golden calf, "This is your god, O Israel, who brought you up from the land of Egypt" (Exod. 32:4), he and the other Israelites misdirected their worship. No wonder, then, that God's prohibition of idolatry was so often accompanied by the assertion that *He* is their God, the one who brought them up from Egypt

(Lev. 19:4; 26:1, 13; Deut. 4:19–20; Isa. 45:18–21). He will not share His praise with another.

In our pluralistic culture it has become somewhat fashionable to say that even idolaters worship the true God in the best way they know. Unfortunately the Bible does not share that assessment. One of the clearer contrasts between true and false deities occurs in 2 Kings 18–19, which records the assembling of Sennacherib's army against Hezekiah. The Assyrians warned the inhabitants of Jerusalem that none of the other nations had been able to withstand Sennacherib's invasion, specifically noting that their gods had not been able to protect them (18:32–33; 19:10–13). "Do not let Hezekiah or your God deceive you," they said. "Have any other gods or any other kings been able to avoid destruction?"

After being reassured of the Lord's promised deliverance by the word of Isaiah, Hezekiah brought Assyria's threats to Him in prayer. He said, "O Lord, the God of Israel, who art enthroned above the cherubim, Thou art the God, Thou alone, of all the kingdoms of the earth. Thou hast made heaven and earth. Incline Thine ear, O Lord, and hear; open Thine eyes, O Lord, and see; and listen to the words of Sennacherib, which he has sent to reproach the living God. Truly, O Lord, the kings of Assyria have devastated the nations and their lands and have cast their gods into the fire, for they were not gods but the work of men's hands, wood and stone. So they have destroyed them. And now, O Lord our God, I pray, deliver us from his hand that all the kingdoms of the earth may know that Thou alone, O Lord, art God" (19:15–19).

Judah's polytheistic neighbors were worshiping in vain, seeking the favor of deities who could not deliver them from their enemies. They were not gods; they were only the work of men's hands. Only the living God, the Creator of heaven and earth, is truly sovereign over the nations, and He reminded Sennacherib of that reality in the prophetic proclamation recorded in this same chapter (19:21–28). God then demonstrated His sovereignty by dispatching an angel to kill 185,000 Assyrians in a single night. Later, Sennacherib himself was killed while worshiping in the house of his god, who was powerless to act in the king's defense (19:37).

Passages like these treat idolatry as a sign of a hardened heart, not a searching one. That is the same point Paul made in Romans 1:18–25, where he argued that idolatry resulted from humanity's refusal to honor God as the Creator. Those who follow false gods today, just as then, "suppress the truth in unrighteousness" (1:18), and they need to be reconciled to the living God through His Son, Jesus Christ.

The Lord Is God, and I Am Not

Submission to God as the Creator carries with it the acknowledgment that we ourselves are finite. That may not sound like a difficult thing to admit, but, as seen in a subsequent chapter, we are proud creatures who tend to exalt ourselves above God. That pride may be seen not only in our disobedience but also in our theology. For example, the apparent contradiction between a good God and the reality of evil, arguably the most significant theological problem of the twentieth century, has encouraged more than one pot to bring charges against the Potter (Rom. 9:19–20).

Because of the pride with which we resist the sovereign God, He occasionally needs to remind us that He is in charge. That was the lesson given to Job and his friends, who thought that in this life righteous people would always be rewarded and sinful people would always be afflicted. When Job was afflicted, his friends naturally concluded he must be a sinner. Arguing that he had not sinned, Job thought that God had afflicted him wrongly. In the midst of his distress Job essentially asked God to meet him in court so he could be vindicated (Job 9:19–33; 13:18–28). This went on for quite some time until God finally spoke for Himself, and His question got right to the point. "Where were you when I laid the foundation of the earth?" (38:4). Asking Job to recount the details of creation, God reminded the finite man of his limitations. As Job learned, there will always be many things we do not understand, but we are never in a place to tell the Creator that He is wrong.

God Is Distinct from His Creation

As the one who spoke the universe into existence, God is by nature distinct from it. The polytheists surrounding Israel had associated various heavenly orbs with the gods, but Genesis demonstrates that these things are not in any way divine. They glorify God and reveal aspects of His nature, but they are not themselves part of His being.

This issue arises not only in response to polytheism, but also in response to contemporary process theology, in which God essentially functions as the soul of the universe and offers possibilities for creative transformation through His presence in the cosmos. Process theologians regard God as both transcendent and immanent, but they also believe He is essentially related to the world, bound to it by nature. The Genesis account describes a God who, though intimately aware of His creation, remains distinct from it.

People Function as God's Vice-regents over Creation

Since God retains all ownership rights to His creation, He governs it and occasionally parcels it out as He sees fit. As already seen, He created people as His vice-regents, stewards who will represent His rule over the rest of creation. Again, that principle contradicts both the ancient polytheist and the modern naturalist. We do not live just to toil in a god-filled world, nor do we live by chance in a godless one. We live and work as representatives of the living God, who created us for His glory.

2

The Debate over Human Origins

Until they retired in Arizona in the late 1960s, Grandma and Grandpa Thomas used to drive every year from Chicago to visit us in Phoenix. I still smile at the memory of those visits—listening to Grandpa's stories as he sat with his pipe, watching Grandma pretend to swim out in the pool, taking them on tours through the desert, and picking oranges together in the backyard. One night we all gathered in the living room to play Password. It was the home version of a popular TV game show in which contestants paired off and tried to guess a "password" as their partners gave them one-word clues (usually synonyms). The clue-givers were given narrow cards on which the passwords had been disguised using different colors of ink. They slid the cards into "secret" sheaths equipped with red plastic windows, through which the words could be clearly seen. Since each team worked on the same word, we could learn not only from our partner's clues, but also from our opponents'. If the password was "automobile," Dad might say "car." If Mom guessed, "truck," then Dave might say, "smaller," and Carol (naturally) would guess the word correctly.

On this particular night Grandpa's clues just didn't fit. Mom would offer a hint like "crochet," and Grandpa would follow it with something like "sailboat." On the next word Carol's clue would be "tree," and

Grandpa's would be "asphalt." As his partner, Grandma started to become angry with him, but he was just as perplexed with everyone else's clues as we were with his. He was looking at the same letters on the same card, but somehow he saw different words! Apparently looking through that red plastic window didn't help him as much as it did the rest of us. We had a good laugh about some of Grandpa's clues, but eventually we had to play a different game. It's pretty hard to play Password when you can't agree on the word.

Sometimes important conversations end up the same way. What seems perfectly obvious to one person might not be so plain to others. It may even be laughable. I've seen debates in which the participants cited such radically different "facts" that I thought I was playing Password with Grandpa. Such confrontations don't usually bring understanding or compromise, for there is not enough shared meaning for the participants to believe they are playing the same game. Both sides return to their likeminded friends, shaking their heads in bewilderment at their opponent's folly.

The subject of this chapter, the origin of humanity, has occasioned lots of conversations like that. Many people study this issue diligently and engage in thoughtful dialogue, but others (too often those with the loudest voices) dismiss their opponents as mindless dolts who must not be able to perceive the evidence. Unfortunately they all seem to have made the same mistake. They apparently think we're trying to read a common password through a shared set of red plastic windows, and they're assuming that somebody just doesn't get it. They don't realize that windows come in all sorts of colors, causing those who look through them to decipher the password differently.

We laughed at my grandfather that night because his clues seemed irrelevant and absurd. Some university students laugh at creationists for the same reason, just as seminarians laugh at evolutionists. But would we have found it so amusing if Grandpa had been looking at his words through a blue window instead of a red one? Probably not. Hopefully we would have checked the rules to determine which color to use. We would have tried to agree on a proper method for playing the game. And that is where we need to begin our discussion of origins.

THE NATURE OF OUR ASSUMPTIONS

None of us approach this (or any other) issue with an entirely open mind. If we did, we would have no way of interpreting the evidence that is before us. In the categories described by Nicholas Wolterstorff, we all operate with certain "control beliefs"—convictions about the sorts of theories we will find acceptable. We measure new data or theories against these control beliefs. When they are incompatible, we seek to restore equilibrium by revising or discarding the theory, looking differently at the data, or somehow modifying our control beliefs.[1]

Control beliefs vary according to our knowledge and experience, and they are particularly shaped by the communities with which we are associated. Most of us take part in many different communities simultaneously, customizing the central ideas provided by each one as we strive for equilibrium and consistency. Returning to the metaphor used in the first chapter, our observations of the world around us arrive like new participants in an old conversation. They may have a significant impact on the conversation's future direction, but for the moment they are interpreted in the context of what has already been said. For each of us, that preceding conversation provides a window through which we peer at the password. That doesn't mean we can never agree on the word, but it does mean that arguments about empirical evidence will not get very far until we identify our core beliefs or admit to our assumptions.

Here are a few of mine. I am a theist, which means that I believe in one God, distinct from this world as the Creator of all things, who is not restricted by time or space. I believe that He can act directly in our world by the word of His power and that His providential rule oversees every event, great or small. I believe the sixty-six books of the Old and New Testaments constitute the inspired word of God and are inerrant. By this I mean that when all facts are known, the Scriptures in their original autographs will be seen to be wholly true (in accord with reality) in everything that they affirm.[2] As a realist, I believe that "all truth is God's truth." When all facts are known, science, history, and every other field will be harmonized with the properly understood revelation of God in the Bible. However, as a *critical* realist, I recognize that all facts are not now known,

19

and some interpretations of Scripture presently thought to be true (just like accepted theories in other fields) may turn out to be incorrect.

One of the most common control beliefs among scientists is naturalism, the belief that "nature is a permanently closed system of material causes and effects that can never be explained by anything outside of itself."[3] Judge William Overton's written opinion on the 1982 Arkansas trial, in which creationists sought equal access to school classrooms, reflected this naturalistic bias when he described what he believed were the essential characteristics of science: (1) It is guided by natural law; (2) It has to be explanatory by reference to natural law; (3) It is testable against the empirical world; (4) Its conclusions are tentative, that is, not necessarily the final word; and (5) It is falsifiable. Overton argued that creationism is not science, because "it depends upon a supernatural intervention which is not guided by natural law."[4] Other than the idea that the conclusions of science should be tentative, each of these points reflects an assumed philosophy of naturalism. Even the idea that science should be falsifiable, if it refers to empirical falsifiability, demonstrates a naturalistic assumption.

One does not have to be an atheist to share Judge Overton's perspective, which some critics refer to as "scientism." Many have argued that the scientific community simply operates best under these guidelines, either by precedent or necessity. They contend that giving attention to ideas like special creation or even intelligent design would jeopardize science's quest for understandable explanations and manageable solutions to the world's problems. It would nip technological advancement in the bud by giving premature, supernaturalistic answers to important questions. Some scientists resolve the issue by considering themselves "methodological naturalists" but not "metaphysical naturalists." In other words, they try to explain the world without appealing to God, but they are open to the idea that God exists. While I appreciate the fact that these folks recognize their limitations, I don't think the problem can be resolved quite that easily. First, methodological naturalism has many of the same effects as metaphysical naturalism. Whatever the system is called, it still excludes God from the scientific arena. Second, methodological naturalists may be able to separate their religious faith from their working philosophy, but I fear that their followers will be more consistent, perhaps joining the ranks of those who use the scientific method as an atheistic assertion.

The fact remains that philosophical assumptions can be extremely influential in this discussion, even though most participants never take the time to think about them. Many men and women with earned Ph.D.'s in physical or life sciences are fine technicians who have never studied the philosophy of science. Even if they have, they may still be operating under the assumption of naturalism. I attended a debate in which a well-known philosopher of science was asked why he was a naturalist. Looking as if he had just been splashed with cold water, he stammered, "Well, I . . . I just am one." Let's see if we can answer that question a little more thoroughly.

The naturalistic scientific method is the product of several relatively recent philosophical and theological trends. First, theological discussions about the nature of language in the late medieval era produced a desire for unequivocal descriptions of reality, which ultimately reinforced the value of mathematics as the ultimate model of expression. Second, the idea that God's handiwork should demonstrate perfection and rationality, together with the Greek notion of order, produced the expectation that nature was homogeneous, uniform, and symmetrical. Third, a homogeneous, rational universe that was described perfectly by mathematics came quite naturally to be seen in mechanistic terms, with all natural phenomena being explainable in terms of mechanical causes. When these foundational concepts, which had existed separately for centuries, were brought together in the seventeenth century, they formed the heart of the scientific method.[5]

That is a quick summary of some complex ideas, but the bottom line is fairly simple. The scientific method is based on a philosophy, namely, naturalism, that has a history. Most of its presuppositions were originally theological, making it especially ironic that naturalistic science eventually helped push theology aside. The child, having grown up, has evicted the grandparent, and that's another story worth telling.

Theology has long operated with four primary sources, described by some as a "quadrilateral." These sources are revelation, reason, tradition, and experience. Most evangelicals quickly note that, of the four, revelation is primary, but certain topics make us turn to the other sources. For example, we rely heavily on tradition to identify the books properly included in the biblical canon, and we appeal to reason and experience when interpreting biblical texts about the earth's orientation to the sun. In the seventeenth century the Roman Catholic Church appealed to tradition to understand those texts, and that is why they treated Galileo as a heretic.[6] Their reassertion of tradition came in reaction to Reformation emphases on the priesthood of believers and *sola scriptura*, but in retrospect the Galileo affair ultimately helped consolidate the Protestant victory. For both Protestants and chastened Catholics, tradition will never again occupy such a strong, formal place of power. We still use it, but it has been relegated to secondary status.

Unfortunately history has seen the same thing happen to the authority of Scripture. Arguing that God must have created the universe in an orderly, intelligible manner, Christian apologists argued that the truths of the faith must be consistent with other intellectual disciplines. Those truths, it was thought, must therefore be defended rationally. At the same time, theologians continued to develop a rich "natural" theology, identifying God's attributes through the order of creation. These arguments seemed helpful, but they produced some problems. First, if Christianity simply reproduced what could already be known through reason, then it was essentially redundant and unnecessary, and it came to be treated that way.[7] Second, it has been said that the religion married to science today will be a widow tomorrow. When evolutionary biologists (and after them, quantum physicists) argued that the world was not ordered, but random, natural theology was widowed.[8] These developments, together with the rise of biblical criticism, helped reason take the spotlight while revelation limped off the stage. Religion still had a place in this world, but it was not as prominent, and it had to accommodate itself to the new order of things. It could speak of meaning, morality, and feelings of dependence, but not of causes, creation, or divine intervention.

Unhindered by tradition or revelation, reason has directed the course of philosophy, science, and even most theology since the Enlightenment. The late twentieth century, however, has brought talk of mutiny. In the aftermath of two world wars and an unprecedented chronicle of human suffering—much of which existed alongside superior education and technology—contemporary philosophers have declared the Enlightenment project dead. The optimistic humanism of modernity has given way to the cynical individualism of postmodernity. With that shift in the philosophy of Western culture, Americans have become increasingly skeptical about previously trusted authorities and are in many ways questioning the authority of reason. People are beginning to prefer both/and to either/or, and the scientific claim to objectivity is widely regarded as a myth. As reason moves out of the spotlight, we are left with an empty stage. It still echoes on occasion with the ideals of earlier generations, but those aims are like cut flowers in a vase. They are pretty to look at, but they have been separated from their roots, and they will eventually shrivel and die.

That being the case, many science books contain as many cut flowers as a florist's shop. Modernistic optimism still thrives as scientists hope to bring lasting benefit to humanity, and the Enlightenment project lives on. However, we should not expect the flowers to last indefinitely. Postmodernity has not yet influenced the natural sciences as extensively as it has history and literature, but its compatibility with contemporary physics has been widely recognized, and one can see its impact on recent discussions of scientific method. When the rational flowers of biology start to wilt, we can expect new and creative theories to gain a wider hearing.

Whether any of those theories will take seriously the role of the Creator remains to be seen, but theists have at least some basis for optimism. We cannot be much more alienated from the scientific establishment than we are already. Most scientists currently assume some form of naturalism and expect theories to be advanced on the basis of reason and empirical evidence. Since those "control beliefs" establish the ground rules for acceptable dialogue, theists have a difficult time fully participating in the conversation. We can bring rational arguments against the naturalistic models of others, but we cannot produce wholly naturalistic models of our own. Likewise, since fully developed theistic models depend in some way on tradition or revelation, they cannot be advanced through reason alone. In short, theists cannot really follow the rules of the game, and naturalists don't want to reevaluate them. We want to stop and talk about which color window to use, but the other players have focused the discussion on which password they see on the other side.

If the rules of the biological game demand that players explain the world apart from God, then theists will have to be disqualified. Having not so quietly exited the field, we take our seats on the sidelines and watch the contest. From that vantage point we can see that those who still try to play the game are failing, but they have convinced themselves they are succeeding. We call attention to their failure, but only to criticize the futility of the game itself. As it is now played, this is a game no one can win. Perhaps our criticisms and the exasperation of some of the players will eventually be significant enough that the rules will be reconsidered, but only time will tell. For the moment, we must sit, watch, and occasionally protest.

THE VIEW FROM THE SIDELINES: AN ASSESSMENT OF NATURALISTIC EVOLUTION

Having already been banished to the sidelines, we will not accomplish much by continuing to squawk about the rules. As long as those still playing the game are convinced that it's going well, they are unlikely to amend the rule book. It is time to adopt a different strategy.

The critique that follows will attempt to stay within the rules. There will be no appeals to revelation, theism, or Christian tradition, and there will be no unverifiable assertions about fluctuating constants or illusions of age. We will grant, for the sake of argument, the naturalistic assumptions behind contemporary evolutionary models, and we will offer reasoned criticisms of those models. It is still a view from the sidelines, but these are good seats, and we can see some parts of the game better than the players can.

Prebiotic Evolution

The most well-known and widely debated aspect of evolutionary theory has been Charles Darwin's concept of natural selection, which seeks to explain how all living things may have developed from a common ancestor. Since that development depends on the prior existence of the ancestor, our consideration of natural selection will have to await the answer to a more basic question: Where did life come from?

Darwin himself spoke of "some warm little pond" in which appropriate organic compounds were exposed to light, heat, and electricity, eventually producing proteins. Those proteins would have experienced further chemical reactions, and eventually the process would yield very primitive, single-celled organisms that would begin to carve out niches for themselves in the environment of the early earth. This has been called "prebiotic evolution" (evolution prior to life itself), "chemical evolution" (since it involves chemicals, not living things), or "abiogenesis" (beginnings from nonlife).

For decades, scientists have attempted to simulate the processes through which the first living organisms may have developed. The most famous such experiment was reported by Stanley Miller and Harold Urey in 1952. Trying to recreate the conditions thought to be present on the primitive earth, Miller had mixed an "atmosphere" of methane, ammonia, and hydrogen gases in a large flask containing an "ocean" of boiling water and the "lightning" of sparking electrodes. After keeping the apparatus boiling and sparking for a week or so, Miller found amino acids in the water. Since amino acids make up proteins, it looked as if Miller had traced the first step in the origin of life from nonlife.

In retrospect the original event was more complicated than its recreation. Miller and those who followed him conducted prebiotic simulations using varying mixtures of purified chemicals under controlled conditions, and they may have biased the results by choosing combinations that would yield the desired product rather than those that were more scientifically probable. For example, they did not allow oxygen gas to enter the flask, but it appears as though oxygen was present in the early atmosphere. In his popular television special, "Cosmos," Carl Sagan noted that oxygen would prevent the desired chemical reactions from going forward. With oxygen present, he said, the experiment "produces only smog—a backward step." Sagan justified the exclusion of oxygen by observing that oxygen comes from plants and could not have been present before plants had evolved. But plants are not the only source for molecular oxygen. Since oxygen is also formed through the photodissociation of water (its breakdown by ultraviolet light), it was almost undoubtedly present in the atmosphere of the early earth. Charles Thaxton, Walter

Bradley, and Roger Olsen have estimated that the primitive atmosphere may have contained as much as one percent oxygen, enough to make spontaneous chemical evolution impossible.[9] The presence of oxygen has also been substantiated by geological studies, which reveal oxidized minerals in the rock layers below the first forms of life.

To restate the point, a certain type of atmosphere—one without oxygen—*must* have existed on the early earth for prebiotic evolution to have taken place. However, it appears as though those conditions existed only in the laboratories of certain scientists.[10] Had those researchers truly simulated the atmosphere of the early earth, they would have ended up with nothing more than smog-filled flasks.

There is another problem. Biochemist Michael Behe has noted that amino acids, if formed, would not be likely to join together in a "warm little pond." Not only do amino acids typically dissolve in water, but the presence of water makes it extremely difficult for them to join together and build a protein. Some scientists have suggested rather imaginative scenarios through which the water might have been removed, but these have not found much support in the scientific community.[11]

If amino acids and even proteins did form spontaneously, they would have had a hard time surviving. The energy sources (lightning, heat, and ultraviolet light) that may have helped create these fragile molecules could just as easily destroy them, and reactions with other substances in the ocean or the atmosphere would also challenge their durability. Survival would be important, because it might take awhile for these chemicals to find their future partners. Imagine trying to find a blind date at a party filled with strangers. Nobody can bring the two of you together, and neither of you knows what the other looks like. Your only hope is to mingle and ask each person's name. If it is a small group of people, chances are that you will locate each other fairly quickly. If the party filled a gymnasium, it would take a little more time, but you would still have a reasonable chance. But the party is not in a living room, or even in a crowded gymnasium. Standing shoulder to shoulder, partygoers fill the continent, and you wish you had at least learned the color of your date's hair. The party is crowded, but from your perspective it is too "diluted"—you and your intended are such a small part of the crowd that you will probably not find each other. For all practical purposes, the two of you are lost among billions of other individuals. That is the situation confronting advocates of abiogenesis. Thaxton, Bradley, and Olsen concluded that "in the atmosphere and in the ocean, dilution processes would dominate, making concentrations of essential ingredients too small for chemical evolution rates to be significant."[12]

Some theorists have tried to get around this predicament by suggesting ways in which the appropriate chemicals may have become more concentrated. Perhaps the "prebiotic soup" was evaporated, frozen repeatedly, or condensed on bubbles of foam. Returning to our analogy of the blind date, these models essentially ask all the party guests to stand closer together. That might bring you nearer to your partner, but you are also closer to everybody else. The concentrating mechanisms condense not only the chemicals we hope to see combine, but also the impurities, making it more likely that each of our two molecules will eventually leave the party with the wrong crowd.

That unhappy prospect raises another important point. If the blind dates don't find each other, the party is as good as over. With prebiotic evolution, unless the right molecules are in the right place at the right time, nothing significant will happen. As an informational code governing the development and operations of each cell, DNA is much more than a complex molecule; it is an *ordered* molecule. It has *specified* complexity. Its pieces have to be in their proper places for it to do anything. Merely complex molecules can be produced by adding energy to a system (as in Miller's famous experiment), but Thaxton, Bradley, and Olsen have argued that mere energy would never be sufficient to overcome "configurational entropy" and produce order except through some sort of mechanism. At present, no such mechanism has been found. They concluded, "Either the work—especially the organizational work—was coupled to the flow of energy in some way not yet understood, or else it truly was a miracle."[13]

All told, each stage of prebiotic evolution faces an apparently insurmountable hurdle. Even when scientists develop a model through which one such obstacle may be overcome, they are challenged by enough others that we should not expect a genuinely naturalistic solution anytime soon. Behe has suggested a different analogy, comparing the prebiotic experimenters to researchers attempting to prove that a groundhog could safely run across a busy freeway.

> Just as there is no absolute barrier to a groundhog crossing a thousand-lane highway during rush hour, so there is no absolute barrier to the production of proteins, nucleic acids, or any other biochemical imaginable, natural chemical processes; however, the slaughter on the highway is unbearable. The solution of some prebiotic chemists is a simple one. They release a thousand groundhogs by the side of the road, and note that one makes it across the first lane. They then put a thousand fresh groundhogs in a helicopter, fly them to the beginning of lane two, and lower them onto the highway. When one survives the crossing from lane two to lane three, they helicopter another thousand to the edge of lane three. Proponents of the RNA world, who start their experiments with long, purified, investigator-synthesized RNA, fly the groundhogs out to lane 700 and watch as one crosses to lane 701. It is a valiant effort, but if they ever reach the other side, the victory will be quite hollow.[14]

The obvious difficulty of "crossing the highway" has caused some scientists to conclude that there never was a "warm little pond" on this planet. Fred Hoyle and Chandra Wickramasinghe have argued that life arrived on this planet from outer space. Others, including Francis Crick, have suggested that this "colonization" may have taken place by design. As I write, I have before me a newspaper article describing a new theory that organic molecules, perhaps even living organisms, arrived in our atmosphere from disintegrating cosmic snowballs (like miniature comets). Even the more orthodox evolutionists like Daniel Dennett admit they cannot disprove these kinds of proposals.[15] They quickly add that different species may still have evolved here even if life itself originated somewhere else, but the point remains: It is so difficult to explain how life arose on earth through natural processes that even some naturalists have given up on the effort. Life apparently could not have come from nonlife on this planet, they reason, so it must have come from nonlife somewhere else.

Others are much more optimistic, perhaps even irrationally so. When it was concluded that recently discovered microbe fossils were 3.5 billion years old—a billion years older than life had been thought to exist on this planet—biologists appreciated the fact that the evolution of various species had a longer time period in which to operate. However, they also recognized that significantly less time was now available for the origin of life itself, which seems to have occurred almost as soon as the earth had cooled.[16] Carl Sagan reacted with optimism. Since it happened so quickly here, he reasoned, prebiotic evolution must not be as difficult as we thought it was. He concluded it probably happened on other planets as well.[17] Stuart Kauffman's suggestion is just as startling. Perhaps molecules contain an inherent tendency toward self-organization, a drive toward complexity that would explain the development of life from nonlife without any real mechanism.[18]

Some people will go to unusual lengths to explain the origin of life from a naturalistic perspective. As we watch from the sidelines, can we be blamed for thinking that our ideas are at least as defensible as theirs? When intelligent people see life on earth as the fruit of cosmic colonization, is belief in an intelligent Designer really so laughable?

Biological Evolution

Until the mid-nineteenth century, about the only way one could explain the complexity of the living world was to attribute it to divine creation. As we have seen, William Paley took that route, comparing nature to a watch, the existence of which demands a watchmaker. Those who were less comfortable with theistic explanations had little alternative but to wait for someone to suggest a naturalistic model. Their wait ended in 1859 with the publication of Charles Darwin's book, *On the Origin of Species by Means of Natural Selection, or the Preservation of Favoured Races in the Struggle for Life*. Richard Dawkins has said that "Darwin made it possible to be an intellectually fulfilled atheist."[19] Those hoping to explain the biological world apart from God now had their champion.

Darwin's explanation was quite simple, and it began with the observation that the members of a given species are not identical. If one member happened to possess characteristics that gave it some advantage over the others in the competition for limited resources, it would probably survive longer and produce more offspring than those who lacked those qualities. For example, a male bird with more colorful tail feathers might have an advantage over his peers in the competition for mates. Since he would have the opportunity to mate more frequently than his less-gifted companions, he would probably have more offspring than they. If the little ones are ultimately as successful as their father, eventually the species would be more heavily populated by individuals with more colorful tail feathers.

In the same way, if an individual possessed characteristics that brought it some disadvantage, it would probably die sooner and produce fewer offspring than the others. The females might like our friend's colorful feathers, but they may not be the only ones to pick him out of a crowd. Since predators, too, might find him easier to spot, the feature that seemed to be an advantage may turn out to be a hindrance. Whether a characteristic is an advantage or a liability depends on external features such as the environment, the behavior of predators, and the nature of the competition. Darwin called this process "natural selection, or the survival of the fittest," and he thought it could explain the development of all living things from a single (or at most a few) common ancestor(s).

Darwin recognized that physical traits were inherited, but he didn't understand the genetic mechanism behind that process any better than others of his day. In fact, Darwin believed that physical characteristics acquired during an individual's lifetime could be passed on to offspring. The study of genetics has forever disproven that notion, but it may help explain some of Darwin's optimism with regard to the adaptability of species. If species changed in direct response to their environment, one would expect evolution to take place more quickly than if they must await the arrival of a lucky genetic mutation. However, awareness of genetics caused scientists in the early twentieth century to modify Darwin's theory. The result, dubbed neo-Darwinism, recognizes that new physical features can arise only through genetic mutations. They will survive or disappear under the pressure of natural selection, but their origin must be genetic.[20]

If all living things evolved from a common ancestor through three or four billion years of mutations, we are all essentially distant cousins. Critics have often misunderstood the theory as teaching that humans descended from apes, but evolutionists do not really believe that. They argue that humans and other primates have followed different evolutionary branches from a common ancestor that was neither man nor monkey.

If these common ancestors were ever plentiful on the earth, one might expect to find their fossilized remains. Popular hopes for the discovery of "missing links" (more accurately called transitional species) have not been realized. Still, most neo-Darwinists believe they have identified enough distant relatives of modern species in the fossil record to substantiate their model. Others have argued that the model needs some fine-tuning. Most notably, paleontologists Stephen Jay Gould and Niles Eldredge suggested that the fossil record presents a challenge to those they call ultra-Darwinians. Traditional neo-Darwinism expects species to be continually evolving, but Gould and Eldredge argued that such changes do not generally show up in the fossil record. Instead, species apparently experience long periods of equilibrium in which there is no evidence of evolutionary change. When such change does take place, they said, it probably happens on the fringes of an established population, where environmental differences would be profound enough for mutations to be beneficial. A distinct species could develop fairly rapidly in such conditions, especially if some geographic change split the original group into two separate populations. The new species would then show up in the fossil record after persisting for many generations and somehow becoming reunited with the ancestral species (at least reunited enough for fossils of both kinds to be recovered). This theory, which is called "punctuated equilibrium," does explain the fossil record better than traditional neo-Darwinism. As Gould and Eldredge recognized, fully differentiated fossils are discovered routinely, while those showing gradual change are not.

Advocates of punctuated equilibrium have raised excellent criticisms of the prevailing evolutionary model. But they have little patience for creationists and do not appreciate the way their view has been used to discredit evolution in general. They still believe all living organisms evolved from a common ancestor through successive genetic mutations, and they still believe the process was random, not directed. They differ from traditional neo-Darwinists only in their explanation of a mutation's survival in particular populations. However, without reopening the issue of presuppositions, it is important to note that their observations do not rule out the possibility of intelligent design. Only their assumptions do.[21]

One of the arguments made by Gould and Eldredge was that patterns of large-scale change in evolutionary history call for a better explanation than the one provided by the traditional model of gradual evolution. Such large-scale changes, in which profound differences exist between species thought to be near relatives, have been called expressions of macroevolution. The examples often cited include the evolution of whales and bats from terrestrial mammals, cases that are made more difficult by their abrupt appearance in the fossil record. Creationists question whether macroevolution ever really takes place, but they universally affirm the reality of microevolution. This refers to the small-scale changes that take place through natural selection in the history of living organisms. As understood by creationists, microevolution may at times produce distinct species, but the differences between them remain relatively small. From the perspective of traditional neo-Darwinists, all evolution is microevolution, since it always takes place in small steps, never in big leaps.

Whether they believe it happened gradually or in fits and starts, evolutionists believe that natural selection can ultimately explain all the diversity of the biological world. Their models were originally developed on the basis of physical comparisons between species, and they continue to be defended the same way. Animals have observable similarities and differences, and the fact that orangutans resemble the kid who used to steal your lunch money might make you think they are related. But contemporary evolutionists argue that the similarities go beyond outward appearances, citing genetic and embryological comparisons that find patterns of resemblance at the most basic levels. There are some striking similarities, but these are not without their problems.

For example, light and dark bands of varying width run the length of chromosomes, and they are arranged in distinctive patterns. The banding patterns on human chromosomes strongly resemble those of chimpanzees. In fact, most differences between them could apparently be resolved by taking the incompatible portions and simply inverting them. Chimpanzees have forty-eight chromosomes, while people generally have forty-six, but corresponding banding patterns indicate that two pairs of the chimpanzee chromosomes may have fused together to make a single pair in humans. This evidence certainly suggests some kind of relationship between humans and chimpanzees, but it also presents a difficult question. As geneticists Lane Lester and Ray Bohlin have pointed out, humans and chimpanzees are not the sort of creatures in which one would expect chromosomal rearrangements to become established. Since such changes so often result in sterility, only an unusually small percentage of them can ever be passed to a second generation. It is possible that "small, isolated, fast-breeding, inbred populations" would allow chromosomal changes to become entrenched, but humans and apes "have a low reproductive rate, late sexual maturity, few offspring, long life span, and high competitive ability."[22] If people and chimpanzees evolved from a common ancestor through chromosomal rearrangements, one wonders how that could have happened with creatures like us. That question becomes even more difficult given the relatively short period of time in which it is supposed to have taken place.

Even if models can be proposed to resolve this particular puzzle, other studies seem to have undercut the common perception that similar species must be closely related. Michael Denton argued that "homologous" characteristics—those that are very much alike even in different species— may be similar only in their final appearance. Embryologically "homologous structures are arrived at by different routes."[23] Like an overweight neighbor's "beer belly" contrasted with the swollen stomach of a pregnant woman, similar physical structures are sometimes attained through entirely different means.

Embryology has presented evolutionists with a new set of problems, but meanwhile some of their old problems remain unresolved. Darwin knew that for his theory to succeed it had to explain the gradual development of complex organs like the human eye. Richard Dawkins addressed that issue for sixty pages in one of his popular books, arguing that the many varieties of eyes could have evolved easily through small changes over a long period of time.[24] Dawkins suggested that the first step in the evolution of vision would have been sensitivity to light in the body surface of an organism, leading eventually to a particularly light-sensitive spot, then to a rudimentary cup eye, a pinhole eye, and the development of a lens. One stage would lead to the next through small (microevolutionary) changes, and each one would be functional, helpful, and advantageous to the organism. Darwin himself had offered a similar explanation, arguing that the eye was not too complex to be explained by gradual evolution.

Such arguments make it seem as though the problem of complex organs has been resolved, but it has not. First, even after a century and a half of evolutionary explanations, many systems still have not been adequately explained. It is still difficult to imagine how such things as feathers (with their unique molecular structure and their intricate arrangement of hooks and barbules), the avian lung (through which air flows in only one direction), the wings of bats (forelimbs that would have been unserviceable as either hands or wings until fully developed), or the amniotic egg (which differs radically from that of amphibians) could have developed gradually. It is just as difficult to explain how some mammals gradually developed an elaborate means by which to suckle their young underwater, or how some species of parasites and insects could arrive at their highly specialized behaviors.[25]

Second, the arguments used to explain complex organs like the eye have focused on anatomy, and that is no longer adequate. The relatively young field of biochemistry has revealed that the chemical processes involved in the life of an organism are far more complicated than Darwin or anyone else might have imagined. For example, biochemist Michael Behe has argued that the biochemistry of vision is fabulously complex. Since physiological processes ultimately take place at the molecular level, anyone attempting to describe the evolution of an eye would have to go far beyond the explanations offered thus far. Behe concluded, "Now that the black box of vision has been opened, it is no longer enough for an evolutionary explanation of that power to consider only the *anatomical* structures of whole eyes, as Darwin did in the nineteenth century (and as popularizers of evolution continue to do today). Each of the anatomical steps and structures that Darwin thought were so simple actually involves staggeringly complicated biochemical processes that cannot be papered over with rhetoric."[26]

Behe has argued that many systems demonstrate "irreducible complexity," meaning that they cannot lose any component part and still perform any useful function. Like a mousetrap, which needs all its pieces if it is to work, these biochemical processes could not have resulted from gradual, successive changes. So how did they evolve? Behe's survey of scientific literature concluded that nobody even attempts to answer that question.[27]

Evolutionists have not addressed the evolution of complex biochemical systems, focusing their efforts on the more easily observed anatomical features that had first intrigued Darwin. If they ever take up the more difficult task of explaining how organisms really work, they will be confronted with systems that appear to be irreducibly complex, making it doubtful that naturalistic explanations about gradual change will ever be sufficient to explain them.

These arguments do not *disprove* evolution, but they do suggest the theory faces real obstacles that may be insurmountable unless some allowance is made for intelligent design. Critics will immediately respond that this approach calls for nothing more than a "god of the gaps"—a deity thought to do the things we are currently unable to explain, but one whose role grows smaller with every scientific discovery. That criticism assumes that naturalistic science is progressively filling in the gaps, but my point is that some of the gaps are too big to be filled.

Allowance for intelligent design would require a meeting of the rules committee for the biological "game," but this view from the sidelines suggests that that meeting is long overdue. As long as the rule book expects participants to offer purely naturalistic explanations for the existence of all living things, it looks as if the players will have a hard time of it. On the other hand, some of them are confident they have succeeded, and they celebrate the victory by denying the existence of God. Dawkins, for example, has written, "In a universe of blind physical forces and genetic replication, some people are going to get hurt, other people are going to get lucky, and you won't find any rhyme or reason in it, nor any justice. The universe we observe has precisely the properties we should expect if there is, at bottom, no design, no purpose, no evil and no good, nothing but blind, pitiless indifference."[28]

In light of the questions that remain, Dawkins's conclusion seems premature. One might also call it foolish (Ps. 14:1), but that is a topic we'll take up later.

It is time now to turn away from the game and its naturalistic players so we theists can talk about something among ourselves. To this point our critique has been mostly negative, simply arguing that evolutionary theorists are unable to explain the world apart from God. If they continue to deny the possibility of intelligent design, they will not be able to explain adequately the scientific evidence. However, those of us who believe in biblical authority have additional data to consider. How are we to understand God's revelation on this topic? What does the Bible have to say about the origin of people?

CONVERSATIONS ON THE SIDELINES: THE BIBLE AND THE ORIGINS DEBATE

As we have seen, naturalists may explain the origin of living things in several different ways (neo-Darwinism, evolution from space, complexity theory, punctuated equilibrium, etc.). Theists have offered various explanations of their own, and this portion of the chapter attempts to evaluate them.

Theistic evolutionists agree with Darwin that all living things have descended from a common ancestor, but they say natural selection alone is not sufficient to explain the process. They affirm many of the criticisms that have been directed toward neo-Darwinism, but they believe the obstacles discussed above could easily be overcome by a nudge from the sovereign God. Theistic evolutionists will likely disagree among themselves as to how frequent and how strong such nudges must have been, and they may also disagree about how "open-ended" the process is. Some will want to say that God in His providence is moving things forward to a predetermined end, and others will say the outcome is still uncertain as God creates possibilities to be acted on by His free creatures and the forces of natural law.

What theistic evolutionists do share in common is criticism. Some theists treat them as traitors, while naturalists often ridicule their "god of the gaps." Neither characterization seems fair. First, many of these men and women are trying hard to integrate their religious beliefs with contemporary science. Second, as noted above, some of the gaps are big enough that God may need to fill them. However, several questions will need to be answered if we are to assess their position biblically.

1. Does the Bible teach (or allow for) the concept of common descent?
2. Does the Bible teach (or allow for) the idea that the earth is billions of years old?
3. Did animals get sick and/or die before Adam's sin?

Theistic evolutionists who wish to use biblical authority would have to answer yes to each of these questions. By contrast, *progressive creationists* would answer yes to questions 2 and 3, but they would say no to question 1. Progressive creationists believe that God worked directly to create particular organisms over a long span of time. They would affirm the likelihood of microevolutionary change within those "kinds" (if we are to use the term from Gen. 1:24–25), but they would reject macroevolution from one "kind" to another, let alone the idea that all living things came from a common ancestor. Progressive creationists recognize from the fossil record that many species became extinct before people arrived on the scene, but they also recognize the relative absence of transitional species, concluding that God must have continually introduced new creatures.

Historic creationism, a relatively new model in spite of its name, handles these questions in the same way as progressive creationism. It might even be regarded as a form of progressive creationism, but it does have a different twist. John Sailhamer, the primary advocate of this position, has argued that Genesis 1–2 describes the creation not of the entire universe but the creation of the Promised Land.[29] From this perspective the text says nothing at all about the age of the rest of the earth, nor does it comment on animal life outside the land. It does teach, however, that Eden (the Land of Promise) was created in six twenty-four hour days, and it rejects the idea that humans have descended from other species.

Young-earth creationists would answer no to all three of the questions above. They argue that God created all living things in distinct "kinds" (no common descent), that He completed His creation in six literal days followed by a seventh day of rest, and that there was no sickness or death prior to the Fall. Advocates of this position often defend "creation science," which attempts to prove a very young age for the earth (between six thousand and thirty thousand years). Creation scientists argue that the geological phenomena typically regarded as evidence for earth's long history are actually the very recent consequences of the flood in Noah's day. That approach adds another phrase to our vocabulary—"Flood geology." Proving that the earth is very young would destroy the theory of evolution by natural selection, and many young-earth creationists believe their scientists have done exactly that.

We must consider a wide variety of issues if we are to make a choice between theistic evolution, progressive creationism, historic creationism, and young-earth creationism. At times it seems ridiculously complicated, especially when someone asks a simple question like the one my five-year-old posed recently: "Daddy, how long ago were dinosaurs alive?" I'll tell you what I told him shortly, but first let me tell you why.

The Meaning of Genesis 1

Genesis 1 describes God's creation of all things in a sequence of six "days." Historic creationists wish to limit the scope of creation to the Promised Land, and that seems fairly persuasive with regard to Genesis 2 and the establishment of the Garden, which has similar boundaries to the land God described to Abraham.[30] However, the references in Genesis 1 to the heavens, the stars, the sun, and the moon seem much more universal, even if the vocabulary can be understood in a more localized way (speaking of the "sky" instead of the the "heavens," for example).

Many interpreters have argued that the "days" of Genesis 1 should be understood as literal, twenty-four-hour days, noting that any other explanation would probably never have been considered if it had not been for the intrusion of science. Alternative interpretations are not simply modern inventions, since even Augustine (A.D. 354–430) questioned whether Genesis 1 was to be understood literally, but it does seem natural to read these as literal days, especially if one considers the use of "day" (*yôm* in Hebrew) in other contexts. It can occasionally refer to a longer period of time (as in Isa. 61:2), but whenever this word is used with a number, as many interpreters have noted, it denotes a literal, twenty-four-hour day. Further, since Exodus 20:9–11 bases the workweek on the pattern established in Genesis 1, we might expect the weeks to be of equal length.

However, we have to be careful not to beg the question. Even if other texts always refer to twenty-four-hour periods when speaking of numbered "days," Genesis 1 may be an exception. Patterns of usage do not constitute inviolable rules. In addition, one must consider the genre of those other texts. Since they are typically historical, they would help guide the interpretation of the Creation narrative only if it too is intended as literal history. If Genesis 1 is of a different genre, then those other examples are not as helpful. In the same way, the Law's pattern of six workdays and a Sabbath need not relate to the length of the days themselves, but simply to the cycle of work and rest. The fact that God does not continually follow that pattern in His own activities already erodes any precise comparison, so we should be careful not to stretch the point of Exodus 20:9–11.

Against the idea that these are twenty-four-hour days, Genesis 2:4 reflects back on the entire Creation week by referring to "the day that the LORD God made earth and heaven." If the first use of "day" after the description of the creation week uses the term nonliterally, one should be careful not to claim too much about the most "natural" reading of the text. Further, we recognize that our own days are determined by the earth's rotation and its orientation to the sun. If the sun was not created until the fourth day (Gen. 1:16–17), what does that say about the "literal" meaning of days one, two, and three?

Another interpretation has suggested that each "day" refers to an age or an era. Some have argued that the man's naming of the animals must have taken much longer than twenty-four hours, but Genesis 2:20 places it between his creation and that of the woman, both of which took place on the same "day" according to 1:27. If each day was a time period of indefinite length, the naming of the animals (and the Creation itself) would not have to be so rushed.

This interpretation has been quite popular, but it has some serious problems. If each "day" is a long span of time, then the earth had been created and was actually sprouting vegetation and bearing fruit long before the sun was placed in the heavens. Since life as we know it is dependent on the sun's rays, this scenario certainly does not help harmonize Genesis with modern science. Some interpreters have offered creative solutions to this problem, suggesting that the earth's vapor canopy made it impossible to see the sun or that it did not regulate time until the fourth day, but such attempts neglect the fact that the lights were both "made" and "placed in the expanse" on the same day (1:16–17).

Another problem facing the day-equals-age theory is one that it shares with the twenty-four-hour-day interpretation. Genesis 1:11–12 describes the creation of plants on the third day, but 2:5–9 implies that plants were not actually growing on the earth until Adam was created on the sixth day. It is possible that chapter 2, focusing on the origin of humanity, describes the more local creation of a garden in the land where the people were to dwell, but it may also be that we do not need to harmonize chapters 1 and 2 quite so specifically.

Part of the problem may be that too much attention has been focused on the meaning of the word *day*. If the passage itself assumes the genre of an epic poem, then the definition of a single word will not be as important as the composition of the passage itself. Umberto Cassuto saw the presence of poetic meter and a pattern of numerical harmony (revolving around the number seven) as evidence that Genesis 1 was written in an elevated poetic form. He also cited Akkadian and Ugaritic literature in which significant works were completed in seven consecutive days as a mark of their perfection. Perhaps Genesis 1 followed an accepted literary framework to portray God's creation as a perfect construction project.[31]

The text's frequently observed balance between the first three days and the last three days reinforces this possibility. Light was made on the first day, and the lights (the sun, moon, and stars) were made on the fourth. The waters below and the waters above were separated by the expanse of heaven on the second day. On the fifth, the waters below were filled with fish and the expanse was filled with birds. On the third day God brought about the creation of dry land and plants, and He filled that land with plant-eating creatures (including people) on the sixth day. God may have followed this pattern in six literal days or even in six ages, but the arrangement of the days, which causes such problems for both the twenty-four-hour and the day-equals-age interpretations, fits the idea of a literary framework very nicely.

This explanation has a number of advantages. First, if it is true, then we do not have to try to harmonize the order of the creative "days" with Genesis 2 or with contemporary science. In this view God's actions were not necessarily described in chronological order. Second, other scientific tensions would be eased by the fact that Genesis 1 makes no comment about the age of the earth (though other texts may still have some bearing on that issue). Third, this view would contribute to our understanding of Genesis 1 as a broad argument against the gods of other nations—not only did the God of Israel create the things that other nations worshiped; He also performed the creation as a perfect work, the greatest construction project of all time.

Seen from this perspective, Genesis 1 presents a message much like that of Job 38:4–7, where God used figurative language to describe His creative work. "Where were you when I laid the foundation of the earth? Tell Me, if you have understanding. Who set its measurements, since surely you know, Or who stretched the line on it? On what were its bases sunk? Or who laid its cornerstone, when the morning stars sang together, And all the sons of God shouted for joy?"

Other generations of interpreters may have misunderstood these statements, but we recognize that the earth does not have a literal "foundation," "bases," or a "cornerstone." We see that God compared the earth to a building and Himself to a builder. He directed its construction from the very beginning. It is worth noting that this passage poses no threat to inerrancy, because the metaphorical statements (even if misunderstood by some later interpreters) should have been apparent to the original readers.

The literary framework interpretation of Genesis 1 makes similar claims. Like Job, the author has described a true theological concept, using a genre that should have been recognized by the original readers. They would not have speculated on the length of the days, nor would they have worried about the timing of the events. They would have recognized that the days were arranged into two sets of three, and they would have gotten the point about the nature of God's construction project. At the same time, they probably enjoyed other literary allusions that we have not yet discovered.

But that is the major difficulty with this approach. Attractive as it may be, we don't really know enough to prove it. (At least I don't!) The cultural distance separating us from the ancient Near East results in many unanswered questions, and until additional studies answer them, we are left with some uncertainty. For example, was the literary model of a seven-day construction project common enough in the culture to form a recognizable pattern? How would it affect our reading of Genesis if some of these extrabiblical texts also relate seven-day patterns to something different, such as fertility cycles? Cassuto's examples apparently arrange the days in three sets of two. Genesis arranges them in two sets of three. Is that difference significant? Those kinds of questions would have to be answered before we can advocate the literary framework interpretation with much confidence. Until then, we should be content to wait, avoiding dogmatic statements and hoping for further insight.

So far we have not yet ruled out any of the theistic options regarding human origins, and I have not yet answered my son's question about the dinosaurs. Since the twenty-four-hour-day interpretation may be correct, young-earth creationism still remains viable. In the same way, since the literary framework intepretation may be correct, either progressive creationism or theistic evolution may prove to be true. Historic creationism also remains a possibility, though I am less comfortable with its treatment of Genesis 1. Perhaps another issue will make it easier for us to narrow the field.

The Historical Adam and the Creation of Eve

Genesis 2 provides a closer look at the origin of humanity, describing the creation of the first man and woman as separate works of God. He made the man of dust from the ground (2:7), and the woman from one of his ribs (2:22). Though some will say that the account seems legendary, the Scriptures provide no reason to doubt the historicity of this narrative. Unlike chapter 1, which provides textual clues that might support a nonliteral interpretation, Genesis 2 (beginning in verse 4, after God's day of rest signals the end of the Creation week) seems to operate in the same historical genre typical of the rest of the book.

If we are to understand this text as genuine history, there seems to be no way around the fact that God created Adam and Eve directly out of the materials described. The "dust" used to make the man was soil from the earth—whatever some theistic evolutionists may hope, the text simply does not describe organic molecules combined through prebiotic and biological evolution. The animals are made of the same material (2:19), and they share the same animating breath (2:7; 6:17; 7:15), but there is no hint here that we all share a common line of descent. In fact 2:18–19 may imply that the animals were made after the man, not before him. In the same way, the woman was fashioned out of the man's rib. She was a new creation, not a transformed hominid from the community on the other side of the hill.

Even if theistic evolutionists accept the direct creation of humanity, they may have a difficult time with the creation of animals in 2:19. It is conceivable that this was an additional, special creation simply for Adam's benefit as God prepared him for a spouse. Those who think Genesis 1 describes a chronological history may need to take this approach, because that chapter mentions the creation of animals before that of people (1:25). Another possibility is that 2:19 summarizes something God actually did earlier, restating it for the purposes of this more focused account. There might have been clearer ways to express it, but this interpretation of Genesis 2 would not be inconsistent with a more literal reading of chapter 1 (or, for that matter, with the idea that animals lived before people).

Genesis 2 poses problems for all the models, but it is easier on young-earth creationism and progressive creationism than on theistic evolution. It will permit a theistic evolutionary approach that allows for the special creation of humanity and perhaps a few animals, but such an approach might be identified more accurately as a version of progressive creationism. Those who wish to argue that God helped all living things evolve from a common ancestor will have difficulty squaring this view with Genesis 2.

This issue has significant bearing on one's view of sin. According to Romans 5:12–19, sin and death entered the world through Adam's rebellion in the Garden. If he was not a historical figure, then Paul's argument has no basis in fact. That same text raises another issue dividing young-earth creationists and progressive creationists. If death came through Adam, could animals have died before the Fall?

Animal Death and Adam's Fall

Observing that "through one man sin entered into the world, and death through sin" (Rom. 5:12), young-earth creationists argue that animals could not have died before Adam's sin brought death into the world. Since no species became extinct before the creation of people, dinosaurs must have lived alongside Adam's descendants, and some may have even made it onto Noah's ark. If they were not all there, how could Adam have named "every beast of the field" (Gen. 2:20)?

Progressive creationists respond by reading further in Romans 5:12, noting that "death spread to all men, because all sinned." Adam's sin, they maintain, had a direct effect on people, but many species of animals (including dinosaurs) were long gone before humans arrived on the scene. From this perspective, Adam named all the animals present in his day, or perhaps only those God prepared for that occasion.

This discussion has the potential to turn silly in a hurry, but we can avoid that mistake by recognizing that the biblical passages in question are written by, for, and about people. They do not address the mortality of animals. We do not find animals nibbling at the Tree of Life, nor do we see them described as having by nature what humans would receive only by faithful obedience and the grace of God, namely, eternal physical life. They were given plants for food (Gen. 1:30), and some writers have argued that there were no carnivores until after the Flood (9:3). But if that is the case, what was Abel doing with flocks and sacrifices of their fat portions (4:2, 4)? Were the animals kept only for clothing and sacrifice? Wouldn't his offering have been followed by a ceremonial meal (as later readers would certainly have expected)? Others will turn to Romans 8:19–21, which speaks of all creation waiting eagerly for the day of our final redemption, when it will be "set free from its slavery to corruption." This apparently constitutes a reversal of God's curse on the ground (Gen. 3:17), and one might expect that that day, highlighted by our resurrection, would also signal the end of all animal death. But here we must recognize that the blessings of salvation have different implications for humans than for animals. According to Isaiah 25:6–8, the day that the Lord "swallows up death for all time" will feature a lavish banquet. The restored people of

God will enjoy "aged wine" and "choice pieces with marrow"—apparently it won't be vegetarian. Isaiah may have been using a familiar image to convey the idea of a wonderful meal, one that will actually consist of, say, pasta salad, but at the very least we need to admit that the death of animals is not seen as a problem in this verse.

Other passages from Isaiah may signal the eventual end of animal death by referring to carnivores one day grazing and eating straw (11:7; 65:25). That surely presents a picture different from the brutal fight for survival currently witnessed in the animal world. It may be that human sin has produced animal suffering and death, perhaps even evidenced by God's clothing of the newly fallen Adam and Eve in garments of skin (Gen. 3:21). However, biblical descriptions of sin's consequences, like those of salvation's blessings, focus on persons, not animals. Possibly animals got sick and died before people were even created, and if so, then progressive creation remains a viable option.

The Contribution of Biblical Genealogies

The most famous attempt to determine the date of earth's creation came from the Irish bishop James Ussher, who added up the lifespans noted in biblical genealogies and concluded that God created the world in 4004 B.C. Cassuto has argued that the lifespans are more symbolic than historical, and that suggestion needs to be considered further, since even young-earth creationists admit gaps in the record and are unwilling to follow a chronology based on a strictly literal use of the lifespans.[32] However, we need to exercise caution on this issue. The correspondence between the genealogies and the Bible's historical narratives suggests that, though something more may also be in view, the genealogies do intend to record historical data. We may not be able to use them the way Bishop Ussher did, but we dare not reject them altogether. As a result, no matter what we say about the existence or extinction of animals before the creation of people, we should maintain a relatively recent date for Adam's arrival.

If the biblical texts are inconclusive on the broader question of animal life, how are we to decide between the various theistic explanations? Perhaps in the end it will hinge on one's response to contemporary science.

Theistic evolutionists, following the pattern of the common-sense realists, generally accept the observational conclusions of mainstream
scientists while rejecting their naturalistic assumptions. Progressive creationists are somewhat more skeptical, rejecting most arguments about
transitional species while accepting those for an older earth. Young-earth
creationists differ with the scientific establishment on so many different
fronts that little love is lost between the two camps.

Science and the Age of the Earth

In the old game Red Rover, children hold hands in two parallel lines, facing one another across an open field, and the teams take turns calling out,
"Red Rover, Red Rover, send (so and so) right over." The child whose
name is called is expected to let go of his friends, run across the field, and
try to burst through the opposing line. Naturally, he or she aims the attack on one of the weaker links in the chain, smashing between two smaller
kids who might be expected to have a hard time hanging on to each other.

In this chapter we have already tested some of the weakest links of
naturalistic evolution, barging into their ranks as they have debated various mechanisms for the origin of life and the development of species. We
are now approaching an area of their line in which they seem to stand
shoulder to shoulder like a Roman phalanx.

It would require far more space than we have available to assess fully
the scientific evidence regarding the earth's age, but the main point can
be summarized fairly plainly. I don't know of any scientists who believe
the earth is only a few thousand years old unless they have the prior theological agenda of reconciling geology to Genesis. Even some of evolution's
most outspoken critics agree that the earth is ancient. That does not mean
the "creation scientists" are necessarily wrong, but it does mean their view
is not very popular among scientists.

That situation may change. A new generation of young-earth creationists, led by well-trained scientists like Kurt Wise and Steve Austin, may
eventually expose enough weaknesses in the phalanx to require changes
in the prevailing old-earth paradigm. So far, however, that has not happened. Instead, creationism has a reputation for arguments that not only

bounce back from the other team's line but weaken the appearance of their own.

For example, when confronted with geological evidence for an older earth, young-earth creationists sometimes respond with the observation that God created things with an appearance of age. Adam did not begin life as an embryo, they reason, and Jesus turned water into fermented wine, not grape juice. It was brand-new, but it looked old. This argument, sometimes called mature creationism, is impossible to refute, but irrefutability is as much its weakness as its strength. The argument that the earth only *appears* old puts an end to any further conversation, but it certainly does not contribute to the mutual understanding of scientific evidence.

Many creationists also argue that estimates of the earth's age rely on circular reasoning. As they see it, evolutionary hypotheses cause paleontologists to assign certain dates to fossils and the rock layers in which they are found. Those dates are then used to support the evolutionary hypotheses that began the whole process. In actual fact, there is quite a bit more to it than that. Geologists employ a variety of dating techniques, only one of which (faunal succession) takes fossils into consideration. Further, other methods, such as radiometric dating, are far more reliable than is often supposed.[33]

Other popular arguments have included the surprisingly slight accumulation of cosmic dust on the moon (not nearly as much as one would expect if it has been out there for several billion years), the shrinking size of the sun (the rate of which suggests that the sun would have been bigger than the earth's orbit when the solar system is supposed to have formed), and the discovery of human and dinosaur footprints in the same strata near Glen Rose, Texas. These would all offer strong support for a young earth if they were true, but they're not. The argument about moon dust relies on outdated and inaccurate measurements of dust accumulation in the earth's atmosphere, and scientists have known about the correct figures since the early 1960s. The sun's size fluctuates, so arguments assuming a standard rate of shrinkage are, ironically, overly uniformitarian.[34] As for the "human" footprints, it now appears as though they, too, came from a dinosaur.

I don't mention these examples in order to make young-earth creationism look bad. I genuinely appreciate the work of those who are seriously trying to reconcile science with the Bible as they understand it, but I fear for those who so routinely repeat inaccurate arguments they have heard from others. More careful young-earth creationists have already abandoned these arguments in favor of others that I have not described, like the rapid fossilization apparently taking place after the eruption of Mount Saint Helens. Such studies may prove fruitful and may eventually help establish the idea of a young earth, but at this point arguments for an older earth continue to carry the day.

Conclusion

After considering the biblical and scientific merits of young-earth creationism, progressive creationism, historic creationism, and theistic evolution, we can offer only tentative conclusions. The biblical text fits either young-earth or progressive creationism most comfortably. Some theologians say theistic evolution is possible so long as it allows for the special creation of humanity and the animals mentioned in Genesis 2.

Our discussion would seem to lean toward some combination of progressive creation and theistic evolution with the special creation of humanity. The relatively recent creation of people, however, is not easily harmonized with current theories in paleoanthropology, the study of human fossils. Researchers argue that the genus *Homo* evolved from australopithecines around two million years ago, leading to *Homo habilis*, then to *Homo erectus*, and, just over a hundred thousand years ago, to *Homo sapiens*, thoroughly modern humans. Some who support the biblical account may find it encouraging that modern humans did not show up until fairly recently. However, we should probably find it difficult to regard any members of the genus *Homo* as nonhuman, and that presents an obstacle. Many of us prefer to follow the implication of the biblical text and posit a relatively recent history for people, but the conclusions of paleoanthropology suggest that people have existed for two million years.

Before stumbling too severely over this issue, we should note that the establishment of these categories and the classification of fossils is apparently not as consistent or rigorous as one might hope. Smooth transitions may be created by exaggerating the human qualities of *australopithecines* or understating those of *Homo erectus,* and fossil fragments are often classified on the basis of age, not morphology.[35] The uncertainty of this field of study, combined with the fact that many of our conclusions have been tentative to this point, suggests that the safest position is probably to wait and see how the conversation progresses. That is one reason so many theistic critics of naturalistic evolution refuse to take a position regarding the age of the earth. Recognizing that capable people on both sides have devoted their careers to this issue, they are content to await "the survival of the fittest." The other reason many prefer to remain silent is that they want to turn the debate toward more winnable issues. The young-earth portion of our Red Rover line has been attacked so frequently that others may no longer want its members on the team. I, for one, am not ready to give up on them, because I admire their commitments, and their efforts may eventually pay off. However, I, too, would prefer to see contemporary discussions turn to the more winnable (and more significant) issue of intelligent design.

Now, about that conversation. . .

"Daddy, how long ago were dinosaurs alive?"

"I'm not sure, Ben, but it was probably a long, long time ago."

"Did some people get to see them?"

"Probably not. It looks like they all died before any people got to see them. Some of our friends think people did see them, and they may turn out to be right. But either way, I'm happy they're not here now."

"But it would be fun to see them in the zoo." (You can tell he hasn't seen *Jurassic Park*!)

A FINAL WORD

Much of this chapter consisted of a view from the sidelines. We watched as the players tried to explain the world apart from God, and our observations reinforced the conclusion that something is wrong with the game. This last part of the chapter has been more like a sideline strategy session. Most of the arguments in this section will seem irrelevant to those currently playing the naturalistic game, but our conversation has not been directed toward them. If it clarifies a few things for the folks on the sidelines, that will be sufficient.

Before we move on to some other issues, however, we pause for one more look at the game. As we watch them play, we know it is not just about biology. Most of the players will tell you it is about the meaning of life. Michael Denton, himself an agnostic, stated the issue plainly.

It was the overriding relevance to fields far removed from biology that made the Darwinian revolution in the nineteenth century so much more significant than any other revolutions in scientific thought. . . . The entire scientific ethos and philosophy of modern western man is based to a large extent upon the central claim of Darwinian theory that humanity was not born by the creative intentions of a deity but by a completely mindless trial and error selection of random molecular patterns. The cultural importance of evolution theory is therefore immeasurable, forming as it does the centrepiece, the crowning achievement, of the naturalistic view of the world, the final triumph of the secular thesis which since the end of the middle ages has displaced the old naive cosmology of Genesis from the western mind.[36]

If that secular thesis is flawed, perhaps the old cosmology was not so naive after all. We have already seen Richard Dawkins's statement that Charles Darwin made it possible to be an intellectually fulfilled atheist. When addressing the philosophers of his own day, the apostle Paul appealed to a different source of fulfillment. "The God who made the world and all things in it, since He is Lord of heaven and earth, does not dwell in temples made with hands; neither is He served by human hands, as though He needed anything, since He Himself gives to all life and breath and all things; and He made from one, every nation of mankind to live on all the face of the earth, having determined their appointed times, and the boundaries of their habitation, that they should seek God, if perhaps they might grope for Him and find Him, though He is not far from each one of us; for in Him we live and move and exist" (Acts 17:24–28).

3

Created in the Image of God

"I KNOW THE BIBLE teaches it, and I suppose it's important, but I don't know what it means."

If that is the way you have approached humanity's creation in the image of God, you need not be embarrassed. You're probably in the majority.

Most students of the Word of God recognize that people have been made in God's image. They might know that it is mentioned in the Bible's first reference to people (Gen. 1:26–27), and they may have even used the concept to support the sanctity of life or the dignity of humanity. At the same time, even some of the most mature believers cannot explain precisely what it means to be made in God's image. And if they can explain it, they may not realize that very few people outside their own tradition agree with them.

Even the "professionals" face this problem. Theologians and commentators have long recognized the importance of humanity's creation in God's image, but they have also long disagreed about what it means. In fact, so many explanations have been offered that whole books and doctoral dissertations have been written simply surveying the various opinions! That does not mean we will never know the truth about this particular issue, but it does mean that we should not jump to conclusions. There are too many other voices in the conversation.

SOME POSSIBLE VIEWS

Image as Rational and Moral Capacity

Recognizing that people are made in God's image but that animals apparently are not, many interpreters have understood the image of God as some attribute that makes us more like God and less like animals. We are often thought to be unlike "brutes" by our ability to reason, love, and act morally (not just by instinct), and many have argued that God shares those same features. Reinforced (especially within the Western church) by the doctrine that God does not have a body, those who follow this approach to the image of God often suggest it consists simply of mind, emotion, and will.

It may be that people differ from animals in these ways (though many dog owners will argue that it is only a matter of degree), and it certainly is true that our moral choices should reflect God's own character (Lev. 11:44–45), but the Bible never associates intellectual or emotional capacities with the image of God. One might also ask why these capacities have been suggested so frequently. Following the logic of the argument, one might just as easily conclude that the image of God consists of self-awareness, creativity, or aesthetic sensibilities.

On a more positive note, this view does have an answer for one of the more puzzling issues related to the divine image. Certain biblical texts suggest that all persons exist in the image of God, while others treat the image as something that needs to be restored in salvation. Genesis 9:6, stating a commandment long after sin had entered into the world, reads, "Whoever sheds man's blood, by man his blood shall be shed, for in the image of God He made man." In the same way, James 3:9 notes the inconsistency between using one's tongue both for praising God and for cursing people, "who have been made in the likeness of God." From these texts we may conclude that all people, even after the Fall, are made in God's image. By contrast, other New Testament texts seem to treat the image of God as something that is exemplified in Christ (2 Cor. 4:4; Col. 1:15) and needs to be restored in people (Rom. 8:2; 2 Cor. 3:18). That need for renewal implies that the image was lost or damaged in some way through the Fall. Those who understand the image of God as humanity's moral or rational faculties often address this tension by suggesting that our abilities have been diminished as a consequence of sin. They then treat the growth of knowledge or moral character as a central focus of the Christian life, which leads eventually to the full restoration of the image.

An older solution to the same problem has been to distinguish between God's image and His likeness. Both terms are used in Genesis 1:26 ("Let Us make man in Our image, according to our likeness"), and many in the early church argued that fallen people retained the *image* of God but needed to be restored to His *likeness*. Those who held this view also emphasized the need for growth in one's moral character (God's likeness), while regarding rational ability as an essential aspect of one's being (God's image).

Unfortunately for this view, Genesis seems to use the words *image* and *likeness* almost interchangeably. Both terms are used in 1:26, but a summary of humanity's creation in 1:27 uses only *image* and a similar summary in 5:1 uses only *likeness*. Both terms show up again in 5:3, but in reverse order from 1:26 and with the prepositions transposed ("in His own likeness, according to His image"). Also, humanity's creation is summarized again in 9:6 using only the term *image*. It appears as though either word in isolation or both words in tandem may say essentially the same thing. They are not differentiated in rabbinic texts, and a similar pattern has been observed with the ancient Aramaic counterparts for the two original Hebrew words, which are used together on the inscription of a recently discovered statue. On the basis of this kind of evidence, it is inappropriate to distinguish between image and likeness. It is probably also inappropriate to use these terms to speak simply of rational, emotional, and moral capacities.

This whole approach not only lacks direct biblical support; it also builds on premises that are not universally accepted. Not everyone approves the assumption that God's image is nonphysical, particularly in the Eastern churches, which have placed less emphasis on the distinction between material and immaterial aspects of humanity. Even some in the West have argued that the image relates primarily to the body, perhaps in some feature such as upright posture. As for the tension between the apparent loss of the image and its retention, a number of interpreters simply favor one side or the other. Some have seen the image of God as a universal human condition related to existence, while others apply the phrase only to those who are rightly related to God.

Image as Community

Some of the most important voices in this discussion have argued that the preceding views are too individualistic. Emphasizing the language of Genesis 1:27 ("God created man in His own image, in the image of God He created him; *male and female* He created them" some suggest that the relationships between men and women demonstrate God's likeness. They also note that God voiced His intention to create people while speaking of Himself in the plural ("Let Us make man in Our image," 1:26), and they argue that the relationships between people reflect the relationships within the Trinity. As social creatures, all persons have the capacity to reflect God's image in this way, but sin has fractured our society. Reconciled relationships restore the divine image, and the harmonious community of the church demonstrates His character most fully. This interpretation owes much to Karl Barth, and, perhaps reflecting the importance of relationships in modern life, is quite popular among contemporary theologians. To assess it, we need to take a more careful look at the language of Genesis 1.

God spoke in Genesis 1:26 as if to others ("Let Us make people in Our image and according to Our likeness"), but the next verse describes Him acting alone ("God created people in His own image"). Some have understood the first statement as a "plural of majesty," speaking of God in plural terms because of the greatness of His being, but grammarians use that category only in the case of nouns, and these verses also include plural verbs and pronouns. A better suggestion treats this as an expression of self-exhortation (as perhaps in 11:7 and 2 Sam. 24:14), but this option cannot explain the equally problematic plural reference in Genesis 3:22, where God said, "Behold, the man has become like one of Us." These texts are related closely enough to suggest that they be treated in similar ways, and the most popular solutions do that by understanding the plural language more literally.

Modern biblical scholars have reached a near consensus in the belief that God was addressing a heavenly council, not unlike the pantheons of the surrounding nations. As monotheists, some early Jewish interpreters thought this council consisted of angels, but one of the oldest and most popular Christian explanations treats it as an early reflection of the Trinity. Both views have their difficulties. Nowhere else in Scripture are angels given such a prominent role in the creation of people, and Genesis comes too early in the progress of revelation for us to think the original audience would have seen this as an expression of plurality in the Godhead. The inclusion of a heavenly council of some sort may add to the polemic pattern of Genesis, however, as it reveals God to be exalted over all even in the heavens, and what was originally understood as an angelic court could be recognized through the lens of further revelation as a divine one.

Even if God did speak of Himself as heading up a heavenly council in Genesis 1, the connection between that fact and the creation of people as male and female remains unclear. Would such a council demonstrate the social nature of God, reinforcing the idea that people reflect God's image in their relationships, or is this just another way of highlighting His sovereign authority? I would favor the latter. God's authority, not His social nature, serves as the major theme of the chapter, and that theme is also present in other verses that use the plural language (3:22; 11:7).

But why would 1:27 mention the sexes except to associate sexual differentiation with the divine image? This reference may introduce the concept of fruitfulness through reproduction in the next verse, or perhaps it explicitly includes both men and women in the blessing that immediately follows creation. The latter option seems better in light of the repetition of this pattern in 5:2. But, however it is used, this reference to the sexes does not provide an obvious explanation for the meaning of the divine image. God made people in His image, and He made them male and female, but His image may not consist of male and female complementarity. If it did, other problems would be raised. For example, if God's likeness is seen in the relationships between men and women, is it *only* seen in those relationships? In what sense do *individuals* bear the image of God (9:6)? How about groups of men or groups of women, especially in the broader context of the church? As we will see, there is a sense in which God's image is manifested in the corporate relationships of the church (Col. 3:10), but that cannot be traced to the creation of humanity as male and female or the presence of a heavenly council in Genesis 1. We must seek a better interpretation of creation in God's image.

Image as Dominion

The most popular position among biblical scholars is the most distinctive of all. The other interpretations we have examined treat the divine image as a point of similarity between people and God, and they define it by identifying the shared attributes. This model explains the divine image not as shared form or faculties, but as shared function. People are like God in that they have been given the authority to rule as His representatives.

Looking at ancient literature from the nations surrounding Israel, many scholars observe potential parallels between the way it describes kings and the way Genesis 1 describes people. Some ancient kings, like idol statues, were viewed as "images" of their gods, suggesting that their rule embodied divine authority. They represented the gods and were apparently thought to resemble them in some ways. In a similar fashion, some kings would set up images of themselves in conquered lands—physical representations of the ruler to be venerated by the new subjects. To honor the king, one would honor his image.

The parallels certainly are appealing. Since people were created in God's image and were immediately commanded to rule over the rest of creation (Gen. 1:26, 28), this may be another way of saying that God had given them unique authority to rule as His representatives. God has established His image in that humanity has been created to rule, and the rest of creation honors the King by honoring His image. Those who favor this interpretation generally speak of people "as" the image of God rather than "in" the image of God, and some will defend this as an acceptable option in light of the grammar of the original Hebrew text. From this perspective, any loss of our status as God's image occurs in a misuse of human authority after the Fall, and its restoration demands appropriate submission to God's rule.

This tie between image and authority finds better support in Genesis

1 than does the tie between image and community discussed earlier. The authority of God serves as the primary theme of the chapter, and the vice-regency of humanity is emphasized as a consequence of Creation. But it is not without its problems. First, the Hebrew prepositions preceding "image" and "likeness" in 1:26 and 5:3 are much more commonly used to introduce a point of comparison ("according to the image") than to suggest an equation ("as the image"). This difference should not be overstated, because the New Testament uses both phrases (compare 1 Cor. 11:7 with James 3:9 and perhaps also Phil. 2:7), but the Genesis text suggests that we have been created according to a divine pattern, not simply to fulfill a divine function. A second problem is that advocates of this view seem to neglect the physical similarities between ancient images and the gods or rulers they represent. They have identified an important concept in associating the divine image with our vice-regency under God, but they have overemphasized the distinction between form and function. The point of Genesis seems to be that people are to rule as God's representatives because they are in some sense like Him.

That conclusion demonstrates that the most central question remains. In what way are we made like God? What do we have in common with Him that would allow us to exercise divine authority? Some interpreters have argued that this question cannot be answered from the Bible, that we can know only the consequence of the divine image (reigning), not its content. Finding our way carefully because of such warnings, we turn now to the content of the image.

IMAGE AND GLORY

We rightly want to avoid suggesting that God has a body, for He has revealed Himself as Spirit (John 4:24) and has forbidden the worship of physical images (Exod. 20:4). At the same time, we must question the assumption (so common to the interpretations discussed above) that the image of God must not be physical. The word translated "image" in Genesis almost always refers to some physical object that has been crafted to resemble a particular person or thing. In fact a study of biblical usage alone suggests that "image" and "likeness" in Genesis 1:26–27 refer to humanity's physical resemblance to God, just as the same terms in 5:3 likely describe Seth's physical resemblance to Adam. Would the author of these verses have ruled out a physical interpretation of the image? Did he not have some notion of God's appearing? After all, Moses saw *something* move past when God showed him His back on the mountain (Exod. 33:23). Would the Israelites have automatically ruled out a physical interpretation of the image? What did they see when God descended on the holy mountain (19:18) or the tent of meeting (Num. 11:25; 16:19)?

Most interpreters assume prematurely that the image of God is non-physical, and they also seem to have missed an important observation. In Genesis 1 people are not the only ones created to have dominion. According to verse 16, the sun and the moon were formed to rule over the day and the night. A different verb is used here than in verses 26 and 28, but it is the same word used of humanity's dominion in Psalm 8:6. The sovereign God has appointed governors. The sun rules over the day. The moon rules over the night. And people rule over the earth.

This observation suggests the intriguing possibility that people were created to share a particular ruling quality with the sun and the moon, namely, the divine glory. Compared to the shining of the sun or the stars in later texts,[1] the glory of God is a manifestation of physical light or brilliance that was commonly associated with His sovereign rule. Lexically it carries the notion of weightiness or authority, seen in the absolute dignity of the divine throne room or the splendor of its earthly imitations (Gen. 45:13; Ps. 24:8; 104:1–2). God made His glory visible to Israel in the pillar of cloud and fire, and the people trembled as they stood at a distance and said, "Let not God speak to us, lest we die" (Exod. 20:18–19). As the mediator between them and the Sovereign, Moses was granted greater access, but even he, after asking to see God's glory, was told that he could not see God's face and live (33:18–20).

God imposed limits on what Moses could see, but the experience was still transforming. After he had been in God's presence, Moses' face shone with glory as he mediated God's rule to the people (34:29–35). After witnessing this, how might the people have pictured Adam, created to mediate God's rule over the earth while enjoying unbroken fellowship with his Maker? One early Jewish tradition held that even Adam's heel shone brighter than the sun, with his face more radiant still, for he had been made in the image of God.

The idea that humanity's creation in the divine image initially included a luminous body may be supported by Ezekiel 1:26–27, where God is revealed in glorious human contours: "Now above the expanse that was over their heads there was something resembling a throne, . . . and on that which resembled a throne, high up, was a figure with the appearance of a man. Then I saw from the appearance of His loins and upward something like glowing metal that looked like fire all around within it, and from the appearance of His loins and downward I saw something like fire; and there was a radiance around Him." The word translated "appearance" in this passage is the same as that rendered "likeness" in Genesis 1. We were made to look like God, and when Ezekiel saw Him, the prophet said He looked like one of us, but as on fire. He was ablaze with divine glory.

The possibility that the divine image is found in humanity's investiture with glory is strengthened by Psalm 8:3–6: "When I consider Thy heavens, the work of Thy fingers, the moon and the stars, which Thou hast ordained; what is man, that Thou dost take thought of him? And the son of man, that Thou dost care for him? Yet Thou hast made him a little lower than God, and dost crown him with glory and majesty! Thou dost make him to rule over the works of Thy hands; Thou hast put all things under his feet." This devotional commentary on Genesis 1 seems to interpret image in terms of divine glory. Dominion, which in Genesis follows from creation in the image of God, here follows from coronation with glory and majesty. Indeed, coronation is the placement of a *luminous* crown, a corona, upon the head of one who is to rule! Psalm 8 suggests that this is precisely what God did when He created people in His image. The sovereign God is "clothed with splendor and majesty," covering Himself "with light as with a cloak" (104:1–2), and He apparently chose to crown His creation in similar fashion.

There are a number of other texts, both in the New Testament and in Jewish tradition, which link the image and glory of God much more explicitly.[2] They both support and clarify the interpretation we are developing here, but only through a process that has been described as "mirror-reading." We have already mentioned the fact that some portions of the

New Testament anticipate the renewal or restoration of the divine image, and these texts illustrate a much broader biblical tradition that treats salvation as a renewal of creation. Since such descriptions of restoration reflect back on the created ideal, they serve as mirror-like commentaries on the original. By looking at what they expected to be (or believed had been) restored with creation's renewal, we see what they thought was lost when creation was marred by sin. We will turn to those New Testament texts shortly, but first it will be helpful to survey the tradition in which they operate.

SALVATION AND THE RENEWAL OF CREATION

The creation described in Genesis involved the divine imposition of order on chaos. It reached its zenith with the pair in the fruit-filled Garden, experiencing God's blessing and living in fellowship with him. When sin entered into the world, all that began to unravel, like a knit sweater coming apart stitch by stitch, until the only way to salvage it was to start over. The man was banished from the garden into which he had been gently placed. He lost his life and returned to the dust from which he had come. Chaotic waters covered the earth in a flood, and the creation was undone.

The Flood gave way to ordered seasons and a new covenant as God essentially started over with a righteous remnant, Noah and his family. He gave the people a renewed mandate to fill the earth, reminded them of their creation in His image, and promised never again to destroy the earth with a flood. Like Adam, Noah began to cultivate the soil, and the creation was renewed.

Following this same pattern, one might say that the children of Israel moved from bondage and wilderness wanderings into an Edenic land, a place flowing with milk and honey in which they might enjoy communion with God. "The LORD will make you abound in prosperity, in the offspring of your body and in the offspring of your beast and in the produce of your ground, in the land which the LORD swore to your fathers to give you" (Deut. 28:11). But they were not just the sons and daughters of Abraham; they were also the sons and daughters of Adam, and sin cost them their garden too. Dragged into exile, they lost their dominion, their land, and their corporate worship of God. Their prosperity became deprivation, and even the once benign passing of morning and evening became cause for terror (28:66–67). When the judgment came, Jeremiah described it as a complete undoing of creation. "I looked on the earth, and behold, it was formless and void; and to the heavens, and they had no light" (Jer. 4:23). This allusion to Genesis 1:2–3 shows that everything had gone back to the beginning.

From that perspective, when God demonstrates faithfulness to His covenants by bringing restoration, that salvific act constitutes a new creation. The prophets looked forward to the day when the wilderness will become a fertile field and the people will again live peacefully in their promised land. Joy and gladness will return to uninhabited streets when God restores "the fortunes of the land as they were at first" (Jer. 33:10–11). In a vivid reenactment of Genesis 2:7, God will breathe His Spirit into those who have been slain, giving them resurrection life and returning them to the land (Ezek. 37:1–14). Their salvation will be a "starting over," but it will not ignore earlier history. It will be based on earlier covenant promises, and it will be a restoration of the way things were supposed to be, a renewal of the created ideal.

THE HOPE OF GLORY

Perhaps because of their focus on corporate life in the land, the Old Testament prophets had little to say about the divine image in their promises of restoration. Like the covenant promises, the promised renewal was largely national in scope, but the anticipation of a righteous remnant meant that it had an individual dimension as well. Not only will the nation one day be what *it* is supposed to be, but also individuals within it will be what *they* are supposed to be. That idea seems to have occasioned more discussion of personal transformation and the renewal of the divine image, and several different interpretations circulated in the communities of early Judaism. Most understood the divine image in a physical sense, and some identified it as investiture with divine glory.[2] Others who did not speak directly of the image did refer to Adam's lost glory and the luminous body to be restored to the righteous in resurrection.

Daniel 12 characterizes this focus on individual transformation by describing the resurrection of people to either eternal life or judgment (12:2). The former will be raised in radiant bodies. They "will shine brightly like the brightness of the expanse of heaven, and those who lead the many to righteousness, like the stars forever and ever" (12:3). Jesus later alluded to this passage when He said that "the righteous will shine forth as the sun in the kingdom of their Father" (Matt. 13:43). In other words, they will be *glorified*.

Some Jewish commentators thought this transformation came through the Law, either in its arrival at Sinai or its fulfillment within the community (2 Baruch 51:3, 10).[3] In the New Testament, Paul too looked forward to the restoration of God's image and personal glorification, but he said it was not through the Law but through the Holy Spirit (2 Cor. 3:7–18). Believers in Christ are to experience a transformation that surpasses that of Moses. It is permanent, more glorious, and no veil is required.

The transformation begins with the self-revelation of God in the proclamation of the gospel. "For God, who said, 'Light shall shine out of darkness,' is the One who has shone in our hearts to give the light of the knowledge of the glory of God in the face of Christ" (4:6). Paul himself had experienced this light quite literally, having been met by the exalted Christ on the Damascus Road. For most others the illumination of the heart is more figurative—the blindness of our unbelief and the hardening of our mind has been removed (3:14; 4:4). We are not restricted, as was Moses, to a glimpse of God's back as He passes by. Instead we are invited to contemplate His glory as we behold the face of Christ. We have been granted unhindered access to God through the gospel.

If Moses was transformed by what he saw, how much more shall we be changed by this intimate relationship with God! Paul said that believers "are being transformed into the same image"—the image of the exalted Christ, the object of our meditation. Christ is Himself "the image of God" (4:4; Col. 1:15), representing the invisible God more completely than Adam ever could. After all, He is the One in whom "all the fullness of Deity dwells in bodily form" (Col. 2:9), the One who eternally existed "in the form of God" (Phil. 2:6), and who is "the radiance of [God's] glory and the exact representation of His nature" (Heb. 1:3). Since He is the image of God, for us to be conformed to Christ's likeness is to be renewed in the pattern of the original. It is to become what we were supposed to be. "If any man is in Christ, there is a new creation" (2 Cor. 5:17).

This transformation is made possible by Christ's reversal of Adam's rebellion. Adam, the first man, though he was made in the image of God, desired equality with God and was judged for his prideful disobedience. Christ, the last Adam, though He was the image of God, did not cling to His equality with God and was exalted for His humble obedience (Phil. 2:6–10). The first Adam was made like God, but fell. The last Adam was God, but was made like those who were fallen (except that He had no sin). He became like us so that we could once again become like him. The first Adam undid creation. The last Adam restores it.

If conformity to the image of Christ constitutes the renewal of the image of God, what constitutes conformity to the image of Christ? Paul describes it in two parts: a future transformation of one's body and a present transformation of one's character. The former should not be surprising in light of what we have already seen. Paul stood in harmony with his tradition in arguing that the bodies of believers will be glorified in resurrection. This will take place as a consequence of the work of Christ. "For our citizenship is in heaven, from which also we eagerly wait for a Savior, the Lord Jesus Christ; who will transform the body of our humble state into conformity with the body of His glory [or, His glorious body], by the exertion of the power that He has even to subject all things to Himself" (Phil. 3:20–21). Having become like us in His incarnation and death, Christ enables us to become like Him in resurrection (Rom. 6:5). As a result, our bodies may be buried "in dishonor," but they will be "raised in glory," with the result that we will "bear the image of the heavenly" (1 Cor. 15:43, 49; also see Col. 3:4).

In Romans 8:11–25 Paul looked forward to the resurrection as the experience through which we would finally be glorified with Christ. It is the hope of our salvation, our "adoption as sons," "the redemption of our body" (8:23). Since God has "predestined" certain persons (the elect) "to become conformed to the image of His Son," He initiates several steps toward that end: "and whom He predestined, these He also called; and whom He called, these He also justified; and whom He justified, these He also glorified" (8:29–30). When we are glorified as the conclusive aspect of God's saving work, we will finally be conformed to the image of Christ, and the hope of the gospel will be fulfilled. "And it was for this He called you through our gospel, that you may gain the glory of our Lord Jesus Christ" (2 Thess. 2:14; see also Heb. 2:10).

From this perspective we certainly "exult in hope of the glory of God" (Rom. 5:2), but our hope does not look only to the distant future. One of the central features of Paul's theology is the idea that believers already experience some aspects of the coming age through the presence of the Spirit, who acts as a down payment on the things to come (2 Cor. 1:22; 5:5). We look forward to a final salvation in the future in which we will be resurrected and spared judgment, but in another sense we have already been saved and have already been given new life by the Spirit (Rom. 5:9–10; 8:11; Titus 3:5). In the same way, our conformity to Christ's image does not just await the future transformation of our bodies, for believers already share in Christ's glory now through the Holy Spirit (2 Cor. 3:18; 4:17).

I have some balding friends who have jokingly suggested that their shining scalps increasingly reflect the glory of God. But the present transformation described by Paul is primarily spiritual and ethical, not physical. In fact, the body seems to be going the other direction! "For we who live are constantly being delivered over to death for Jesus' sake, that the life of Jesus also may be manifested in our mortal flesh" (4:11). "Therefore we do not lose heart, but though our outer man is decaying, yet our inner man is being renewed day by day. For momentary, light affliction is producing for us an eternal weight of glory far beyond all comparison" (4:16–17). Paul's body was being destroyed, but he recognized that he was becoming more Christlike as a result of his sufferings. His character was being transformed. This took place not just through persecution, but also through "putting to death the [sinful] deeds of the body" and walking "according to the Spirit" (Rom. 8:4, 13). As we are empowered by the Spirit to model Christ in our behavior, we are transformed into His likeness.

This present transformation is seen not just in individuals, but also corporately in the church. Paul wrote in Colossians 3:9–11, "Do not lie to one another, since you laid aside the old self with its evil practices, and have put on the new self who is being renewed to a true knowledge according to the image of the One who created him—a renewal in which there is no distinction between Greek and Jew, circumcised and uncircumcised, barbarian, Scythian, slave and freeman, but Christ is all, and in all."

The salvific renewal of the created ideal, here described as a "new man," involves a community without boundaries. As in Ephesians 2:15, ethnic and social barriers have been set aside to make a new creation in Christ, and Paul exhorted his readers to live in accord with this new pattern. When those in the church refrain from lying, stealing, arguing, and abusive speech and treat one another with love, humility, compassion, and patience, they corporately demonstrate Christ's character. The church is renewed in the image of the Creator in a process that will continue until His coming (4:13).

Paul expected the image of God to be restored through the Spirit, who conforms us to the image of Christ. This begins with sanctification, the spiritual and ethical transformation of individuals and the church, and it will be completed in the future with glorification, the transformation of our bodies in resurrection and our final conformity to Christ's likeness. We will thus demonstrate His glory. As Seyoon Kim wrote, "Paul describes redemption in Christ in terms of a new creation, a restoration of the image and glory of God and of life which have been lost to mankind through the fall of Adam."[4] Herman Ridderbos, another Pauline scholar, stated, "To be created or transformed into the image of Christ does indeed mean to share anew (just as the original man) in the glory of God."[5]

One might even argue that the restoration of this image results in renewed dominion. Paul did not make the connection explicit, but he said believers will judge both the world and angels (1 Cor. 6:2–3), and he implied that our resurrection will result in restored dominion. In 1 Corinthians 15:25–28, Paul treated the description of human sovereignty in Psalm 8 as a promise that will not be fulfilled until all enemies, including death, are placed under Christ's feet. With the general resurrection in the future, that last enemy will finally be defeated, and God will have given us the victory in our Lord Jesus Christ (1 Cor. 15:57). As the last Adam, Christ's triumph will be our own, and the dominion described in Psalm 8 will be restored.

Paul's treatment of the subject coheres well with Hebrews 2:8, which also alludes to Psalm 8 while describing our present dominion as incomplete.

"For in subjecting all things to him, He left nothing that is not subject to him. But now we do not yet see all things subjected to him." "Not yet" implies that we will see that level of authority someday through Christ, who has already been crowned with glory and honor in His resurrection (Heb. 2:9). The pattern suggests that believers will receive renewed dominion through glorification, just as Christ did, calling to mind the millennial expectation that the martyrs will come to life and reign with Christ for a thousand years (Rev. 20:4).

Not surprisingly, Paul also recognized a present aspect to this restored authority. Christ has already been raised from the dead and has been seated at the right hand of the Father, "far above all rule and authority and power and dominion, and every name that is named, not only in this age, but also in the one to come" (Eph. 1:20–21). We who were once the helpless servants of sin have in regeneration been raised up and enthroned with Christ (2:6). Thus the down payment on our resurrection is also the down payment on our restored dominion. Our reinstatement will not be complete until we are glorified, but having been reconciled to God, we now "reign in life" as Christ's representatives (Rom. 5:17; 2 Cor. 5:20), and we are expected to live more holy lives as a result (Col. 3:1–5). One might also see the Great Commission as a renewed creation mandate in the sense that worldwide evangelism will "fill the earth and subdue it" for the kingdom of God (Gen. 1:28; Matt. 28:18–20).

In the first part of this chapter we concluded from Genesis 1 that people were created to be like God in some way and that this similarity resulted in dominion. We are now prepared to be more specific. If Paul's vision of the restored image accurately reflects the original creation, we may conclude that *the image of God consists of humanity's investment with God-like glory and the moral capacity to reflect His character while ruling the earth as His representatives.*

We had several clues from the Old Testament as to the association between image, glory, and dominion, but the reference here to moral capacity comes primarily from the Pauline texts that describe our present sanctification as a renewal of the divine image. Those same verses suggest a problem that has not been fully addressed to this point. We see that believers are restored to the image of God both now and in the future, but what about those who do not know Christ? In what sense may they be said to be in His image?

DEFACED, BUT NOT ERASED

If humanity's conformity to the image of God must be restored in salvation, then sin must have damaged the created ideal. At the same time, that damage must not have been complete, for, as we have seen, some biblical texts describe all persons as made in the image of God (Gen. 9:6; James 3:9). Even Paul, who had so much to say about our re-creation, described man quite broadly as "the image and glory of God" in 1 Corinthians 11:7.[6] For this reason one may say that the image of God has been defaced, but not erased. It has been tarnished, but not destroyed.

Like many Jewish interpreters before him, Paul described the loss of divine glory. He wrote in Romans 1:22–23, "Professing to be wise, they became fools, and exchanged the glory of the incorruptible God for an image in the form of corruptible man and of birds and four-footed animals and crawling creatures." The "exchange" here consists of a turn to idolatry, but in the process the people are said to have abandoned the glory of God. This is an apparent allusion to Psalm 106:20 and Jeremiah 2:11, where Israel is said to have exchanged "their" glory for an idol. Paul restated the idea in Romans 3:23, where he wrote, "All have sinned and lack the glory of God."[7] By contrast, we who have been freely justified by faith now rejoice in the hope of its restoration (3:24; 5:2).

If the glory has been lost, then what has been retained? There remains the capacity to demonstrate God's likeness, even when that capacity is not fully realized. Unbelievers retain the ability to make moral decisions (even if they continue to make them wrongly). In the same way, their bodies, though fallen, still give testimony to the Creator who designed people to reflect His glory. Likewise, all persons retain the capacity to rule as God's vice-regents in spite of the fact that we committed mutiny through sin, essentially transferring our allegiance to another god (2 Cor. 4:4). In short, though sin prevents us from fully demonstrating God's likeness, something special remains about people. We were made in the image of God.

THE DIGNITY OF HUMANITY AND
THE SANCTITY OF LIFE

The Internet enables people from all over the world to carry on continuous "conversations" regarding an unlimited number of topics. One of the discussions I followed a couple of years ago began when a theistic evolutionist was attempting to explain the transition from animal to human life. "What makes people unique," he said in the course of his argument, "is the fact that we have been given the breath of life."

We theologians are so frequently accused of straying into matters of science that we particularly enjoy seeing scientists drift into the realm of theology. Naturally, it didn't take long for me to join the conversation. Armed with several verses in which animals are said to have the breath of life (for example, Gen. 6:17; 7:15), I suggested that the difference between animals and people must be found in something else.

Another participant ventured the idea that only people have immortal souls, but there are difficulties with that idea as well, mostly in the area of definition. The conversation drifted toward self-awareness, abstract thought, and other cognitive abilities thought to be uniquely human. These seemed like helpful suggestions, but a more skeptical scientist raised a difficult question. "Why are we so confident that animals don't have similar abilities? Might they be just a little bit self-aware? Might they feel just a little of what you feel?" They might, of course, but science provides no way of knowing. That brought the conversation back to theology. What makes people unique? The Bible teaches that we are unique because we have been made in the image of God.

Discussions like this are not simply academic. Sometimes wrong conclusions have horrific consequences. For example, Helga Kuhse, who directs a center for bioethics in Australia, asked whether the sanctity of human life can really be defended. "Here we should note that I shall not, when speaking of the sanctity of life doctrine, be using the term 'sanctity' in a specifically religious sense. While the doctrine may well have its source in theology, I am not concerned with the question of whether or not the doctrine is true to some theological tradition or other, but rather with the question of whether it can be defended on non-theological grounds."[8] In other words, can one argue that all human beings have inherent dignity and unique value without appealing to some sort of divine authority?

I would suggest that from a biblical perspective, one cannot. People are unique not because they think differently than chimpanzees (though they probably do), and human lives are valuable not because they contribute to a better world (though they probably do that too). People have inherent dignity and unique value because they have all been made in the image of God. Since every person has been created according to the divine image, every human life becomes sacred. Just as David would not lay a hand on Saul as God's anointed (1 Sam. 24:10), so we should not murder (or even curse) those who have been made in the image of God (Gen. 9:6; James 3:9).

This becomes a very important point in bioethical discussions like those taking part between Kuhse and her peers. If one assumes a naturalistic philosophy, which regards humanity as unique only in the sense that we have reached a higher stage of evolutionary development, those who are less capable may easily be regarded as less valuable. On the other hand, if one believes that human dignity comes from God, one who seeks to honor God will honor those whom He has made in His image. The difference is especially apparent when considering those whom our society views as least valuable: the poor, the terminally ill, the elderly, the unborn, and the handicapped (Ps. 82:3–4; Prov. 14:31). Kuhse concluded that it would be right to kill patients painlessly, including handicapped infants, if their lives were not judged by others to be pleasant ones. This is not unlike a *Newsweek* essay, in which a woman argued that a severely handicapped man, Henry, should be put to sleep in the same manner as her suffering cat. In response to that article I found myself in rare agreement with Derek Humphry of the Hemlock Society, who said that "to kill Henry, even out of mercy, would be murder in the worst degree."[9]

I should probably add that my feelings on this issue are colored not only by my theology, but also by my experience. Our oldest son, Steve, had open-heart surgery when he was just eight months old. Unfortunately, some countries, doctors, and even some parents would not have allowed him to have that operation, even though it was necessary to save his life. Steve has Down Syndrome, and too many people think that lives like his are not worth saving.

My temptation as a proud dad has always been to talk about the things that Steve enjoys doing, how quickly he learned to read, or how sincerely he loves the Lord, to try to convince others that his very happy life was worth saving. On the other hand, my job as a theologian is to say simply this: His life was worth saving because he has inherent dignity as a human being in the image of God. The same is true of little boys who never will learn to read and those whose lives don't look happy at all.

The treatment of the handicapped raises another important implication of the approach taken here toward the image of God. If the image of God consists simply of our rational, emotional, and volitional capacities, then certain severely handicapped persons (like anencephalic infants, for example) evidently lack God's image and may be judged less than human. People who lose those capabilities would lose something of their humanity, perhaps forfeiting inherent human rights. By contrast, I have argued that even our bodies have been formed in God's image as they have been made to reflect His glory. Since all persons still have the potential to be fully conformed to Christ's likeness and to act as vice-regents over creation, either in this life or the next, all human life is valuable.

In the West this basic affirmation of life is continually challenged by dehumanizing technologies and a disproportionate emphasis on comfortable lifestyles. Elsewhere the obstacles are different, but the essential issues remain the same. In 1997 I made a trip to India, where so many people crowd the streets of cities that human life is too easily regarded as of little value. Cattle and cobras are often worshiped as gods, while many of God's vice-regents live in desperate poverty. When so many have "exchanged the glory of the incorruptible God for an image in the form of corruptible man and of birds and four-footed animals and crawling creatures" (Rom. 1:23), the results are devastating.

Whether in India or America, the basic problem remains the same, as does the basic solution. Sin has prevented our world and the people in it from fulfilling the Genesis ideal, but if anyone is in Christ, there is a new creation. Glory is restored to the common, dignity to the dishonored, and dominion to the oppressed, but only through the gospel of Christ, who is the image of God.

4

The Material Aspect of Human Nature

WHEN I WAS IN COLLEGE, I worked part-time at a health club. We had all kinds of people there, and on any given day I would see all sorts of bodies. When the doors opened at six in the morning, Roger would be waiting. He was one of our success stories, a tall, forty-something businessman who had lost 150 pounds and now looked as lean as a long-distance runner. His bald head and arms were tanned from weekends on the golf course, and he always began his workout with half an hour on the stationary bike.

The morning aerobics crowd would be kicking to the music by eight o'clock, trying to keep up with their instructor, Becky—five feet two inches of muscle and spandex who never weighed as much as Roger had lost, even when she was pregnant. About the same time I was usually working with Alan, the eighty-year-old former campaign manager for one of our state's most powerful politicians. He wanted to get into shape, but his body seemed headed the other direction. He moved slowly and took lots of rest breaks, so I got to hear some great stories.

The more serious weightlifters would start showing up after lunch, and they would stay until late afternoon. Many of them hoped to work out with Doug, a professional football player enjoying the off-season. He was an impressive figure—six foot six, 285 pounds, with dark, flowing hair reaching the tops of his shoulders. His arms were almost twenty inches around, but his waist was about thirty-six, and he could run like a cheetah. When Doug moved through the room, he left envy in his wake.

The members at the health club came in as many shapes as Jello (and some with as many jiggles), but they were all very conscious of their bodies. You could see it when they glanced at the mirrors around the room, sucking in their stomachs and flexing their muscles when they thought no one was watching. They wore clothes that accentuated their most impressive features and obscured their most embarrassing ones, and they always worked just a little harder when they had an audience.

By contrast, my Christian friends and I, who were probably just as body-conscious as anyone, always talked as if we weren't. We spoke of "changing hearts" and "saving souls," and we used phrases like "the real me" as if that were somehow different from our bodies or distinguished from our behavior. We laughed about those who seemed so obsessed with their bodies, but in retrospect I fear that we may have made an equal but opposite mistake. If folks in the health club act as if they are nothing more than bodies, we in the church sometimes act as if we are nothing more than souls. Some Christians actually treat the body as if it were the source of all sin and evil, and that is just as unbiblical as worshiping oneself in the mirror. Where is the balance? I believe it must begin with a biblical analysis of the body, and that takes us once again to Genesis.

LIFE IN DEPENDENCE ON GOD

After God formed the man from the dust of the ground, He "breathed into his nostrils the breath of life; and the man became a living being [literally, a living soul]" (Gen. 2:7). Many theologians use this text to support the idea that people consist of both material and immaterial parts, and they often describe this as God's giving a soul (or spirit) to Adam. I support the idea that people have both material and immaterial aspects, but that is not taught in this text. Here, as a result of God's action, the man "became a living soul." The "living soul" is not a piece of him; it *is* him! He is, as a whole person, a living being.

Genesis 2:7 describes the initial impartation of God's life-giving breath, through which He sustains every person and animal on earth. This is a new and foreign concept to many of us, but it really is quite simple when you think about it. Today we have extremely sophisticated ways to determine whether someone has died, but our ancestors resolved the issue quite simply. Is he breathing? If so, then he's alive. If he's not breathing, then he's dead. The presence or absence of breath provided a clear test for the presence or absence of life. Put that together with the idea that God alone is sovereign over life and death, and you can see how God would be regarded as the Giver and Taker of breath. If God gives a person (or an animal) breath, then he will live. If God takes the breath away, he will die.

The most common word in the Old Testament for God's life-giving breath is the Hebrew *rûaḥ*. This word is used elsewhere to refer to the wind, the breath (or spirit) of an individual, or the Spirit of God. Some commentators and translators have distinguished sharply between these referents, and that may be appropriate in places, but several verses make those distinctions difficult. For example, Genesis 1:2 speaks of the *rûaḥ* on the surface of the waters. Is that the wind or the Spirit of God? The same difficulty exists in the New Testament with the Greek word *pneuma*. In John 3:8 Jesus said that the *pneuma* blows where it wishes, and He compared that to those who are "born of the *pneuma*." We tend to translate one as "wind" and the other as "Spirit," but we probably overlook Jesus' association of the two images. Old Testament theologian Walther Eichrodt has appropriately summarized their interrelationship.

> *Rûaḥ* has retained at all times—and in this it is akin to the Greek πνευμα—the meaning "wind," denoting the movement of air both outside Man in Nature, and inside him, his own breath. Just as, in ancient popular belief, the wind was regarded as something mysterious, the bringer of life and fertility, so at an early stage primitive Man observed that breath also was an indispensable bearer of life, the origin of which he could not explain. Just as Man only comes to life in the first place because God breathes into him his own breath of life, so in order for him to succeed during life the *rûaḥ* must not be impaired or dwindle away, or, if it does vanish, it must return to him. Moreover, even the animal kingdom is called into existence by the same vital principle. Hence every

living thing in the world is dependent on God's constantly letting his breath of life go forth to renew the created order; and when its vital spirit from God is withdrawn every creature must sink down in death.[1]

Genesis 2:7 uses *nišmâ*, the more specific word for breath. That difference has caused some commentators to say that the man received a "breath of life" unlike that given to the animals. That interpretation neglects the fact that every other Old Testament text referring to God's animating breath, whether seen in people or animals, uses either *rûaḥ* by itself or both *rûaḥ* and *nišmâ* in synonymous parallelism. There seems to be no distinction between people and animals with regard to this concept. For example, Genesis 6:17 refers to both people and animals as "all flesh in which is the breath [*rûaḥ*] of life." Psalm 104:29–30 also uses *rûaḥ* alone while illustrating the creation's dependence on God's breath: "Thou dost hide Thy face, they are dismayed; Thou dost take away their spirit [or 'Thy Spirit'[2]], they expire, and return to their dust. Thou dost send forth Thy Spirit, they are created; and Thou dost renew the face of the ground." Job used the two Hebrew terms in synonymous parallelism when he vowed to speak the truth for the rest of his life. "For as long as life [*nišmâ*] is in me, and the Spirit [*rûaḥ*] of God is in my nostrils, my lips certainly will not speak unjustly, nor will my tongue mutter deceit" (Job 27:3–4). The same parallel is employed three more times in subsequent chapters. "But it is a spirit [*rûaḥ*] in man, and the breath [*nišmâ*] of the Almighty gives them understanding" (32:8). "The Spirit [*rûaḥ*] of God has made me, and the breath [*nišmâ*] of the Almighty gives me life" (33:4). "If He should determine to do so, if He should gather to Himself His spirit [*rûaḥ*] and His breath [*nišmâ*], all flesh would perish together, and man would return to dust" (34:14–15). Judging from this parallelism between *rûaḥ* and *nišmâ* in Job and the use of *rûaḥ* alone in texts describing both people and other living things, animals and people are animated by the same life-giving breath of God.

As you read through these examples, you may have noticed that "spirit" is occasionally capitalized. The translators seem to have had some difficulty deciding whether this animating breath should be identified with the Holy Spirit of God, and they apparently did not arrive at a consistent answer. The term is ambiguous, but it appears as though a later more fully Trinitarian understanding of the Spirit depends heavily on this fundamental concept of the life-giving breath.

The unfamiliarity of these ideas may leave the reader a little confused, but for our present purposes the main point may be stated plainly: We are utterly dependent on the Spirit of God for our very lives. He sustains us by the unconditioned exercise of His power. He is the one who "kills and makes alive, who brings down to Sheol and raises up" (1 Sam. 2:6), so none of our worries can add a cubit to our lifespans (Matt. 6:27). As Eichrodt has stated, our life is "a gift of grace, which can at any time be revoked, from the one who is the living Lord over the spirit of life."[3]

MY BODY AND ME

One night, while my children were getting ready for bed, I flopped on the couch to watch our beloved Texas Rangers take on their rivals, the Seattle Mariners. Such peaceful moments don't last long in our home, and I had only been seated for a couple of minutes when I was joined by four bouncy, giggly kids in pajamas, ready for bed, but not ready to sleep. Juggling for position, Danny asked, "Dad, could you please move your arm? It's in my favorite spot."

"You mean *I'm* in your spot. Sorry, but I got here first."

"You're okay, it's just your arm. You're stretching it out across my favorite spot."

"But isn't my arm part of *me*?"

"Sure it is, but you can move it. Please?"

Finding his logic persuasive (as usual), I moved my arm. He made himself comfortable, and I had something to think about while we watched the game. What is the relationship between my limbs and my self? Danny acknowledged that my arm was part of *me*, but it was somehow distinct from *me* too. I could still move *it*. He seemed to regard the trunk of my body as more central—I wasn't actually *sitting* in his spot, so *I* was okay. On the other hand (no pun intended), sometimes even my trunk seems distinct from the real *me*. *I* have spoken of *it* in the last sentence, treating it as an object distinct from myself.

If my arm is *me* when someone punches it ("He hit me!") or when I fall and hurt it ("I hurt myself"), why is it at other times *not me* ("My arm's asleep!")? The feet seem even more isolated, perhaps because we are conscious of them only when there is a problem ("Feet, don't fail me now!"), or maybe because they're usually so unsightly that we would rather not be closely related. Actually, it may simply be a matter of distance. We tend to place our "selves" pretty much right behind the eyes. (Wanting the children to look me in the eye, I might say, "Look at me!") The farther any body part is from that spot, the easier it is to objectify it or treat it as distinct from our selves. It may also be that we more easily objectify the more expendable parts of our bodies, and limbs are more expendable than heads or trunks.

Any way you look at it, however, our language seems inconsistent. The child's response to ridicule treats the body as "the real *me*." "Sticks and stones will break my bones, but words will never hurt me." Broken bones will hurt *me,* but wounded emotions will not? Don't my feelings reflect some aspect of my self?

I am not suggesting we change the way we talk about our bodies. If we only referred to our whole selves, medical doctors, choreographers, and tailors (to name just a few) would find it impossible to do their jobs. However, we do need to recognize the ambiguity with which we speak of ourselves, and we need to evaluate whether we really mean what we say. Is there a distinction between my body and *me*? Is the body the real *me*? Is there something to *me* besides (or inside!) my body?

MONISM VERSUS DUALISM

It has been fashionable in recent decades for both theologians and scientists to speak of *wholistic* (or *holistic*) models of the human person. A wholistic model maintains that people cannot be divided into constituent parts, like soul and body or immaterial and material, but can only be viewed as whole creatures. Those who come to that conclusion might also be called monists, because they believe that human nature (and perhaps even all of reality) consists of a single essence. Monists come in several varieties, so we'll start by recognizing the two extremes. Idealistic monists believe that everything is essentially immaterial (or spirit), and materialistic monists believe that everything is essentially matter.

Most of the naturalistic evolutionists discussed in chapter 3 are also materialistic monists, believing consciousness to be nothing more than the product of chemical reactions in the brain. Marvin Minsky summarized this position well: "The brain is just hundreds of different machines ... connected to each other by bundles of nerve fibers, but not everything is connected to everything else. There isn't any 'you.' "[4] Research on brain physiology lends some credibility to Minsky's conclusion. Since many emotions and memories can be triggered by electronically stimulating specific portions of the brain, mental experiences are apparently linked to physiological events. However, physiology cannot explain all our thought processes. As neurosurgeon Wilder Penfield has stated, "There is no place in the cerebral cortex where electrical stimulation will cause a patient to believe or to decide."[5] Still the materialistic monists (also called pancorporealists because they believe that "all is body") believe they have explained enough mental states to conclude that the mind is the brain.

Ultimately, materialistic monism is based on faith. (Or should we say unfaith?) Its advocates admittedly cannot prove there is no "ghost in the machine" of the human body, but it is a reasonable conclusion, given their naturalistic assumptions. Those who do not share those assumptions are not so easily persuaded.[6]

The modern scientific climate has increased the popularity of materialism, but idealistic monism has not disappeared. It thrives in the teachings of some popular New Age advocates who believe that matter is a creation of the mind and that all things share a common spiritual essence. This view has been called "panpsychism" because it maintains that "all is spirit." Marianne Williamson provided a good example of it. "Old Newtonian physics claimed that things have an objective reality separate from our perception of them. Quantum physics, and particularly Heisenberg's Uncertainty Principle, reveal that, as our perception of an object changes, the object itself literally changes. The science of religion is actually the science of consciousness, because ultimately all creation is expressed through the mind. Thus, as *A Course in Miracles* says, our greatest tool for changing the world is our capacity to change our mind about the world."[7]

In a similar way Shirley MacLaine demonstrated her belief in the unity of all things when describing her experience in an Andean mineral bath. "Slowly, slowly, I became the water. . . . I was the air, the water, the darkness, the walls, the bubbles, the candle, the wet rocks under the water, and even the sound of the rushing river outside."[8]

Such statements violate the common sense of people who recognize that there are real differences between themselves and objects, and Williamson's appeal to Heisenberg only shows that a little awareness of physics can be a dangerous thing. Heisenberg's Uncertainty Principle does not show that we have the power to change objects by looking at them differently; it only shows that we are unable to determine the velocity and location of subatomic particles at the same time.

Some monists find a middle ground between the extremes of materialism and idealism, contending that the common essence of all things is both material and immaterial. From this perspective (known as "dual-aspect monism"), nothing is pure matter (not even rocks) and nothing is pure spirit (not even God). David Steindl-Rast, a Roman Catholic with decidedly New Age (he would say "new paradigm") leanings, represents this view. He wrote, "For me spirit and matter are two sides of the same coin, two interwoven aspects of reality."[9]

This perspective resolves some of the difficulties of both materialism and idealism. Reality consists of more than just matter and more than just spirit. Further, both matter and spirit are real and necessary. Dual-aspect monism is thus more consistent with both our observations and our common sense, but it leaves some major theological problems unresolved.

Materialists teach that people do not survive death in any way, for they are nothing more than physical bodies. Idealists believe that something survives a person's physical death, but eventually it will merge with the universal spirit, in which there are no individual entities. Since dual-aspect monists believe that no immaterial part of anything can be separated from the physical, they too teach that no part of the individual person will survive death. The only thing that continues to exist is what has always existed, that absolute immaterial and material reality we call God (or nature).[10] Steindl-Rast wrote, "When you die, you're dead. Time's up for you, therefore there is nothing 'after' death. Death is by definition that after which there is nothing. Time's up; your time has run out. Someone else's time may go on, but your time's up. There is no 'after' for you."[11]

These monistic options are in opposition to the traditional Christian doctrine of eternal life, which anticipates continuing personal existence after death. They are also inconsistent with the idea that God exists as a transcendant, personal Being who has no body. For these reasons, one does not find conservative Christian theologians advocating monism, at least in such universal terms. However, many Christians have (inconsistently) embraced a monistic model of human nature, describing people as body/soul unities and denying any kind of "Greek dualism."

Dualism teaches that there is not just one kind of reality, but two. Material and immaterial, physical and nonphysical, or body and soul, these dual essences come into contact with one another but remain distinct. Historically, many dualists understood the difference between soul and body as the difference between good and evil. Second century Gnostics, for example, believed that all matter was created by a powerful "demiurge" who existed in opposition to God. Therefore any physical thing, including the human body, was considered inherently evil. In a similar way the philosopher Plato (428–348 B.C.) regarded the body as inferior to the soul, which must be freed from the body at death in order to reach its true goal.

Early in the history of the church, many influential theologians thought Plato's basic principles were biblical, especially those that addressed the nature of humanity. They maintained that only the soul, not the body, existed in the image of God, and they viewed it as the real essence of an individual person, that which directs the body and is inherently immortal.

In recent years this dualistic approach to human nature has drawn sharp criticism. Arguing that the Hebrews understood people in a wholistic sense, the critics say that Platonic dualism has distorted the biblical text and has skewed the church's approach to ministry for centuries. Anthropological dualism has been blamed for the privatization of religion, the rise of modern secularism, the separation of social and religious issues, the physical exploitation of people, the abuse of the environment, the failure of missions, and the trivialization of the gospel.[12] At the same time, theological treatises on the body have become fashionable, and biblical scholars regularly emphasize the wholistic anthropology of the Semitic mind. The Jews would never have accepted any form of dualism, they say, because they placed so much emphasis on the body that personal identity apart from it would have been inconceivable.

Some dualists may have gone too far, and they may have allowed their emphasis on the soul to keep them from obeying biblical principles about social justice, but their critics err in the other direction. If there is no division at all between soul and body, if the immaterial and material aspects of a person share an inseparable unity, then nothing more than a memory survives physical death. A dual-aspect monism, even if applied only to people, has essentially the same effect as materialism. In materialistic monism, the mind is the brain. If the brain is in the grave, the mind no longer exists. In dual-aspect monism, the mind is distinguished from the brain, but inherently tied to it. Again, if the brain is in the grave, the mind shares the same fate.

For this reason, all the biblical passages about the afterlife stand against a purely wholistic view of human nature. If any aspect of a person survives physical death, then dualism has to be true. Some have attempted to get around this difficulty by treating the promised resurrection as an individual's complete re-creation. God will raise a person from the dead in the sense that He will make a new soul/body unity to replace the one that perished, and this new copy will share the memories and experience the rewards of his or her prototype. Would it be selfish to say that I don't find much hope in that arrangement? When facing death, is my comfort nothing more than the expectation that some other individual will eventually experience bliss in my stead? In what sense will death and Hades give up the dead (Rev. 20:13) if their graves remain occupied for eternity?

Others suggest that we will receive resurrection bodies immediately upon death, thus continuing to exist as soul/body unities. I don't believe this is correct, but it is important to note that even this model demands some kind of dualism. As John Cooper has stated, "[According to this view] at death a person passes immediately from existence in one body to existence in another. In this formulation we have one self-identical person and two bodies. The one person is therefore separable from the earthly body, which is dualism by definition."[13] Not only does this view fail to maintain the wholism it intends to preserve, but it also teaches a "resurrection" that leaves the graves occupied, and that would be no resurrection at all.

RESURRECTION AND THE BODY

We do not have the space available here to fully develop the New Testament teaching on the resurrection of the body, but this doctrine contributes so much to our understanding of human nature that some comment is required. We will look primarily at 2 Corinthians 5 and 1 Corinthians 15.

Second Corinthians 5:1–10 addresses Paul's immediate expectation, and that makes it particularly relevant for our discussion of monism and dualism. When Paul spoke of the "earthly tent" in verse 1, he was describing his physical body, which was deteriorating through persecution (4:16). That suffering may actually have pushed Paul toward the conclusion that he would likely die before the return of Christ. Earlier he seems to have been expecting to be one of those who would still be alive at the rapture (1 Thess. 4:17; 1 Cor. 15:51–52), but here he showed no such confidence, expecting to be raised up and presented alongside the Corinthian believers (2 Cor. 4:14). Confronting the possibility that his body would be "torn down," Paul recognized that he would have a more permanent "building from God, a house not made with hands" (5:1). Jesus had described His own resurrection body in similar terms (Mark 14:58), and the emphasis seems to be on its divine origin. God is the one who builds this house.

In the present dwelling, the apostle groaned with discomfort, longing to be "clothed over" with his resurrection body. This refers to the immediate bodily transformation of believers who will be alive at Christ's coming. When their perishable, mortal bodies suddenly become imperishable and immortal (1 Cor. 15:53), it will be as if people put on new bodies over old ones. The suffering apostle longed for that day, hoping that the Lord would return in his lifetime. If that happened, Paul would "put on" the new body without having to "take off" the old one in death. That way he would remain "clothed" and would not be "found naked" (2 Cor. 5:3). As he wrote in verse 4, Paul did not want to be "unclothed" by death before the return of Christ. His obvious preference was to remain "clothed," that is, that "the mortal may be swallowed up by life" in immediate transformation.

Paul observed (5:5) that God had been preparing him and other believers for that glorious future, having already provided the life-giving Spirit "as a pledge." The Spirit brings life by His presence, and His present work of regeneration serves as the down payment on His future work of resurrection (Rom. 8:11). With that initial installment of eternal life in mind, Paul was of "good courage" even with the knowledge that "while we are at home in the body we are absent from the Lord" (2 Cor. 5:6). He was able to rest in the fact that God had promised eventual resurrection and had already begun to fulfill that promise with the coming of the Spirit.

In the meantime Paul hoped for the imminent return of Christ. If that did not happen, his second choice was "to be absent from the body and to be at home with the Lord" (5:8). The only remaining possibility, that Paul would remain "at home in the body" and be "absent from the Lord," would certainly be acceptable (Phil. 1:21–24), but Paul was anxious to be in the presence of his Savior, even if it meant death at the hands of his enemies. Either way, whether he stayed "at home" in the body or was "absent," Paul hoped to be pleasing to Christ (2 Cor. 5:9).

By referring to the body as a "tent, house, building, or dwelling," and then describing it as a suit of clothes that one can put on or take off, Paul plainly endorsed some form of dualism. Death separates the physical body from the part of a person that immediately enters the presence of the Lord. Moreover, by describing that separation from the body as a state of "nakedness," Paul used a term made familiar by Plato and other Greek philosophers to describe the disembodied state.[14]

The thought of life without bodies seems foreign to us, and it remains difficult to answer the many questions that arise concerning that kind of existence. How can we be in Christ's presence—indeed, how can we *be* anywhere—unless we have some kind of body? What about the fate of unbelievers? Can one experience physical punishment without flesh? We may be helped here by the realization that angels, as localized spirits, apparently abide in the presence of God without bodies (Luke 24:39; Heb. 1:14). Furthermore, demons, who are fallen angels, will experience genu-inc suffering and affliction for all eternity (Matt. 25:41; Rev. 20:10). Revelation 6:9–11, even if elements of it are to be understood figuratively, speaks of "the souls of those who had been slain because of the word of God, and because of the testimony which they had maintained," being visible beneath heaven's altar. What is more, each of these martyrs was given a white robe and told to "rest a little while longer," presumably awaiting the triumphal resurrection (see Dan. 12:13). The Bible contains other examples of persons who were visible even in the intermediate state (1 Sam. 28:14; Matt. 17:3; Luke 16:23). That may be some kind of temporary visibility (again like angels), or it may be that souls retain some kind of form we do not understand. We simply do not know. But we do know at least one thing about the intermediate state: Believers who die before the return of Christ will enjoy conscious existence in His presence even while their physical bodies decompose in the grave.

We also know that one day those graves will be emptied. Many in the Corinthian church must have denied that at one time, because a portion of Paul's first letter to them vigorously defends the resurrection of believers. His argument is based on the idea that salvation without bodily resurrection would not be salvation at all, and death would still be the victor (1 Cor. 15:21–28, 53–57). Christ came to provide eternal life, and we will not experience that if our bodies remain forever dead. If the dead are not raised, Paul reasoned, then apparently Christ has not been raised either (15:13), for Jesus' resurrection demonstrated that His death had forever paid the penalty for sin (Acts 2:24; Rom. 6:9). If we remain under that penalty by not being raised, even though we have believed in Jesus, that would mean His death was not efficacious and He was not resurrected. "If Christ has not been raised," Paul concluded, "you are still in your sins" and the gospel is a lie (1 Cor. 15:17). On the other hand, if Christ has truly been raised, then His death really did break the power of sin and we can expect to be raised along with Him. That, of course, was Paul's confident judgment. "But now Christ has been raised from the dead, the first fruits of those who are asleep" (15:20).

For our salvation to be complete, our bodies will need to be transformed. As Paul said in verse 50, "flesh and blood cannot inherit the kingdom of God." We should avoid reading too much into that phrase, for Paul apparently saw the problem not with our physicality, but with the fact that our bodies continue to suffer from the consequences of sin. They are mortal, so they need to be made immortal (15:53–54). They are weak, so they need to be made strong (15:43). They do not fully manifest the image of God, so they need to be glorified (15:43; Rom. 8:18–23).

One might ask why God would go to so much trouble. If believers enjoy communion with Him even before the resurrection, why bother to bring their bodies back into the picture? Apparently bodies are not required for genuine worship of God, but bodies are required if He is to be worshiped the way He intended. If salvation renews the creation and restores people to God's original design, bodies will have to be included.

Further, if the consequences of sin are to be reversed, occupied graves present a problem. Paul expected the body that is buried to be raised, and he demonstrated that belief by comparing the process to the germination of seeds. The same body is sown perishable but raised imperishable (1 Cor. 15:42), sown in dishonor but raised in glory, sown in weakness but raised in power (15:43). It is sown a "natural" body, but raised a "spiritual" one (15:44), just like the body of Jesus (Phil. 3:21).

We are familiar with Jesus' empty tomb, but it is easier to imagine the resurrection of someone after three days than after three millennia. What becomes of a body that has been cremated, devoured, or decomposed? Medieval artists frequently portrayed animals regurgitating human limbs as the resurrected dead (missing those very parts) scampered out of their graves. In the same way, many theologians supposed that the bits of matter composing human bodies could not be digested by any other creature, leaving them perpetually available for recombination at the last trumpet. We recognize that the situation is more complex than that. The molecules that make up our bodies helped compose a wide variety of other organisms before we came along. Even now, the body continually renews itself, sloughing off old cells and replacing them with new ones, so that we have used and discarded far more molecules than we currently possess. And who knows what has become of them? Some body (or some plant) may be using them once again.

Perhaps one of the oldest answers remains the best. There will be enough identity between the old and the new to say legitimately that the graves have been opened, but God will re-create whatever He must. In fact, the concept of creation *ex nihilo* ("out of nothing"), which frequently shows up in contemporary discussions of human origins, appears to have been first articulated as an answer to the puzzle of resurrection. If necessary, God will make some of our parts out of nothing.

But that does not resolve our problem. We entered this lengthy discussion of the resurrection while considering the relationship between personal identity and the physical body. Is the body such an essential part of *me* that I no longer exist apart from it, or is there some part of me that continues to exist even when separated from the body? Our look at 2 Corinthians 5 helps affirm the latter (dualistic) position. However, this same passage should also caution us against the Platonic idea that we need to escape our bodies. The body is not an evil or inferior entity, but a vital part of us that must be restored for salvation to be complete. We come then to a balance between extremes. The body is an *important* part of our humanity. We won't be saved *from* it, but *with* it. Still, since a great number of humans (namely, all who are deceased) currently exist without bodies, the body is not an *inherent* part of our humanity.

Like most people, I was born with two kidneys. Though *I* am able to talk about *them* as distinct parts, just as I do when talking about my arms and legs, they are important parts of *me*. I would be in pain if you punched one of them. However, if that same kidney were removed, it would be distinct not only from *me*, but also from my body! If I donated it to my brother, that organ would no longer be a part of me. It would now be a part of *his* body, a part of him. If you then punched that same kidney, *he* is the one who would be in pain. In the meantime, I would be missing something, for *I* would no longer *have* that kidney. However, it is conceivable that he could later give it back. In that unusual circumstance, I would once again be able to describe the kidney as a part of *me*!

The situation appears to be similar with the intermediate state. Believers currently in God's presence can say, "I no longer have a body. It is not now part of me, but it will be once again." Without the body, as without some piece of it, they are not all they were created to be. But they do not cease to exist, nor do they cease to be human. However, apparently they will cease to struggle with sin, and that leads us to another issue.

THE RELATIONSHIP BETWEEN SIN AND THE BODY

The apostle John wrote, "Beloved, now we are children of God, and it has not appeared as yet what we shall be. We know that, if He should appear, we shall be like Him, because we shall see Him just as He is. And everyone who has this hope fixed on Him purifies himself, just as He is pure" (1 John 3:2–3). If persons become finally pure and cease sinning when they see Him, does that mean that those who see Him when they enter the intermediate state have separated from sin by separating from the body? If so, that would seem to support the Gnostic brand of dualism, in which material things (bodies included) are inherently evil. Further, since so many of our sins relate to bodily pleasures (gluttony and sexual immorality, to name two), might it be appropriate to say that the body drives me toward things that *I* do not really want to do?

We must be careful not to get too far ahead of ourselves at this point. Since we have yet to discuss the Fall and the nature of sin, it would be premature to consider topics like the struggle between "flesh and Spirit" in this chapter. That will be reserved for chapter 10. For now, a more basic response will have to suffice.

The Bible views all things, bodies included, as good in their creation but corrupted through sin. God was pleased with what He had made (Gen. 1:31), and material things were all part of His original plan. When used in accord with God's creative intention, they remain good. If misused, they can function as instruments for evil. Paul wrote, "For everything created by God is good, and nothing is to be rejected, if it is received with gratitude; for it is sanctified by means of the word of God and prayer" (1 Tim. 4:4–5). He made that statement to answer teachers who thought believers needed to abstain from certain physical pleasures. They were forbidding marriage and telling their followers to avoid particular foods, sounding something like the early Christian ascetics who treated sexuality as a consequence of the Fall. Paul said these things were created by God "to be gratefully shared in by those who believe and know the truth" (4:3). Food and sex can obviously be misused, but they are good gifts of God when used appropriately.

In the case of sexuality, that appropriate use centers on heterosexual marriage. Paul said it is "unnatural" when men and women pursue sexual relationships with members of their own sex, and that may be what he had in mind when he spoke of unbelievers' bodies being "dishonored" (Rom. 1:24, 26–27). Likewise, it is contrary to God's design when people fall into heterosexual promiscuity, incest, adultery, or fornication (1 Cor. 5:1; 6:9–10). No matter what the nature of one's temptation, God's expectation remains consistent—people should enjoy sex in the setting of heterosexual marriage, but in any other context they must abstain.

Fortunately, even bodies that have been misused can be "washed" and recommitted to the service of Christ (1 Cor. 6:11). Paul told his readers that they were to abstain from immorality (1 Thess. 4:3) and glorify God with their bodies (1 Cor. 6:20). We are to stop making our bodies instruments of sin, offering them instead to God as instruments of righteousness (Rom. 6:13; 12:1). In so doing, we are "putting to death the deeds of the body" and experiencing sanctification through the Spirit (6:19; 8:13).

The Christian ascetics who subjected their bodies to rigors in the service of Christ were driven not just by their desire for holiness but also by their anthropology. Many held to a Platonic dualism, which encouraged them to escape the confines and demands of their physical bodies. Others were actually driven by a more monistic belief. Tertullian, for example, believed that body and soul were so closely related that one could refine the soul by disciplining the body.[15] Both sides probably reflected the common Greek ideal of self-control. Believing that young men possess an inordinate amount of body heat, which causes the blood to boil into the foam of semen, they thought personal maturity corresponded with the ability to "keep the temperature down," as it were, and demonstrate self-control.

One of Augustine's lasting contributions is his firm reminder that our problem is not with youthful bodies, but with sinful hearts. We all desire physical pleasures, but our problem is more than physical. The body's desires can be satisfied either appropriately or inappropriately as it evidences the choices of the heart (Mark 7:15, 21–23). However, that does not mean the body itself is purely neutral. Under the control of sin, we grow accustomed, even addicted, to certain pleasures, developing a craving that is often both physical and emotional. One could even call it spiritual in a sense, because the addiction functions as an enslaving power.

We are complex people, and our sin has not been confined to a single aspect of our being. That means it would be wrong to think of our bodies (or their pleasures) as the source of evil or to see them as doing battle with the rest of us. We possess a dualistic nature, but those two parts live (and sin) together.

IMPLICATIONS

Looking back on this discussion, we see that the body should not be denied (as in monistic idealism), denigrated (as in Gnostic dualism), or dehumanized (as in monistic materialism). It should instead be treated with dignity as an important part of a whole person made in the image of God.

These mortal bodies of ours are weak and dependent on the Spirit of God for life. "For He Himself knows our frame; He is mindful that we are but dust. As for man, his days are like grass; as a flower of the field, so he flourishes. When the wind has passed over it, it is no more; and its place acknowledges it no longer" (Ps. 103:14–16).

These principles characterize both the rich and the poor, the powerful and the weak. The life of the wealthy businessman is just as fragile as that of the indigent, regardless of their relative access to healthcare. We live not by self-preservation, but by the grace of God. Our common nature may be frail, but it also carries inherent dignity. That means we should respect the bodies of all persons, even if they do not respect them themselves.

The Humanity of the Handicapped

The doctrine of the image of God demands that we treat all persons with respect, but we sometimes fail to do that because of an improper understanding of the body. As we have seen, people consist of more than just their bodies. However, our society often measures one's "quality of life" on the basis of physical ability. For example, a 1989 court case involved a man who had been paralyzed from the neck down in a motorcycle accident. He could breathe only by means of a ventilator, and he wanted the doctors in his nursing home to remove the machines and let him die. They would not do that, so he asked the courts to decide, and the judge ruled in his favor. In support of his decision, the judge wrote, "The ventilator to which he is attached is not prolonging his life; it is prolonging his death."

Joni Eareckson Tada responded appropriately when she wrote, "That made me, a disability advocate, steaming mad. If that judge had been approached by a poor minority woman who could no longer endure racism, sexism, and poverty, and she wanted to end her life painlessly, the woman would have been refused flat-out. In fact, rather than helping her escape her suffering, she would be offered support in seeking better housing and a job, and placed in a suicide-prevention program. But when a disabled person . . . declares the same intention, people assume he is acting rationally."[16]

As Tada added, rather than making it easier for the handicapped to die, we should try to make it easier for them to live. Karl Barth put it quite well.

A man who is not, or is no longer, capable of work, of earning, of enjoyment and even perhaps of communication, is not for this reason unfit to live, least of all because he cannot render to the state any notable or active contribution, but can only directly or indirectly become a burden to it. The value of this kind of life is God's secret. Those around and society as a whole may not find anything in it, but this does not mean that they have a right to reject and liquidate it. Who can really see the true and inward reality of this type of life? Who can really know whether it may not be far more precious in the eyes of God, or reveal itself as far more glorious in eternity, than the lives of hundreds of healthy workers and peasants, technicians, scientists, artists and soldiers, which the state rates so highly? . . . No community, whether family, village or state, is really strong if it will not carry its weak and even its very weakest members. They belong to it no less than the strong, and the quiet work of their maintenance and care, which might seem useless on a superficial view, is perhaps far more effective than common labour, culture or historical conflict in knitting it closely and securely together. On the other hand, a community which regards and treats its weak members as a hindrance, and even proceeds to their extermination, is on the verge of collapse.

89

The killing of the weak for the sake of others hampered by their weakness can rest only on a misconception of the life which in its specific form, and therefore even in its weakness, is always given by God and should therefore be an object of respect to others.[17]

Abortion

If, as some dualists seem to believe, our humanity is determined only by the immaterial aspect of our nature, then abortion could be justified by the belief that the material "blob of protoplasm" had not yet been joined by a human soul. We will consider the origin of the soul in the next chapter (I will argue that it is propagated along with the body and is therefore never "added"), but our understanding of the body provides a preliminary answer to this argument, one that does not depend on a particular view of ensoulment. In fact, a version of it could even be used by a materialist. Human nature, like the divine image, is seen not just in soul, but in body. That means that human bodies need to be respected, not killed.

As she latches on for the first time to her mother's breast, a newborn infant clearly has a human body. Her life situation has changed significantly since the day before, but she herself hasn't. She had a human body then too. What about the day before that? And the day before that? If we had a continuous videotape of her prenatal development, we would see that this same body has been there all along. It has changed, but nobody has exchanged it. It's the same body at different stages of development, and those stages would be imperceptible unless we played the videotape at high speed. Even if we watched more closely at the end of the eighth week to witness our subject's transition from "embryo" to "fetus," we would not see much of a difference. Every now and then we might think she looks just a little more like her mother, but that is not because new features were suddenly added. In fact, after the union of sperm and egg, nothing is added to the embryo to make it fundamentally different from what it became at that moment. After conception, each stage is just a short step from the one preceding it, and nothing changes in the basic makeup of the unborn baby. If that little girl's human body began at conception, that is when her parents and doctors should have begun treating her with dignity. From that point on, they should be committed to preserving her life, not ending it.

Not everybody sees it that way. One woman presented an interesting argument in a letter to a Dallas newspaper. Acknowledging that unborn babies are living humans, she wrote, "If a child is aborted, its soul goes to heaven. What's so awful about that?" Again, our theology of the body offers some insight. Our belief that someone is bound for heaven does not give us the right to kill him. God has commanded that we not commit murder, and that prohibition reflects the priority of His created ideal. He did not make us just for heaven; He made us for earthly life in its fullness—a bodily existence in which we glorify God and enjoy His blessings. To cut short the life of any individual is to preempt God's design.

It should go without saying that our appreciation for the dignity of humanity also extends beyond the womb. It includes pregnant women, single parents, those who have had abortions, and those whose family members have been victimized. I recall hearing a pro-choice political candidate say, "Unlike my opponent, I'm more concerned about people from birth to death than from conception to birth." But why should we have to choose one concern over the other? Our churches ought to work with crisis-pregnancy centers, postabortion counselors, maternity homes, adoption agencies, parent educators, social-service organizations, and other benevolent agencies to meet the needs of families and give young women a genuine alternative to abortion.

Birth Control

I have argued that physical pleasures are good when used according to God's design. On the basis of Genesis 1:28, one could say that sexuality is designed for the purpose of procreation. God created people and told them to be fruitful and multiply. If they specifically avoid multiplying, are they not violating God's intention?

Other biblical texts suggest that a sexual relationship between a husband and wife should be pleasurable. That is certainly the impression given by a literal reading of the Song of Solomon, and Paul sanctioned the marital satisfaction of sexual desires (1 Cor. 7:1–5). If sex is encouraged for both pleasure and procreation, the real question is whether both purposes must always be in view. Can couples satisfy God's design by primarily seeking pleasure in some encounters and procreation in others?

By answering that question affirmatively, I believe Christians can use birth control with a clean conscience. However, I do need to mention several cautions. First, couples need not reproduce to enjoy a godly marriage, but they should be open to the possibility that God will give them children (by birth or adoption). Since procreation is one of God's purposes in marriage, men and women should enter that relationship with the expectation that they will likely have children.

Second, certain types of birth control should be avoided. If human life begins with the union of sperm and egg, then those who use contraception should seek methods that will keep that from happening. Couples would do well to consult a doctor on this issue, but some methods, like intrauterine devices (IUD's) or "morning-after" pills will allow fertilization while avoiding pregnancy. By preventing the embryo from implanting on the uterine wall, they essentially cause an early abortion. Even birth-control pills have this potential. They are designed to prevent ovulation, but if ovulation and fertilization do happen to occur, "the pill" contains other drugs to prevent implantation.

Third, couples need to be in agreement on this issue. If a woman believes birth control is sinful, yet her husband insists on using it, she would feel compelled to confess the sin to God every time they had intercourse. In a case like that, the "stronger" believer, her husband in this case, should yield to the "weaker," rather than forcing her to sin against her conscience (Rom. 14:13–23; 1 Cor. 8:7–13).

Assisted Reproductive Technologies

If couples discover they are not likely to conceive children on their own, they will also need to agree regarding the potential use of assisted reproductive technologies (ARTs). Technology inevitably gives us more power than we are comfortable exercising, and it always has both helpful and frightening applications. New techniques will inevitably be developed, with researchers asking questions about whether they should have attempted them only after publishing the results of their attempts. In the case of ARTs the benefits are obvious. Infertility specialists often have pictures of babies all over the walls of their offices—babies who were conceived when their parents received some technological assistance. Many people fear, however, that such technologies encourage us to play God.

The natural conception of a child strikes us as the most private act in marriage. No wonder many bristle at the thought of a doctor assisting in that event as a "third party." However, I'm not convinced that it is inappropriate. The many Christian couples I've seen obtain medical help have done so out of deep devotion to one another, and their prayers, like Hannah's (1 Sam. 1:10–18), are directed toward the Lord, not the doctors. It can be frightening to see someone poised atop the slippery slope of technological possibility, but it is just as steep on the other side of the mountain, on the slope of technological denial. If we reject medical intervention in this area, when may we accept it? If treatments encouraging reproduction constitute "playing God," what about those treatments that delay death? Is God not sovereign over both?

In truth no one really "plays God." Only He exercises divine prerogatives. In His providence He has allowed us to do some remarkable things, but He is still the One who brings life into the world. No one can do that apart from Him. That truth does not make every method of assisted reproduction ethical, but it does help redefine the question, which does not concern the sacredness of the territory as much as it does the morality of the action. Having been commanded to multiply and exercise dominion (Gen. 1:28), we have the opportunity to exercise dominion over the way we multiply. The question concerns what we do with our opportunity.

Because the methods are so diverse, we should avoid any categorical acceptance or rejection of all assisted reproductive technologies. Couples need to consider each option separately, making wise choices on the basis of godly counsel and up-to-date medical information. Since this field changes so rapidly, that current information should come from medical specialists, not books. It would be inappropriate for me to assess the available procedures in this format. However, based on our understanding of the human body and the sanctity of life, we can affirm some general guidelines.

First, we need to avoid the excess endangerment or loss of human life. For example, some couples have had doctors create a dozen or more embryos by mixing their eggs and sperm in a culture dish. Since no woman could successfully carry that many embryos to term, they transfer only a few of them to her uterus while putting the rest in the freezer. If need be, those frozen embryos can later be thawed and introduced to the uterus.

We should probably stumble over those words, "if need be." Embryos that couples decide not to use are often simply discarded, and that constitutes a careless disregard for human life. If they are thawed, either for transfer to the mother or for donation to another couple, at the present time only about 50 percent survive that process. We will never be able to eliminate all risks to the survival of the unborn, but until that success rate changes, the freezing of embryos appears to put them at too much risk.

A second general guideline is that couples need to use doctors who are sympathetic to their convictions. In the case of in vitro fertilization and embryo transfer (described in the example above), many couples insist that no more embryos be created than the mother is actually willing and able to carry to term. Most doctors and clinics will gladly honor such requests.

Embryo and Fetal Tissue Research

Assisted reproductive technologies have become far more successful in recent years, largely through the efforts of talented researchers who develop new techniques on the heels of failure. This is where we run into the darker side of that most basic technological question—what is the price of progress?

Doctors may be able to hone their techniques by using animal embryos, but applying those methods to humans will always introduce some unknowns. A blanket ban on embryo research may inappropriately prevent the use of more advanced technologies still deemed "experimental." However, guidelines must be imposed to make sure embryos are treated as living human bodies, and care should be taken to avoid the excess endangerment of human life.

Fetal-tissue research confronts us with the same kind of double-edged sword. Doctors can treat debilitating diseases using chemicals retrieved from aborted fetuses, and that seems like a better idea than discarding (or burying) those bodies. However, we should oppose the use of fetal tissue in medicine for at least two reasons. First, the widespread use of that technology would further institutionalize the practice of abortion. Second, it would at least partially soothe the consciences of those obtaining abortions, convincing them that they were doing a good thing by providing for the improved health of others.

Cloning

Ever since British researchers successfully cloned an adult sheep in 1997, politicians and ethicists have been issuing statements against the application of that technology to humans. They are right to see a distinction between people and animals, for humans alone are made in the image of God, but naturalistic evolutionists will have a hard time holding that line for long. Already some legislators have suggested that researchers should be allowed to clone human embryos so long as they never actually implant them in a uterus—in other words, you can experiment with human life provided you also kill it—so the time will likely come when this technology will be used with people.

If that happens, the resulting human clones would not be soulless automatons. They would have exactly the same genetic material as their "originals" (it doesn't seem quite right to say "parents"), so they would be just like identical twins of varying age. They would have as much dignity as any other human, so it would be utterly irresponsible to think of them only as potential organ donors. Also like everyone else, they would consist of more than just physical bodies. They would be responsible people with a lifetime full of choices, not genetically determined robots.

That being said, human cloning would not necessarily be a good thing. There is such potential for abuse in this technology (for example, creating clones for organ donation or pursuing asexual reproduction) that it should not be pursued.

Organ Transplants

I have said that parts of my body can cease to be a part of *me*. If a shark were to eat one of my feet, the digested material would become part of his body, not mine. I would grieve the loss, but I would not be less human for it, and the shark would not receive characteristics of my personality. Some dual-aspect monists (Jehovah's Witnesses, for example) believe that the immaterial and material aspects of our nature are so inherently bound to one another that the transfer of blood or organs from one person to another also transfers attitudes, emotions, and personal idiosyncrasies. I'm not sure what they would say about sharks, but personalities are not transferred in either case.

Again, we can be separated from our bodies and remain ourselves, and our bodies can deteriorate or be digested without threatening our resurrection. That kind of dualism, which I believe is biblical, allows for the transplantation of organs from one person to another without fear that their personalities will be blended.

The transplantation of organs does present other ethical concerns, however. To keep from damaging the donated parts, doctors prefer to "harvest" them while they are still receiving oxygenated blood—that is, while the donor is still breathing and his heart is still beating. The problem, obviously, is that these are conventional signs of life. That is why organ transplantation generally relies on the principle of "brain death." In such cases the brain stem continues to maintain many bodily functions but the cerebral cortex is almost completely inactive. Since assessments of brain death are not purely objective, on occasion the removal of organs is the cause of death.

Such thoughts make us yearn for a simpler day, when the presence of breath provided an obvious sign of life. At the same time, knowing that people can sometimes be resuscitated after they stop breathing makes us appreciate more modern determinations of death, even if they sometimes make it difficult for us to recognize life's boundaries. I have friends whose infant daughter was described by doctors as "95 percent brain dead." She had had multiple surgeries and was kept breathing by a ventilator, but her condition was not improving. After losing any hope of recovery apart from a miracle, the parents eventually reached the painful decision to remove the machines. With tears all around the room, she lay dressed in white on her daddy's lap as the doctor removed the vent. Freed from the tubes, she took about half a breath and was gone. In retrospect, my friends say they are not really sure when she died. Was it that agonizing morning when they said good-bye, or was it weeks earlier, when most of her brain shut down after one of the surgeries? It is impossible to say.

Cases like that leave us all vulnerable to what has been called the "bearded-man fallacy." How much of a beard does a man have to have before we agree that he has one? Would a couple of ten-inch hairs dangling from his chin suffice? If not, how many more hairs would he need? What about someone who has to shave twice a day? Does he have a beard by dinnertime? If we linger too long on such borderline examples, we may eventually convince ourselves we do not know exactly what a beard is, and we may be unwilling to say whether a man has one. I would suggest that we can usually tell. In the same way we will usually know when death has occurred or when a life might still be saved. In those instances when we are not sure, we should err on the side of life.

Another controversial issue relating to organ transplants concerns the fact that certain animal organs can be transplanted into people. Many were shocked when doctors placed a baboon's heart into a child, but it is difficult to think of good reasons why they should not have been able to do that. Animal-rights activists protested vigorously because the baboon was killed in the procedure, but the fact that a human life was saved (at least for a while) certainly justifies that action. (Some would call me a "species-ist" for that comment, but isn't that what Psalm 8 teaches?) Setting aside concerns about the life of the donor, what is wrong with humans receiving animal organs? It does not seem different from using prescription drugs derived from their bodies (insulin, for example), and it is no more dehumanizing than using mechanical substitutes (like artificial hearts). In fact, it recognizes that organs made by God work better than ones that are made by hand.

Assisted Suicide and Euthanasia

After all that has been said to this point, I probably don't need to specify too many implications with regard to euthanasia. There is a difference between preserving life and prolonging the process of dying. We seek the former, and not the latter.

There is yet another difference between accepting the inevitability of death and causing death. Again we seek the former, and not the latter. We should try to make people comfortable, and sometimes those same actions may hasten the inevitable. Painkillers, for example, may also slow the respiratory rate, making it more difficult to keep fluid out of the lungs. However, such methods should always be intended to bring relief, not death.

Some people seek to find relief in death, and that presents another problem. Should physicians or family members cooperate when asked to help someone commit suicide? The recent national debate over assisted suicide has often treated it as a distinct act, neither murder nor suicide. In actual fact, it is both murder and suicide. Two people conspire to kill someone. One seeks to kill herself, and that is suicide. The other seeks to kill someone other than himself, and that is murder. As noted in our discussion of handicapped persons, suicidal people need our help—not in committing suicide, but in *not* committing suicide.

Capital Punishment

Many observers wonder why so many pro-lifers favor the death penalty. Aren't these positions incompatible? The biblical text most often used to support capital punishment seems to resolve that problem. "Whoever sheds man's blood, by man his blood shall be shed, for in the image of God He made man" (Gen. 9:6). Life is so valuable that the penalty for taking it is death.

The biblical text justifies the possibility of capital punishment, but it also establishes a pattern for its application. Numbers 35:30 stipulates that no murderer be put to death without the testimony of two or more eyewitnesses, a more exacting criterion than the American judicial standard of reasonable doubt. Apart from that standard, one must ask whether the penalty can be applied consistently and fairly. Some judges and prosecutors are much more likely than others to file capital murder charges, especially against non-Caucasian defendants. Further, no matter what the color of their skin, defendants are many times more likely to be convicted of capital murder if the victim was Caucasian than if the victim was non-Caucasian. That kind of disparity suggests that we are not altogether fair in our application of the death penalty. While we have the right to use it, we should not do so as long as these inequities exist.

The Treatment of Dead Bodies

Our understanding of the body does not favor one method of disposing of human corpses over another, but it does suggest that dead bodies should be treated with respect. The resurrection will occur just as completely with cremation as with interment in sealed vaults, and the sea will give up its dead just as readily as will the dry ground (Rev. 20:13). The Romans did shift from cremation to burial about the time Christian influence was strong, but that change may have been unrelated to the spread of Christianity. Believers have practiced all kinds of burial practices over the centuries, and there seems to be no distinctively Christian method.

Medical schools have long profited from the use of human cadavers. Since the careful study of the human body helps young doctors develop an appreciation for its marvelous design and ultimately contributes to better care for the living, this practice seems justified. However, the bodies should always be handled with reverence for the life that was led through them.

Cosmetic Surgery

It is difficult to find much biblical justification for all the attention we give to our appearance (or, for that matter, to our self-esteem). The Bible does not regard attractiveness as a flaw, but it is not so important as we think. David was apparently handsome (1 Sam. 16:12, 18), but God was much more interested in his heart (16:7). Likewise, Paul and Peter instructed their readers to be more concerned with the cultivation of their character than the adornment of their bodies (1 Tim. 2:9–10; 4:8; 1 Pet. 3:3–4). We need that reminder today as the media surrounds us with images (and expectations) of physical perfection.

Not all cosmetic surgery reflects misplaced priorities, but the ability to change one's appearance is another of those technological gifts that sits unopened in our living room while we try to figure out whether it came from God or the Devil. Maybe it is best to say that this gift is like the body itself—it can be used for good or evil, depending on the heart of the one using it.

5

The Immaterial Aspect of Human Nature

A PORTION OF THE PREVIOUS CHAPTER attempted to demonstrate that each of us consists of more than a physical body. There is an immaterial part of our being that survives death and (in the case of believers) consciously enters the presence of Christ to await the resurrection. I occasionally referred to this as the "soul," following common usage, and I tended to avoid some of the other expressions found in the biblical text—for example, the human spirit (distinguished from the animating breath of God), the heart, the mind, and the "kidneys." This chapter seeks to clarify that terminology and fill in some of the details about our composition as humans.

Just as our discussion of the body had many implications with regard to bioethical issues, this examination of biblical "psychology" affects the way we approach counseling and personal sanctification. Unfortunately, many of the evangelical resources addressing those topics assume models of human nature that are overly simplistic and biblically indefensible. Such faulty foundations often lead to complex and confusing models of the spiritual life. Ironically a more complex (and more biblically accurate) model of human nature yields a much simpler approach to spirituality. To see that difference, we need to begin by considering some of the suggested models.

HOW MANY PARTS DO WE HAVE?

In the last chapter we looked at monistic and dualistic understandings of human nature to determine whether people consist of more than just bodies. That debate is conducted even among non-Christians in areas like philosophy and brain physiology. This chapter introduces a few more models, all of which are essentially forms of dualism because they agree that our material and immaterial aspects are separated at death. The debate over these alternatives is generally confined to the church, and it focuses on the meaning of biblical language.

Paul wrote, "Now may the God of peace Himself sanctify you entirely; and may your spirit and soul and body be preserved complete, without blame at the coming of our Lord Jesus Christ" (1 Thess. 5:23). Many regard this as a straightforward description of human nature. As they see it, Paul desired his readers' entire sanctification, so he mentioned spirit, soul, and body, the three component parts of an individual. This *trichotomous* ("three-part") view can be described in a variety of ways.

Some say that plants consist only of body, an animal of body and soul, and humans of body, soul, and spirit. From this perspective, the soul provides physical life and ceases to exist at death (as in animals), while the spirit (with its rational abilities and immortal life) survives and awaits reunification with the body. A different version of this argument maintains that Adam's spirit died as a result of the Fall, leaving him like an animal. Believers then receive a new spirit (or their spirit comes alive) at regeneration. Another trichotomous model regards the mind as part of the soul (along with emotion and will). From this perspective, the spirit provides God-consciousness, the soul self-consciousness, and the body world-consciousness. The three elements thus represent the spiritual, psychological, and physiological aspects of our humanity.

Such models may look nice on charts for weekend seminars, and they seem to summarize some important points very plainly, but they posit a sharp distinction between "soul" and "spirit" that cannot be justified biblically. When Mary said, "My soul exalts the Lord, and my spirit has rejoiced in God my Savior" (Luke 1:46–47), she was not talking about two different entities within her any more than she was praising two different Gods.

She was using the Hebrew poetical pattern of synonymous parallelism, and she understood "soul" and "spirit" to be different expressions for essentially the same thing—her immaterial being. Similar examples can be multiplied. For example, Job said, "I will speak in the anguish of my spirit, I will complain in the bitterness of my soul" (Job 7:11), and Isaiah wrote, "At night my soul longs for Thee, indeed, my spirit within me seeks Thee diligently" (Isa. 26:9).

Other texts use only one term or the other, but comparing them produces direct parallels. Genesis describes Rachel's death as the departure of her "soul" (Gen. 35:18), but Stephen asked the Lord to receive his "spirit" (Acts 7:59; see also Luke 23:46). Jesus spoke of people consisting of "body and soul" (Matt. 10:28), but Paul spoke of "body and spirit" (1 Cor. 7:34; see 5:3–5; 2 Cor. 7:1). Jesus said His "soul" was troubled as He neared the cross (John 12:27), but John described it as His "spirit" (13:21). Hebrews speaks of "the spirits of righteous men made perfect" in God's presence (12:23), but Revelation pictures their "souls" (Rev. 6:9; 20:4). If the terms are not interchangeable, they at least appear to be referring to the same thing—the immaterial part of a person, which departs the body at death.

The trichotomists also describe the functions of "spirit" and "soul" too distinctively. It is inappropriate to describe the soul as the principle of physical life and the spirit as the principle of spiritual life when they overlap in so many ways. The "soul" can have sinful desires and be purified (1 Pet. 1:22; Rev. 18:14), but so can the "spirit" (2 Cor. 7:1; Ps. 78:8). Mind, emotion, and will cannot be confined to the "soul," for these things are also experienced by the "spirit" (Mark 2:8; John 13:21; Acts 17:16; 1 Cor. 2:11). In the same way, worship is not the sole domain of the "spirit," for it is also enjoyed by the "soul" (Ps. 103:1; see also 62:1; 146:1; Mark 12:30). In light of such texts Wayne Grudem rightly asked, "What can the spirit do that the soul cannot do? What can the soul do that the spirit cannot do?"[1]

Even if they admit that they have only speculated about the ways in which spirit and soul differ, trichotomists want explanations for passages that suggest the difference is real. At the top of their list would be 1 Thessalonians 5:23, which we have yet to address, and Hebrews 4:12, which reads, "For the word of God is living and active and sharper than any two-edged sword, and piercing as far as the division of soul and spirit, of both joints and marrow, and able to judge the thoughts and intentions of the heart." Why would this verse speak of dividing soul and spirit if they were not divisible? In the same way, why would Paul imply that his spirit and his mind could be separated (1 Cor. 14:14), if in fact they are the same?

To understand Paul's statement in 1 Thessalonians 5:23, which describes sanctification taking place in spirit, soul, and body, we need to recognize that other verses speak of the whole person using different terms. Mark 12:30, in which Jesus quoted the great commandment, reads, "You shall love the Lord your God with all your heart, and with all your soul, and with all your mind, and with all your strength." Do we consist of four parts—heart, soul, mind, and body (strength)? Or is it five, adding spirit? Matthew 22:37 has a similar quotation, but strength is not included. "You shall love the Lord your God with all your heart, and with all your soul, and with all your mind." Are we down to three again? If so, which three?

Obviously, such questions do not provide the basis for Paul's exhortation. His point, like that of Jesus, is clear. By multiplying the terms used to refer to the human person, he meant, "Love God with your entire being. Be sanctified through and through. Don't be content with partial commitment or a lackadaisical spiritual life."

In Hebrews 4:12 the author was describing Scripture's ability to pierce through appearances and judge a person's heart. The spirit is not being divided from the soul any more than the joints are divided from the marrow. Both spirit and soul are sliced down the middle, and the bones—joints, marrow, and all—have been split apart. The individual has been opened up, and all that had been hidden has been placed on display like the inside of a filleted fish. Consequently "all things are open and laid bare to the eyes of Him with whom we have to do" (4:13).

Regarding 1 Corinthians 14:14, the fact that Paul experienced something in his spirit that he did not understand in his mind does not mean that spirit and mind (much less spirit and soul) are distinct entities. He simply meant he did not comprehend the words he uttered through the gift of tongues unless they were translated for him. The experience was still beneficial as Paul was refreshed by the demonstrable presence of God's

Spirit, but he desired to be encouraged by the message itself, so he preferred interpretation. By describing this as a blessing received only in the spirit, Paul used the same sort of expression we employ ourselves. When we want to communicate, "I really want to go with you, but I know I should stay home," we might say, "My heart says, 'Go,' but my head says, 'Stay.'" These expressions don't imply that the head and the heart are distinct entities or that the will is located separately from the emotions. They simply mean that we find ourselves torn by conflicting desires. In the same way, Paul described an activity of limited benefit by saying that it aided only part of his being, but that does not mean he regarded that "part" as distinct and separable.

Since so many verses seem to treat soul and spirit interchangeably while so little evidence suggests that they are distinct, most theologians have preferred a *dichotomous* ("two-part") model of humanity. Unfortunately many have understood that to mean that terms like "spirit," "soul," "heart," and "mind" function as simple synonyms, all describing the same thing. They may all denote the same entity—the immaterial part of a person—but that does not mean they all communicate the same idea. Each term had its own field of meaning and its own connotations, so the different words were often used with different emphases. And in fact we use language the same way.

A SURVEY OF BIBLICAL TERMS

One Saturday I sat down at my desk to do some writing while the house was still quiet. I was well refreshed from a good night's sleep, and I faced the day rather lightheartedly, ready to do a little work before getting on to other plans. My wife, Julie, and I were headed to a concert later in the morning, and that sounded like fun. It would be an afternoon and evening filled with country music, which I don't always like, but the tickets were free and so was the baby-sitter, so the day promised delight for the soul! If I could get in a little writing first, it would be that much better.

Sometimes it doesn't take much of a hardship to ruin a nice morning.

In place of its usual "desktop," the screen on my computer displayed nothing but vertical lines, and the sight hit me like a hard kick in the gut.

My spirit sank with the realization that not only would I not be able to write that morning, but if I couldn't access any files, I might lose the work I had done the night before. Repeated restarts didn't make things any better, and my heart began to race as frustration bordered on panic. Every breath became a sigh, and I squirmed in my seat each time the dreaded vertical lines reappeared. I might have raised a hand against it, but I don't know enough about computers to know where a hard slap would help, so I just put it away.

I tried to do some reading, but my mind was too preoccupied to concentrate very well. On the way to the concert, Julie tried to lift my spirits by making pleasant conversation, but that didn't help that nauseous feeling in my stomach. I knew in my heart that the problem wasn't irresolvable, and I reminded myself that it was ridiculously minor compared to the struggles of others, whose souls are in peril every day. Still, it was hard to put on a happy face in spite of the fact that it pained my conscience to feel depressed for something so small. Julie prayed that God would encourage me, and I started to think about getting access to a different computer. By the time we got to the concert, I was much less melancholy, contented enough that I could actually enjoy songs about homesick cowboys and broken hearts.

That story is true, but it's completely irrelevant to our topic. What is relevant, probably too obviously, is the way I told it. I described my feelings using words like "soul," "heart," "spirit," "mind," "conscience," "gut," and "breath" much the same way as they are used in the Scriptures. I even spoke of feeling "melancholy," a word which calls to mind the ancient Greek notion that human emotions are governed by competing "humors," substances associated with different organs. Phlegm, the clear mucus secreted in the respiratory passages, produced the "phlegmatic" temperament—sluggish and impassive, not unlike the way one feels when troubled by the common cold. When blood was the prevailing humor, it yielded a "sanguine" personality—cheerful and colorful, full of life. Yellow bile (choler), secreted by the liver, made one "choleric"—irritable and easily moved to anger. The spleen could produce this as well. Even today, to "vent one's spleen" is to release pent-up anger. Along with the kidneys, the spleen also produced the fourth humor, black bile, which yielded a melancholic temperament—sad and depressed.

The Hebrews, too, associated emotions with bodily organs, but not as specifically. For them, outward emotions and behaviors were linked to "inner" inclinations which were described in the picturesque language of one's inner organs. Those organs, like the limbs of one's body, could be oriented in one direction or another. One's "heart" could be inclined toward good or evil, and one's "breath" (or "spirit") could reflect excitement or despair. We use similar expressions (as my story about the computer tried to demonstrate), but we don't always recognize the earthy connections that helped them make sense in their original context. The next several pages attempt to restore those connections, examining the appropriate biblical terms and their meanings.

Soul

In the Old Testament the English word "soul" usually translates the Hebrew *nepeš* . Like the words for "spirit" encountered in the last chapter (*rûaḥ* and *pneuma*), *nepeš* is associated with breathing, especially in its verbal form. As a noun, it often refers to living (i.e., breathing) beings, describing both animals and people as "living *nepeš* " (Gen. 1:30; 2:7, 19). The Old Testament applies that label to people so frequently that *nepeš* often means nothing more than "person." In fact it even refers to *dead* persons in several places (e.g., Num. 6:6; 19:13), but that is more rare, because *nepeš* usually retains the idea that this person is a living, breathing creature.

Our English Bibles often translate *nepeš* as "person," but most frequently they use "life." That makes sense considering the fact that the threat of death places one's *nepeš* under attack. If the threatened one is delivered, the *nepeš* has been spared—his "soul" (or "life") has been saved. Those who sought to kill Moses were seeking his *nepeš* (Exod. 4:19), and Abram asked his wife to pose as his sister "that my *nepeš* may live on account of you" (Gen. 12:13). When Sodom was destroyed, the angels told Lot, "Escape for your *nepeš*" (19:17), and he asked for immediate refuge "that my *nepeš* may live" (19:20). The sacrifices of the Law protected the Israelites from death, constituting a ransom or atonement for their *nepeš*. (Exod. 30:12, 15; Num. 15:28). Leviticus 17:11 makes the relationship clear—it is the sacrifice of the animal's *nepeš* for the *nepeš* of the worshiper. "For the *nepeš* of the flesh is in the blood, and I have given it to you on the altar to make atonement for your *nepeš*; for it is the blood by reason of the *nepeš* that makes atonement." When the blood of the sacrifice was poured out, its life, its *nepeš*, was given that the life of the worshiper might be spared. Isaiah 53:10–12 uses this language while looking ahead to the death of Christ. "But the LORD was pleased to crush Him, putting Him to grief; if He would render His *nepeš* a guilt offering, He will see His offspring, He will prolong His days, and the good pleasure of the LORD will prosper in His hand. As a result of the anguish of His *nepeš*, He will see it and be satisfied. . . . Because He poured out His *nepeš* to death, and was numbered with the transgressors; yet He Himself bore the sin of many, and interceded for the transgressors."

Jesus gave His life that we might have life, His "soul" that ours might be saved. This exchange provides the ultimate answer to the prayer of the psalmist, who asked the Lord to redeem his *nepeš* (Pss. 69:18; 72:14). Hoping that his life would be spared, he may not have had much more in mind than immediate deliverance from his threatening enemies. Christ, however, provided a way for one's *nepeš* to live forever.

Life demands certain basic necessities, so the *nepeš* naturally desires such things as food, water, and rest. God's provision of these needs brings satisfaction to the "soul." "They were hungry and thirsty; their soul [*nepeš*] fainted within them. Then they cried out to the LORD in their trouble; He delivered them out of their distresses. He led them also by a straight way, to go to an inhabited city. Let them give thanks to the LORD for His lovingkindness, and for His wonders to the sons of men! For He has satisfied the thirsty soul [*nepeš*], and the hungry soul [*nepeš*] He has filled with what is good" (Ps. 107:5–9). When praising the LORD for such material benefits, the psalmist very appropriately said, "Bless the LORD, O my . soul [*nepeš*]" (Ps. 103:1). He is the one who "heals all your diseases; who redeems your life [*nepeš*] from the pit; . . . who satisfies your years with good things, so that your youth is renewed like the eagle" (103:3–5).

True life consists of more than such elemental needs, as the Lord frequently reminds us (Deut 8:3; Isa. 55:1–3; Luke 12:15). For this reason the *nepeš* is associated with more than just physical survival. Even in Psalm 103:3–4, the soul is also commanded to offer praise for the fact that the LORD "pardons all your iniquities" and "crowns you with lovingkindness and compassion." This more abstract use of *nepeš*, in which it does not just mean "person" or "life," but seems to denote one's very being, can also be seen in Genesis 27, where Jacob and Esau contended for the blessing of their father's "soul" (vv. 4, 19, 25). In the same way, one's *nepeš* can cling to that of another person, so that one's life or being becomes dependent on the other. Joseph's brothers meant this quite literally—they were afraid to tell their father that something had happened to Benjamin because they thought the news could kill the old man, and they said, "his *nepeš* is bound to the lad's *nepeš*" (44:30). This is also the language of love letters and romance ballads, but in those cases the dependence of one's soul on another is more figurative (34:3). People today speak of "soul-mates," and that is approximately the same idea— there is a dependent connection between them that extends to the depth of their being.

Many passages of Scripture relate this concept of "soul" to our relationship with God. You might say He wants to be our soulmate. Linking the soul to the "heart," as the core of one's being, He commands His people to love and serve Him "with all your heart and all your *nepeš*" (Deut. 11:13; 13:3; Josh. 22:5; also see Mark 12:30). Nothing is to be held back in our devotion. Likewise, *God's* soul, *His* being, "delights" in His Servant (Isa. 42:1), but "has no pleasure" in those who shrink back from obedience (Heb. 10:38; also see Lev. 26:30; Isa. 1:14).

As one's being, the *nepeš* demonstrates choices ("If it is your *nepeš* for me to bury my dead," Gen. 23:8); desires ("You may spend the money for whatever your *nepeš* desires," Deut. 14:26); and emotions ("My *nepeš* is in despair within me," Ps. 42:6). Further, it can sin ("the sin of my *nepeš*;" Mic. 6:7; see Hab. 2:4), be in distress (Gen. 42:21; see Mark 14:34), or worship ("Praise the LORD, O my *nepeš*" Ps. 146:1). It should go without saying that those are all things that *I* do. My *nepeš*, my "soul," is *me*. It is my life, my being, and its desires, emotions, and commitments, are *my* desires, emotions, and commitments. When God tells us to love Him with all our souls, He means that we are to be devoted to Him with all our being.

The Old Testament does not dwell at length on the topic of life after death, perhaps because Israel's sense of justice and blessing was primarily land-based until about the time of the Exile, when revelation concerning the righteous remnant brought individual (and eternal) justice more into focus. In the same way, the Israelites associated *nepeš* so closely with life (and its salvation with temporal deliverance from one's enemies) that they did not comprehend the "eternal salvation of the soul" as clearly as we do. Still, even if texts describing the deliverance of the *nepeš* from Sheol speak primarily of escape from physical death (Pss. 30:3; 49:15; 86:13; 89:48; Prov. 23:14), others do seem to assume the separability of soul and body. Genesis 35:18 mentions the departure of Rachel's *nepeš* at death, and 1 Kings 17:21–22 describes the resurrection of the widow's son as the return of his *nepeš*. The word may mean nothing more than "life" in either passage, but *nepeš* so often includes a sense of personal identity that here the departure of oneself from the body cannot be ruled out. The same may be said of Job 11:20 and Jeremiah 15:9, which speak of the "breathing out of the *nepeš* " at death.

In the New Testament the word "soul" usually translates the Greek word *psychē*, which has much the same range of meaning as the Hebrew *nepeš*. It speaks of one's life; when Eutychus fell from the window, the others were relieved to hear Paul say, "his *psychē* is [still] in him" (Acts 20:10). As in the Old Testament, one life can be substituted for another in sacrifice. Jesus said, "The Son of Man did not come to be served, but to serve, and to give His *psychē* a ransom for many" (Matt. 20:28). John, too, wrote, "We know love by this, that He laid down His *psychē* for us; and we ought to lay down our *psychē* for the brethren" (1 John 3:16). Like *nepeš*, this word can refer simply to persons, as it likely does in Acts 2:41, 43 (where people are added to the church, not just immaterial souls), or it can describe the interior self. The *psychē* experiences emotions ("a sword will pierce even your own *psychē*," Luke 2:35), worships ("my *psychē* exalts the Lord," 1:46), and makes moral choices ("strengthening the *psychē* of the disciples," Acts 14:22). Believers are told to love the Lord with their whole heart and *psychē* (Mark 12:30).

The New Testament has clear statements about the afterlife, and some of these describe it as the separation of soul and body. Matthew 10:28 reads, "And do not fear those who kill the body, but are unable to kill the *psychē* ; but rather fear Him who is able to destroy both *psychē* and body in hell." Conversely, Revelation 6:9 mentions the conscious, heavenly existence of the *psychē* in the intermediate state.

Even though it can be distinguished from the body in some texts, the *psychē*, *nepeš*, or "soul" commonly describes the totality of one's being. It should never be treated as a distinct entity among several others in human nature. Its centrality can be seen in Proverbs 2:10–11, where both "soul" and "heart" are simply interchangeable with "you": "For wisdom will enter your heart, and knowledge will be pleasant to your soul [*nepeš*]; discretion will guard you, understanding will watch over you."

Unless the Lord returns first, death will one day separate you from your body. Your survivors will treat it with respect for what it was, but that body will not be a part of you again until the resurrection. Nothing like that can be said of the soul. It is not a part of you from which you can be separated. It is you. So is the spirit—but that's another story.

Spirit

Every Friday afternoon during football season, the snare drums of our high-school band signaled the beginning of a pep rally in the gymnasium. Intended to raise our excitement about that night's game, the rally usually consisted of a skit poking fun at the opposing team, some rousing cheers, a few words from the football coach, and the singing of the school fight song. Occasionally the cheerleaders would try to raise the decibel level by appealing to our competitive nature. Turning to one side of the crowded bleachers, they would call out, "We've got spirit! Yes, we do! We've got spirit! How 'bout you?" The students would shout it back to their peers on the other side of the room, and they would go back and forth until one group or the other felt they had shown themselves to be the loudest. "We've got spirit! Yes, we do! We've got spirit! How 'bout you?"

Late in the year, all the department stores play holiday music, prepare elaborate displays, and host special events for the enjoyment of Christmas shoppers. They know that customers delighting in the season will probably buy more gifts than those feeling grumpy, so retailers do their best to nurture "the spirit of Christmas."

Those who gamble on horse racing try to determine which thorough-bred has the most spirit, and Americans cheer fireworks every Fourth of July to celebrate "the spirit of 1776." A particularly kind person might be described as having a sweet or gentle spirit, but someone with the opposite personality is mean-spirited. Such things don't have to be permanent, for our spirits can be broken or revived. Likewise, they can be sad, cheerful, high, or low.

The biblical writers also used the word "spirit" in many different ways, so many that one scholar said the varied use of this term "almost defies analysis."[2] Its basic meaning is "moving air"—"wind" or "breath." The *rûah* as the life-giving Spirit of God animates all of creation. However, the concept broadens to include the breath that we have as a consequence of His breath and the various winds that move us as we conduct our affairs.

God gives life and breath to every creature through His animating Spirit. That breath then provides an indication not only of the presence or absence of life, but also of its fervor. When someone is sad, his breath becomes shallow or is filled with sighs. The psalmist said that his spirit had been overwhelmed and was failing (Pss. 142:3; 143:4, 7). Encouragement or refreshment then restores the spirit. When Jacob heard that Joseph was still alive, he was stunned (literally, his heart grew numb, Gen. 45:26). When they showed the old man the wagons Joseph had sent, his spirit revived (45:27). His breath returned with vigor as he was encouraged by the news. In the same way, when Samson had grown fatigued, his spirit returned after a long drink of water (Judg. 15:19; see also 1 Sam. 30:12).

The breath also provides an indication of one's emotions. The Old Testament writers described anger as a hot flaring of the nostrils. Similarly, a patient person was "long in breath," breathing evenly, while an impatient person was short in breath, clearly agitated (Prov. 14:29). An even-tempered person "ruled his spirit" (16:32), while one whose spirit was without restraint needed to be avoided (25:28). The spirit could be sorrowful (1 Sam. 1:15), anguished (Exod. 6:9), or broken (Prov. 17:22), rendering someone quiet or even inactive. It could then be refreshed (1 Cor. 16:18; 2 Cor. 7:13) and fervent (Rom. 12:11), leading to ongoing service. ("We've got spirit! Yes, we do! We've got spirit! How 'bout you?") Describing another emotion, the writer of 1 Kings said that when the queen of Sheba saw all of Solomon's wealth, "there was no more spirit in her"—it took her breath away (1 Kings 10:5).

When one's spirit is at peace, like the breath in slumber, one is content. However, when one's spirit is restless, sleep and contentment become impossible (Dan. 2:1), and some kind of change is bound to occur. When God moved kings or armies, He "stirred up their spirit" and moved them to action (1 Chron. 5:26; 2 Chron. 36:22).

Thus the breath is not just an outward expression of emotion; it functions as a moving internal influence. A "spirit of jealousy" compels one to distrust (Num. 5:14, 30); a "haughty spirit" is synonymous with pride (Prov. 16:18); and a "spirit of harlotry" led Israel astray (Hos. 4:12; 5:4). This sense of "spirit," in which it represents a compelling inner tendency or emotion, can be hard to distinguish from the use of the same word in reference to personal spirits or demons (1 Sam. 16:14–16; Mark 9:17). In most passages the difference may not be very important, as either kind of "spirit" highlights one's hardness toward God while not discounting responsibility for one's actions.

Likewise, the more positive sorts of "spirits" are often difficult to distinguish from the Spirit of God. He specially gifts people with wisdom, understanding, knowledge, and skill (Exod. 31:3; 35:31; Isa. 11:2; Eph. 1:17), and His presence brings a "spirit of gentleness" (1 Cor. 4:21; Gal. 6:1). By the Spirit of God we are "renewed in the spirit of [our] minds" (Eph. 4:23), and He is no doubt the source of the psalmist's contrite, right, willing, and broken spirit (Pss. 34:18; 51:10, 12, 17). It is probably in this sense that the "spirit of Elijah" rested on Elisha (2 Kings 2:15) and God took "of the Spirit who was upon Moses" and gifted the seventy elders (Num. 11:25). The presence of God's Spirit yields certain gifts and tendencies that can be re-created by His presence in others. This also explains the "new spirit" and "new heart" promised in the New Covenant through the indwelling of the Spirit (Ezek. 36:26–27). The Holy Spirit as God's animating breath brings life and breath to all creation, but He also moves God's people with a compelling inner influence (the new spirit and new heart) and gives them an everlasting relationship with God by His presence (eternal life in regeneration). God's Spirit thus brings assurance to the spirits of believers (Rom. 8:16), but the spirits of others He will cut off (Ps. 76:12). That is why Paul's familiar benediction states, "The grace of the Lord Jesus Christ be with your spirit" (Phil. 4:23; see also Gal. 6:18; 2 Tim. 4:22; Philem. 1:25).

By speaking of the spirit as a moving influence, I do not mean to give the impression that it is somehow distinct from the "real me." We have already seen substantial overlap between the spirit and the soul, and Paul said that only the spirit knows the true thoughts of an individual (1 Cor. 2:11), perhaps because the breath was thought to flow throughout the body (Prov. 20:27). In this sense the spirit also shares much in common with the "heart." It perceives (Mark 2:8), worships (Luke 1:47; 1 Cor. 14:14–15), and demonstrates willful intentions (Matt. 26:41), and the two words are often used in parallel ("my spirit is overwhelmed within me; my heart is appalled within me," Ps. 143:4; see also Deut. 2:30; Ps. 51:10; Isa. 57:15). Since the breath is more visible, it might be appropriate to regard the spirit as the expression of desires and thoughts that are rooted in the heart.

In summary, we use "spirit" in much the same way as the Bible does. We have lost the foundational idea of breath, but we still think of spirit in terms of emotions or tendencies (good or bad), and relate it to life and the vigor with which we express ourselves. We recognize the reality of evil spirits, but we don't confuse that meaning of the word with the others, even if we don't know which kind of spirit causes someone's misbehavior. Finally, we don't usually attempt to distinguish between our spirit and ourselves—the spirit may change like our moods, but it's part of who we are.

Heart

If you had some difficulty understanding the Hebrew idea of breath, it may revive your spirit to know that the concept of "heart" is much easier to grasp. From country songs to love letters and valentines, we speak of the heart in almost exactly the same way as did the biblical writers. We describe others as good-hearted, cold-hearted, soft-hearted, hardhearted, or brokenhearted. We give our hearts to others in love, and our hearts ache when love is lost. We set our hearts on things we want, guard them against things we want to avoid, and turn them away from things we no longer desire. In our hearts we feel emotions, ponder questions, remember events, and make plans. Our hearts may not be as pure as those of the biblical writers, but at least we have the same vocabulary.

It is surprising that traditional models of human nature commonly employ the terms "soul" and "spirit" but leave out the heart, which the Bible mentions more frequently. As the physical organ hidden deep within the chest, the heart is that part of a person that is both central and unreachable. On this point Bruce Waltke wrote, "The hiddenness and inaccessibility of the physical heart give rise to its figurative sense for anything that is remote and inaccessible. The 'heart of the seas' (Jon. 2:3) refers to the sea's fathomless, unapproachable depths and the 'heart of the heavens' is its most unreachable height."[3]

Because it is so inaccessible, the contents of the heart cannot be seen by other persons. We describe some people as especially "transparent," meaning they are very "open" about their thoughts and feelings. Both expressions imply unhindered access to the heart. As the seat of emotion, understanding, will, and conscience, the heart is the center of one's being, the source of all thoughts and behavior.

The heart can produce belief or rebellion (Rom 6:17; Ps. 14:1); integrity or corruption (101:1–5); obedience or obstinance (Heb. 3:12–15). It can be enlightened or blinded (Eph. 1:18, 2 Cor. 3:15); arrogant or humble (Isa. 9:9; Matt. 11:29). It can be fearful (Isa. 21:4; 35:4), astonished (Deut. 28:28), gladdened (Deut. 28:47), or joyful (Ps. 16:9). It can be inclined toward evil or good (Gen. 6:5; Deut. 10:12; Josh. 24:23; Jer. 17:9), demonstrating pride or humility (Deut. 8:14; 2 Kings 22:19). Many of these things can be observed by others, and behavior (more accurately than profession) reveals the inclination of one's heart. Still, we all try to look better than we know our hearts to be, and those who don't know us well might believe the facade. God is never deceived by false virtue or impressed by physical appearances, for He "looks at the heart" (1 Sam. 16:7). Jesus said, "You are those who justify yourselves in the sight of men, but God knows your hearts; for that which is highly esteemed among men is detestable in the sight of God" (Luke 16:15). Even when people continue to praise Him, He knows when their hearts have turned away (Isa. 29:13), and that makes His judgment truly fair (Rev. 2:23).

Depending on what is in our hearts, God's knowledge of their contents can be threatening or encouraging. When falsely accused by others, it is very reassuring to know that God knows our hearts. Paul took comfort in His judgment in such instances, writing, "as we have been approved by God to be entrusted with the gospel, so we speak, not as pleasing men, but God, who examines our hearts" (1 Thess. 2:4). The psalmist also invited His inspection ("Search me, O God, and know my heart," Ps. 139:23), but at times we may not want our hearts on display. Denying both His understanding and our own sinfulness, we often try to conceal our iniquity, making ourselves appear righteous when in our hearts we know better.

Obviously such attempts are futile. The day will come when the Lord will "both bring to light the things hidden in the darkness and disclose the motives of men's hearts; and then each man's praise will come to him from God" (1 Cor. 4:5). It's no use pretending He doesn't know. "For the word of God is living and active and sharper than any two-edged sword, and piercing as far as the division of soul and spirit, of both joints and marrow, and able to judge the thoughts and intentions of the heart. And there is no creature hidden from His sight, but all things are open and laid bare to the eyes of Him with whom we have to do" (Heb. 4:12–13).

When His word exposes our sinfulness, the proper response is, of course, to seek forgiveness. David wrote, "How blessed is he whose transgression is forgiven, whose sin is covered. . . . When I kept silent about my sin, my body wasted away through my groaning all day long. For day and night Thy hand was heavy upon me. . . . I acknowledged my sin to Thee, and my iniquity I did not hide; I said, 'I will confess my transgressions to the Lord'; and Thou didst forgive the guilt of my sin" (Ps. 32:1–5). God's knowledge of our hearts makes His love and forgiveness all the more amazing. He who knows us best loves us most.

As the seat of our deepest feelings, beliefs, choices, and convictions, our hearts become the central focus of biblical commands. Rituals like circumcision and sacrifice are inadequate unless they touch the heart (Deut. 10:16; Rom. 2:29), and God demands that we love and serve Him wholeheartedly (Deut. 11:13; 13:3). We don't do that very well, so His solution ultimately is to replace our hearts (Ezek. 36:26), for God desires His people to love Him with all their heart and all their soul (Josh. 22:5; Mark 12:30).

Heart and soul are not viewed as distinct entities, for they appear too often in synonymous parallelism to allow for that (Deut. 4:29; Ps. 24:4; 73:21; 84:2; Acts 4:32). Yet the terms do have slightly different emphases. The soul, as we have seen, is "me" because it is my life. The heart is "me" because it is the central organ of my being. The spirit is "me" because it is my breath and that which moves me.

Other Anthropological Expressions

The terms used most frequently in the Bible to denote the immaterial aspect of humanity are "soul," "spirit," and "heart," but others occur often enough that they should also be mentioned. Though they are often associated with distinctive bodily organs, these terms do not denote separate immaterial entities. As in English, they describe particular functions or emotions using picturesque language. One feels deep anguish in the loins (Isa. 21:3; Nah. 2:10), and central emotions are expressed by the kidneys (Ps. 73:21; Prov. 23:16; Jer. 12:3; Rev. 2:23). Likewise, the New Testament often uses the Greek word for intestines to refer to feelings (Phil. 1:8; Philem. 1:7). Those idioms might seem odd to us, but we use essentially the same concept when we talk about "gut feelings" or say that news hits us "like a kick in the stomach."

Thinking usually takes place through the soul, spirit, or heart, but the New Testament also attributes it to the mind. The contents of the mind reflect the orientation of the heart, so the mind of the unbeliever is "set on the things of the flesh," is "hostile toward God," and "does not subject itself to the law of God" (Rom. 8:5, 7). Indeed, it is "not even able" to subject itself to God's law (8:7), for it is depraved (1 Tim. 6:5; 2 Tim. 3:8), defiled (Titus 1:15), and blinded (2 Cor. 4:4). It needs to be be opened to the truth (Luke 24:45) and renewed (Rom. 12:2; Eph. 4:23) so it will be set "on the things of the Spirit" (Rom. 8:5–6). We'll discuss the effects of sin in a subsequent chapter, but for now we simply note that the mind is not a neutral entity used by the self. It is an expression of the self.

One's moral capacity can also be expressed through the conscience. As an internal monitor of one's behavior, the conscience condemns evil deeds (Rom. 2:15). When its standards are violated, the conscience is "wounded" or "defiled" (1 Cor. 8:7, 12) or even made insensitive (seared as if with a branding iron, 1 Tim. 4:2). However, it can be purified in Christ, whose forgiveness washes the conscience clean (Heb. 9:14; 10:22; 1 Pet. 3:21). Having been washed, the conscience remains clear through consistent good behavior (Acts 23:1; 24:16).

Summary and Implications

The biblical writers used many expressions to describe the immaterial aspect of human nature. However, when they spoke of one's soul, spirit, heart, mind, or gut, they did not regard those as distinguishable entities any more than we do. The phrases do not denote different parts, but their particular nuances do contribute to the meaning of the biblical text. For example, when David spoke of enemies who pursued his soul (Ps. 143:3), he meant that they were attempting to kill him. Because of them, his spirit was overwhelmed and his heart was appalled (143:4)—he was deeply discouraged. He recalled God's previous acts of deliverance and longed for Him with all his being ("my soul longs for Thee as a parched land," 143:6). Asking for a quick answer, David said that his spirit was failing (143:7). If God delayed, his breath (and his life) would be gone. But David had confidence in the Lord, so he lifted his soul to Him (143:8), entrusting Him with his life.

This perspective on human nature contradicts the trichotomist idea that the soul and the spirit are distinct components of the immaterial part of each individual. It rules out models of sanctification and counseling in which the spirit or the heart, wholly purified or even replaced at conversion, must be expressed through the mind, emotion, and will that abide in the soul. There is no reason to treat the spirit or the heart as distinct from the soul, nor is there reason to exclude from them faculties like mind, emotion, and will, which are so central to the human personality. By locating the "real you" in the spirit, these approaches lean toward anti-intellectualism (if rational thought is a function of the soul), perfectionism (if the spirit is wholly pure), and Gnosticism (if sinful desires reside only in the body or perhaps also in the soul). Further, many make misleading (and ultimately meaningless) statements about demonization, contending that demons can reside in the body or soul of believers, but not in their spirits. Such arguments are rooted more in contemporary tradition than in Scripture, but they have become popular in evangelical churches.

Those who make an overly simplistic distinction between soul and spirit (or between soul and heart) often approach sanctification in a formulaic but complex fashion. Using charts and diagrams, they describe the conflict between different parts of human nature, noting what happened to each at conversion and suggesting ways in which the "real you" can be manifested. A more biblical approach affirms the complexity of human nature—we cannot be neatly divided into parts—while suggesting a much simpler approach to the spiritual life. Love the Lord your God with all your heart. That is, be wholly devoted to Him. Rather than trying to figure out a conflict between different aspects of our being, we should simply aim to love the Lord in every way.

Having discussed both the material and immaterial aspects of human nature, and having considered their temporary separation in the intermediate state and their final reunification in resurrection, we are left with one more question. How did they get together in the first place?

THE UNION OF MATERIAL AND IMMATERIAL (OR THE ORIGIN OF THE SOUL)

We understand the formation of the body in the womb, but what about the rest of the person? Where does the "soul" come from? There have been several approaches to the problem.

The Preexistence Theory

Many people believe in the "preexistence of the soul," maintaining that the immaterial aspect of each person existed in some previous state before its union with the body. This view was popular among Greek dualists and a few early Christian theologians who were heavily influenced by Plato's thought. He believed that souls had become incarnate from the world of Forms, making life here an attempt to return the soul to its proper home. Largely because of the influence of Augustine, this view has not been held by the Christian church since about the fifth century, though versions of it may still be found in Eastern thought and in Mormonism. The current popularity of reincarnation has encouraged belief in the preexistence of souls, but neither concept should be considered a serious option for Christians.

There are many different models of reincarnation, but they share the idea that a person's essence is immaterial, occupying one body after another while striving for moral and spiritual perfection. Many people believe that this system answers the problem of injustice, for the next life brings each individual what he or she deserves. Unfortunately, it also makes any notion of salvation utterly dependent on works, while establishing an impossible standard in perfection. Does that demonstrate justice and compassion? Further, belief in reincarnation encourages social apathy by teaching that everyone is receiving what he or she deserves. It is ironic that some would believe in reincarnation out of a desire for justice, only to perpetuate injustice in society through that belief. Finally, the concept of reincarnation is incompatible with Scripture. The Bible teaches, "It is appointed for men to die once and after this comes judgment" (Heb. 9:27). An individual's birth and death do not continually reoccur in an indefinite cycle. Each is a single event that will not be repeated.

Whether it comes in a package with reincarnation or not, the concept of the soul's preexistence cannot be accepted. It tends to deny the importance of the body through a form of dualistic philosophy that we have already seen is false. The view destroys the true unity of the human race, relating us to one another only by our bodies, which it does not believe are essential to our humanity. In the same way, it ignores the Fall as the pivotal event in human history. (If the immaterial aspect of humanity has always existed, how are those souls who were not present in the Garden of Eden affected by Adam's sin?) The preexistence of the soul finds no support in the biblical text.

The Creationist Theory

Creationism (not to be confused with the alternative to biological evolution) maintains that God creates the soul of each individual and joins it to the body in the womb. He thus creates the soul "immediately" (without the use of secondary agents) and the body "mediately" (through sexual reproduction).

Most Reformed theologians join Roman Catholics in holding this view, and some have argued that it best explains the sinlessness of Jesus. If all persons inherit a sinful nature from Adam, then how did Christ avoid that inheritance unless His soul was created directly by God? Further, since He was made like us, our souls must be created in the same fashion.

Others see a pattern for the creation of humanity in Genesis 2:7, believing this to be the addition of the soul to the body of the man. I have already argued that the passage describes the coming of the breath of life, not the addition of a soul, but it is by no means irrelevant to the discussion. God gave life to the man by His breath, but we do not see that act repeated in His creation of the woman, whom God formed from living flesh (2:22). We should not rely too heavily on silence, but Eve's creation does raise another question. If she was made in such a way as to preserve the essential relatedness of the primal pair, wouldn't the separate creation of her soul damage that relatedness?

The Traducianist Theory

Also known as generationism, traducianism maintains that both body and soul are propagated through sexual reproduction. Most Lutherans hold this view, as do many evangelicals, and they often cite the same issue that concerns many creationists—the transmission of sin. If God creates each individual soul, traducianists argue, then how is Adam's sin passed on to his descendants? Obviously, this is the flip-side of the creationist argument. Creationists say that souls must be created separately to prevent Jesus from being sinful, and traducianists say that souls must be related to one another to explain the sinfulness of the rest of humanity. It may be that neither argument is accurate. If Adam's sin is transmitted not physically, but judicially, it would have no relation to the origin of the soul.

Traducianism does better than creationism at explaining the inheritance of both material and immaterial traits from one's parents, and it better supports the essential unity of the human race. Creationists will counter that their view better accords with the concept of the soul as a nonphysical entity that cannot be divided, but traducianists might regard that notion as too dependent on Greek philosophy. Creationists claim the scriptural support of Hebrews 12:9, which describes God as "the Father of spirits," but traducianists observe that it says nothing of mediate versus immediate creation, even if the verse does imply that God creates human spirits.

Many theologians have abandoned the discussion altogether, considering the issue unimportant and recognizing the lack of clear biblical arguments for either side. We should always seek to retain the biblical priority of certain topics over others, but this debate has found its way into a very practical concern. In spite of the fact that most creationists maintain that the soul is infused at the moment of conception, abortion-rights groups have used creationism to say that we do not know when the soul is added to the body of the unborn baby, thus making it human. While preserving the biblical emphasis on human nature as a complex whole, traducianism removes any theological basis for such an argument. This does not establish the truth of either side, but it does show that the debate is not completely esoteric.

SUMMARY

This chapter has covered some significant issues related to the immaterial aspect of humanity. We have seen that simple assumptions about distinctive "parts" do not do justice to the broad biblical usage of terms like "soul," "spirit," and "heart." These expressions all refer to the whole person or to the immaterial aspect in particular with varying emphases. However, while the biblical terminology may seem relatively complex, the biblical expectation is not. We are to love the Lord our God with our whole being. We have also considered the origin of the immaterial aspect of our nature, finding more support for traducianism than for creationism, while recognizing the biblical emphasis on other issues.

Some of the toughest questions about the relationship between soul and body concern not their union in the womb or their separation in the intermediate state, but their function in human behavior. We tend to follow a biblical pattern in locating attitudes, emotions, thoughts, and choices in the immaterial heart, but we also recognize that all these things are affected by physiological factors like inheritance, rest, diet, exercise, or drugs. If emotions can be changed by mood-altering medications, are they rooted in the soul or the body? If certain behaviors are genetically predisposed, what is the nature of human will? Those are some of the questions to be considered in the next chapter.

6

Human Nature and Human Behavior

On HIS FIRST DAY BACK at the firm after a two-week vacation, Jack's spirit was buoyant. He strode confidently toward his office with a spring in his step and life in his eyes. The black leather of his desk chair felt like the upholstery of a new Ferrari, and Jack couldn't resist a little smile when he hopped in and started to make up for lost time. Don, the paralegal, complimented Jack on his tan, but inwardly he wondered if a vacation alone could explain this kind of change. What happened to the grumpy old guy who used to stare out the window? Had Jack decided to quit the firm? Had he vacationed in Vegas and returned a billionaire? Was there a new love in his life? How long was this going to last?

Mary knew there wasn't another woman, and she knew their fortunes hadn't changed, but she had to admit that something was different about her husband. Jack wasn't as burdened by plans for her aging parents, and his evening conversation had become much more animated. She didn't know if it was the vacation, their new diet, or those sessions he had been having with the counselor, but she felt as if she was seeing a part of Jack she had never seen before.

Jack noticed the change, too, and he liked what he saw. Just months earlier, his self-image had hit an all-time low, and he finally went to see a psychiatrist for depression. That first day back from vacation, Jack had been on Prozac for almost a month. Beyond just feeling well, he felt "better than well." He didn't know what it was that had held him back before, but it was gone now, and he was free to soar. His real abilities were finally evident, and Jack felt like a new man.

Jack's mood had clearly changed, transforming his behavior, but had *he* really changed? Jack was ready to redefine his sense of self, but how much of that mood is really Jack, and how much of it is Prozac? Is this, as Mary thought, a part of Jack that had been previously hidden? Or is it more like the alcoholic who apologizes by saying, "That was the tequila talking"? Does a chemically induced change in my personality represent part of *me* when it is positive, but something foreign to me when it is negative? What is the real me? More specifically, what is the connection between physiology and psychology? If my emotions can be radically affected by mood-altering drugs, are they really rooted in an immaterial soul?

Similar questions arise from the longstanding controversy between nature and nurture as determinants of human behavior. Many geneticists have tended to treat DNA as the essence of the individual, claiming genetic causes for homosexuality, obesity, alcoholism, intelligence, and even infidelity.[1] Are all those things biologically determined? Behavioral psychologists would explain them by appealing to the individual's nurturing environment. John Watson demonstrated this focus in memorable fashion when he wrote, "Give me a dozen healthy infants, well-formed, and my own specified world to bring them up in and I'll guarantee to take any one at random and train him to become any type of specialist I might select—doctor, lawyer, artist, merchant-chief, and, yes, even beggar-man and thief, regardless of his talents, penchants, tendencies, abilities, vocations, and race of his ancestors."[2]

Most participants in this debate seek more moderate positions, attributing behavior to some combination of nature and nurture. Interestingly, however, most tend to ignore the role of personal choice— the very thing Christians usually emphasize. What is the relationship between genetics, upbringing, and moral behavior? How much has our character been determined, and how responsible are we for our choices? What are the social implications?

NATURE VERSUS NURTURE:
ASSESSMENT AND IMPLICATIONS

In 1991 a neuroscientist named Simon LeVay identified what he believed to be a physiological cause of homosexuality. After studying the brains of forty-one deceased men, nineteen of whom were homosexuals, LeVay found that a specific portion of the hypothalamus, the area of the brain that governs sexual activity, was consistently smaller in the homosexuals than in the heterosexuals. He interpreted this to mean that "biology is destiny," a conclusion that immediately grabbed the attention of the national media.

When LeVay published his study, homosexuality was already being widely discussed as one of the most controversial issues of our day. Conservative Christians were speaking against "the gay agenda," and politicians were attempting to define "family values." Radio shows, TV specials, and magazine and newspaper articles were all debating the morality of homosexual practices. Churches wrote position papers on the ordination of homosexuals while businesses discussed whether gay partners should receive spousal benefits. In this context LeVay's study seemed to support the idea that homosexuality was not a moral issue but a physiological one. If sexual preferences result from physical differences in the hypothalamus, how could conservatives continue to think of homosexuality as "unnatural?" Many concluded that it must be similar to left-handedness—not as common as the alternative, but not unnatural, and certainly not immoral.

That argument was received warmly in the gay community, and LeVay became something of a hero to its members. He seemed to provide scientific justification for their behavior and for the feelings many claimed to have had since their youth. The excitement, however, was fairly short-lived. It didn't take long for observers to remember that conditions with physiological causes must also have physiological cures. If we can identify an anatomical structure that makes a person homosexual, might doctors eventually be able to change it and make that same person a heterosexual? If an objective test could detect someone's sexual orientation, would employers and insurance companies have access to that information? Might LeVay's study actually lead to the increased persecution of homosexuals? Letters to the national news magazines began to question the rationale for scientific research on homosexuality. "Who cares where it comes from?" they said. "Just accept people as they are."

The public reacted the same way to later studies that attempted to link homosexuality to a particular gene. Would that research eventually produce genetic therapies to make persons heterosexual? Might babies be selectively aborted if they carry a "gay gene?" Many scientists have been careful to condemn such practices even before they become feasible, and their caution is understandable. Like others who recall twentieth-century history, they recognize the specter of eugenics.

Late in the nineteenth century Herbert Spencer and other social Darwinists believed in the "survival of the fittest" in both biology and sociology. Arguing against government aid to the unfit, Spencer wrote, "If they are sufficiently complete to live, they *do* live, and it is well they should live. If they are not sufficiently complete to live, they die, and it is best they should die."[1] Many of the wealthy, who were not only living but living well, found this philosophy very attractive. It helped them see their advantages as gifts of nature, and they concluded that similar success was unattainable to those less gifted.

Spencer's social Darwinism was too individualistic for many people, especially in an era of labor movements and the social gospel, so a more collective version also came into vogue. It distinguished not between the fitness of persons but of groups, and it was often racist in its implications. Reinforcing the nationalistic concept of Manifest Destiny, the American expression of this view contended that the Anglo-Saxon race was inherently superior to others and would inevitably dominate the world. The First World War caused many to amend that assessment and affirm the superiority of only English-speaking peoples, but the majority of the population continued to see themselves at the highest level of human ability.

The earliest social Darwinists, like Darwin himself, believed that acquired characteristics could be passed on to the next generation. They still did not want to aid unnaturally the survival of those who were less fit, so they discouraged government involvement in social welfare. However, most believed in helping the poor with education, libraries, and other such tools with which they could then help themselves. At the dawn of the twentieth century it was popularly believed that poverty and crime could be virtually eliminated through education in just a few generations.

The rise of Mendelian genetics and the development of neo-Darwinism changed much of that. Recognizing that manifold differences between people have less to do with their environment or upbringing than with their genes, many social Darwinists came to see eugenics as the only way to change society. Rather than burdening their more capable neighbors for generation after generation, they concluded, certain individuals and groups should be discouraged from bearing children. In 1907 Indiana enacted a law permitting the sterilization of "confirmed criminals, idiots, imbeciles, and rapists," and by 1930 similar laws had been passed in about thirty states.[2] These statutes were primarily designed not to punish wrong-doers but to prevent inferior seed from being passed on to another generation. The same principles were directed toward whole groups of people thought by others to be less fit, as eugenic organizations encouraged birth control among selected groups of immigrants.[3]

The eugenic movement was popular on both sides of the Atlantic, but its success was short-lived. Several factors contributed to its decline, but the most significant was the application of eugenic principles in Nazi Germany.[4] The Nazis demonstrated the horror of overemphasizing "nature" as the key to social welfare. Hitler's conception of a "master race" silenced most remaining social Darwinists, and the Holocaust brought a sudden (if temporary) halt to eugenics.

Behaviorism, with its emphasis on nurture seen clearly in Watson's boast about shaping a child's destiny, filled much of the void left behind when biology was expunged from sociology. The behaviorists viewed most human actions as the result of conditioning, so they emphasized environmental or cultural change in their vision for society. In the 1950s the possibility of innate racial differences was virtually ignored, and individuals who a generation earlier would have been dismissed as "feebleminded" came to be seen as poorly trained and in need of assistance. This rather hopeful view of human potential may have been aided by postwar optimism in America, but it did not last. Too many scientists still remembered Darwin.

Even the most consistent behaviorists affirmed the reality of both nurture and nature, but they strongly emphasized the former. The last three decades of the twentieth century have witnessed a sharp turn in the other direction. Animal studies and advances in pharmacology have revealed the role of instinct and physiology in social behavior, while the discovery of DNA has accelerated the investigation of genetics and popularized the idea that each of our essential qualities could be located somewhere in that double helix.

As part of this swing back toward nature as an explanation for human behavior, LeVay's work on the structure of the hypothalamus was one of several studies linking homosexual tendencies to physiological or genetic factors. Critics thought the conclusion of each investigation was overstated. In LeVay's case the anatomical difference he observed could have been explained as either cause or effect of homosexuality. He opted for the former, his critics the latter, and neither side was able to prove its case.

A later study by Michael Bailey and Richard Pillard ran into the same problem. They surveyed homosexual men about the occurrence of homosexuality in their immediate families and found that 52 percent of those who were identical twins had a co-twin who was also homosexual. By contrast, only 22 percent of those who were fraternal twins had a co-twin who was also homosexual, and only 11 percent of adopted siblings were both homosexual. The difference in the percentages was attributed to the difference in the amount of genetic material shared. Since identical twins have the same genetic code, the doctors reasoned, they are far more likely to share sexual orientation than fraternal twins. In the same way, fraternal twins obviously have more in common than adopted siblings.

All that evidence seems pretty straightforward, and many thought it demonstrated a genetic basis for homosexuality. Critics, however, noted several problems. First, most published reports about this study did not mention the fact that the nontwin brothers of homosexuals were homosexual only 9 percent of the time. Fraternal twins share no more genetic information than nontwin brothers, yet homosexuals are more than twice as likely to share their sexual orientation with a fraternal twin than with a nontwin brother. Why? Whatever the answer, it is not genetic. Second, if genetic information is determinative, why aren't the identical twin brothers of homosexuals *always* homosexual? Bailey acknowledged that "there must be something in the environment to yield the discordant twins,"[5] but that answer could just as easily be used the other way. If environment causes heterosexuality about 50 percent of the time (in spite of the genetic code), could it not just as easily cause homosexuality about 50 percent of the time?

Those who seek a clear explanation in either nature or nurture will be frustrated by these kinds of studies. Bailey and Pillard did demonstrate a probable correlation between genes and homosexuality (ruling against pure behaviorism), but that link is not significant enough to be the sole cause (ruling against genetic determinism). Apparently other factors also contribute to sexual orientation.

The same may be said of the social Darwinist's favorite topic—intelligence. In the fall of 1994 Charles Murray and Richard Herrnstein sparked heated debate with their book *The Bell Curve: Intelligence and Class Structure in American Life.*[6] They argued that the United States was experiencing an increasing gap between the cognitively gifted and the cognitively challenged. The most capable people would continue to excel, but those less gifted could be expected to have poorer jobs and more social problems, eventually becoming permanent wards of a custodial state. It was a grim picture, but the most controversial aspect of their thesis was the argument that blacks and Latinos are overrepresented among the cognitively challenged and that Jews, Orientals, and whites (in that order) are more likely to be found among the cognitive elite.[7] Murray and Herrnstein tried repeatedly to distance themselves from charges of racism, and they explicitly rejected eugenics, but critics understandably questioned their consistency, if not their sincerity. Though they formally concluded that intelligence was determined by about 60 percent nature and 40 percent nurture, Murray and Herrnstein argued so strongly against environmental explanations that they seemed to reject them altogether. Their social agenda, which rejected affirmative action and other means of government intervention as counterproductive while calling for a laissez-faire meritocracy, reminded many readers of Herbert Spencer.

Different people do possess different natural abilities, but the variances do not split as easily along racial lines as *The Bell Curve* or the old eugenicists maintained. Murray and Herrnstein's arguments regarding ethnicity relied on questionable data, much of which has been contradicted by other researchers, and apparently they did not adequately differentiate between their subjects.[8] In another era the book might not have received much attention, but it came at a time of high racial tensions and joined the ongoing debate about nature and nurture in popular sociology. It did not resolve either issue, but it did get people talking.

Predictably the public response to *The Bell Curve* frequently followed class lines. Groups thought likely to be in the cognitive elite usually liked it, but those who were likely excluded did not. That reaction provided an interesting contrast to the reception given to Simon LeVay, which was described above. When Murray and Herrnstein argued for nature over nurture, social conservatives (including many Christians) generally agreed with them. When LeVay made a similar point, those same people generally disagreed, arguing for nurture over nature. Everyone clearly prefers studies that support his or her own agenda, but one still hopes for more consistency, or at least more balance.

Both genetic determinism and behaviorism lack that balance. A simple choice of nature or nurture will almost inevitably prove wrong, especially if other factors, like the moral choices of people, are ignored. As discussed earlier in this chapter, God created us as responsible moral agents. We have the capacity to make choices, and we are accountable for the choices we make. The ongoing debate between nature and nurture seems to have neglected those choices, arguing that people are determined by their environment, their genes, or some combination of the two. Ironically, Christians have often neglected *those* factors, arguing that our destiny is established by nothing other than free will.

We must not ignore any of the three. Those who neglect the role of personal choice will have little basis for criminal justice, especially if scientists identify genes that supposedly predispose individuals toward particular crimes. Some guilty persons may not be punished if they can prove their actions were genetically or environmentally determined. At the same time, innocent persons may be punished unfairly. When one's criminal destiny is believed to be inescapable, others may want to euthanize them or at least incarcerate them before they have a chance to harm society.

Conversely, those who neglect the role of biology or environment may not show much compassion toward those whose temptations are different from their own. For example, homosexual behavior seems incomprehensible to many heterosexuals, and those who regard it as a matter of personal choice may find that choice revolting. However, the realization that homosexuals feel differently than I have ever felt, largely because of their biological drives or the way they were treated by their parents, should make me more sympathetic to their struggles. That behavior is not right, excusable, or moral, for the Scriptures forbid homosexual practices (Rom. 1:26–27; 1 Cor. 6:9–10), but biology and environment do make the temptation more understandable.

It is difficult to maintain the balance between nature, nurture, and personal responsibility, especially when deterministic models dominate the philosophical landscape. Those approaches too easily convey the idea that people are puppets, with either biology or upbringing pulling the strings. However, the promise of genetic therapy (or to a lesser degree, operant conditioning) presents the possibility that we can learn to pull the strings ourselves. We are told we can take control of our destinies. Ted Peters has described these approaches as "puppet determinism" and "promethean determinism."[9] The latter, in which the puppet takes control of his own strings, receives its name from the Greek legend of Prometheus, who stole fire from the gods. Puppet determinism errs by neglecting human responsibility and endangering any hope for change. Promethean determinism errs by usurping authority (entering the divine domain) and hoping for too much. The search for a more balanced position brings us back to the creation models discussed in chapter 2. We are not the lowly servants of a divine pantheon, nor are we the machine-like products of naturalistic evolution. We are neither puppets nor puppeteers. We are vice-regents of the sovereign God, exercising responsibility under His providence. We make choices for which we are responsible, but we can never really usurp God's authority or steal fire from His heaven.

As moral agents we are called to demonstrate God's character in our responsible choices. "As obedient children, do not be conformed to the former lusts which were yours in your ignorance, but like the Holy One who called you, be holy yourselves also in all your behavior; because it is written, 'You shall be holy, for I am holy'" (1 Pet. 1:14–16). Rather than excusing certain behaviors as genetically determined, we are to strive for obedience in the power of the Holy Spirit (Rom. 6:19; Gal. 5:16). Rather than counseling others to blame their genes or their parents, we are to help them overcome all such obstacles through faith in Jesus Christ (Matt. 28:18–20; 1 Cor. 6:11; 2 Cor. 5:18–21).

Further, as God's representatives in this world, we are called to demonstrate compassion and social justice. "Learn to do good; seek justice, reprove the ruthless; defend the orphan, plead for the widow" (Isa. 1:17). "I was hungry, and you gave Me something to eat; I was thirsty, and you gave Me drink; I was a stranger, and you invited Me in; naked, and you clothed Me; I was sick, and you visited Me; I was in prison, and you came to Me" (Matt. 25:35–36). Rather than abandoning the poor to the survival of the fittest, we are to remember their needs (Gal. 2:10). Rather than telling them that hereditary feeble-mindedness keeps them from sharing our success, we are to save the children of the needy and help correct the social structures that have oppressed them (Ps. 72:4, 12–14). Rather than pursuing eugenics, we are to have compassion on the disadvantaged and to help them.

From this perspective the sources of our temptations and the causes of our problems are not nearly so important as the manner in which we deal with them. In God's providence, nature and nurture have combined to give each individual a unique set of gifts. Some are more appealing than others, and some may even be exchanged. As responsible moral agents, we must choose what to do with what we have received.

WHAT ABOUT THAT PROZAC?

Human emotions and behavior can be influenced by physiology, environment, and the decisions of one's heart. The Bible clearly affirms that one can have a change of heart (Rom. 6:17; Col. 3:12), and it also recognizes that environmental influences can be changed, at least insofar as one can pursue a new circle of friends or be instructed in the "reparenting" relationship of discipleship (1 Cor. 15:33; 2 Tim. 1:2; 2:22). The modern era, however, has given us the ability to make physiological changes, too, and that presents us with a whole new set of options. We understand ourselves with categories that were unavailable until now, particularly through the discoveries of modern science.[10] Unlike those who came before us, we can alter all three influences on human behavior and emotions.

However, since humans are complex creatures, we cannot always distinguish between physiology, psychology, and spirituality. I remember once telling my wife that I was struggling spiritually, and she told me that what I really needed was a good night's sleep. I think we were both right, because, as ascetics have long recognized, those areas are not necessarily unrelated. And that brings us back to Jack and his Prozac.

Jack's wife said she saw a side of Jack that she had never seen before, and I am inclined to think she was right. That happy, hard-working guy across the table from her each evening really was her husband. He had changed, of course, but he was no less himself.

Jack's own understanding was that his real self had been hidden until he started on the Prozac, but I disagree with that assessment. The old Jack was the real Jack too. He liked himself better on the medication, so he redefined his sense of self to fit that new image, but he should not have so easily written off the man he used to be. Jack was a changed man, but he was simply himself both before and after the change.

It might help to look at a less happy transformation. A couple of years ago, Bill, one of my brightest and most engaging students, fell from a ladder and struck his head. His brain was injured in the accident, but Bill survived by the grace of God. It took him several weeks to regain the ability to speak, but he eventually returned to the campus to finish his final year of training. We all had high hopes that Bill would recover all his abilities, but it soon became apparent that he was a changed man. His cheerful spirit remained—in fact, he seemed even happier than before—but his mind just didn't work the way it had. It took him longer to process new information, he forgot details more easily, and he no longer launched off on tangents or pressed his teachers with hard questions. It would have been a mistake to say he was "really" much more brilliant than he now appeared, just as it would have been wrong to say that we missed the "real" Bill. He *was* the "real" Bill, but he had been changed by the accident. At times we missed the "old" Bill, but we got to know the "new" Bill just as easily, and we love him just as much.

If we can be changed by physical trauma, we can just as easily be changed by physical medication, even if it isn't as permanent. Some women find that their moods are profoundly affected by the use of birth control pills; athletes often demonstrate dramatic personality changes when they abuse anabolic steroids; and Jack seems different when he takes Prozac. Does that mean our emotions are rooted in our bodies and not in our immaterial souls? No, it simply means we think, feel, and act as whole people. We know that body and soul will be divided at death, but we cannot divide them in our own self-analysis. Because physiology is not the only source of Jack's personhood, other factors might change him just as profoundly. He might become depressed after the death of a relative, or the presence of a dear friend might bring out a part of him that others have not seen. If he were to become a Christian, his coworkers would hopefully notice the difference, and he might even find that the fruit of the Spirit would replace the fruit of the pharmacy.

This is not the place to enter into an extended discussion of particular medications. That should be left to the medical doctors. I've used the example of Prozac because in recent years it has caused people to question their sense of self, highlighting an important issue in contemporary anthropology. That issue may be stated plainly by the question, What is the real me?

Based on the discussion presented here, I would suggest we adopt a more flexible notion of the self than we often employ. I have no "true self" somewhere that is distinguished from what I am or what I do. That idea appears to be an unbiblical holdover from Greek philosophy that has become especially unservicable in the modern era. Whether I laugh or cry, succeed or fail, sin or do acts of righteousness, I am the one doing it. Whether I do it under the influence of nature, nurture, or the Spirit of God, it's still *me*. I am changing as each day passes, but I am not becoming more myself (or less). I am the one changing. Like it or not, it's really *me*.

One of the reasons many may be inclined to think of their real selves as distinct from their acting selves is that we don't always like the way we act, and we would like to think we are better than we appear to be. Unfortunately that approach to the question may itself be an expression of our sinfulness, and that is the topic to which we now turn.

7

Sin in the Garden (and in Our Backyards)

For almost a year our five-year-old son had been asking us, "When are we gonna go to the Grand Canyon?" We might be driving in the car, playing catch, or talking about a completely different topic, but every week or two Ben would get a little frown on his face and ask, "When are we gonna go to the Grand Canyon?"

In the summer of 1996 we finally went. Joining what must have been a million other tourists, we marveled at the canyon's immensity, bought the kids souvenirs, and took pictures that will never do the place justice. On our second night there, as we sat down at the picnic table for dinner, my wife, Julie, asked Ben if the Grand Canyon had satisfied his expectations. "You've been wanting to come here for so long," she said. "Is this what you thought it would be like?"

Ben smiled kind of sheepishly, paused just a moment, and said, "I thought you said it was a big cannon."

It had been a simple mistake, but it explained a little boy's prolonged excitement about going to a national park! We thought about how it must have sounded to him when we told him that the "Grand Cannon" was "much bigger than downtown Dallas." He was probably hoping to see them shoot it! When he saw that big hole in the ground, he must have wondered if someone already had!

We felt sorry for our little guy, and we asked him if he was disappointed. "No," he said. "It's just different, that's all. . . but it is a lot prettier than I thought it would be."

Ben handled that situation really well, but it's hard not to be disappointed when life does not match our expectations. People fail to keep their promises, or they surprise us with their selfish behavior, and we become disillusioned. Newlyweds soon realize that married life involves a lot more compromise than they expected, and that new job is never quite as terrific as the recruiter said it would be.

Since an accurate understanding of sin helps keep our expectations much more realistic, a study of human depravity keeps us from being too easily discouraged by the behavior of people (either ourselves or others). You are less likely to be disillusioned when you don't have too many illusions from which to be "dissed"!

The doctrine of sin also clarifies the central problem in theology's most vital theme—the relationship between God and humanity. Those who misunderstand the problem of sin will inevitably misunderstand its solution in the gospel, as false teachers throughout history have demonstrated. The study of sin may not be pleasant, but sin is one of the most important concepts in all of theology. It is also one of the most discussed. Theologians have long debated very detailed questions in the field of "hamartiology," the study of sin. We will consider many of those issues in the next several chapters, but we begin with something a little more basic—a careful reading of Genesis 3, accompanied by a hard look in the mirror.

THE SLIDE INTO DEPRAVITY

Moment of Decision

Before creating Eve, God had given Adam a single prohibition. He was not to eat from the tree of the knowledge of good and evil, lest he die (Gen. 2:17). The name of the tree seems to assume that he knew what good and evil were, and the forbidden fruit associates evil with a particular act, but Adam had not yet performed it or witnessed it. He understood the reality of evil, but he had no experiential knowledge of it. Partaking of the tree would bring that knowledge, amounting to guilt, and it would bring death, the ultimate penalty. Remarkably, temptation made that package look desirable.

The Old Testament's most familiar story opens with the serpent, who was "more crafty than any beast of the field," coming to the woman with a question. "Indeed has God said, 'You shall not eat from any tree of the garden'?" (3:1). The query misrepresented God's prohibition, so Eve attempted to state His will more precisely. "From the fruit of the trees of the garden we may eat; but from the fruit of the tree which is in the middle of the garden, God has said, 'You shall not eat from it or touch it, lest you die'" (3:2–3).

That was not quite right either. God had never said they were not to touch the tree; He had only said they must not eat its fruit. Some have faulted Adam for Eve's misunderstanding, noting that the command had been given before she was created, but the text makes no attempt to assign blame. The issues here are more basic. Eve may have misunderstood God's prohibition, but more importantly, she misunderstood God.

Because God's nature establishes the standard for all that is good and righteous, everything He chooses to create must be good. Further, He is the source of all goodness. James wrote, "Do not be deceived, my beloved brethren. Every good thing bestowed and every perfect gift is from above, coming down from the Father of lights, with whom there is no variation, or shifting shadow" (James 1:16–17). Everything that is good comes from God. Conversely, what does not come from Him is not good. Eve misunderstood that fundamental principle, falling prey to the deception James warned about. Listening to the serpent, she apparently concluded that the fruit of the tree could still be good even if it did not come from God.

The serpent convinced Eve that God was not being totally truthful. "You surely shall not die!" he said. God had forbidden the fruit because He "knows that in the day you eat from it your eyes will be opened, and you will be like God, knowing good and evil" (Gen. 3:4–5). There was some truth to the latter statement, for the fruit would bring the knowledge of good and evil (3:22). However, God and His holy angels know evil only as observers; Adam and Eve would come to know it as guilty participants. The serpent's first point lacked any such subtlety. When he said they would not die, the serpent emphatically contradicted God's warning. He made the whole decision a question of trust. Would Adam and Eve trust God to tell the truth about Himself and His creation, or would they decide that the serpent's opinion was more reliable? From this perspective the decision presents itself as a choice between faith and what has been called "unfaith."[1] Obedience to God demonstrates faith in His goodness and His knowledge, and disobedience demonstrates lack of trust. We become convinced that we know a better way, and following that alternative path constitutes unfaith.

The Turn toward Unfaith

When we respond to God, we either trust Him enough to obey, or we reject what He has to say and try something else. We demonstrate unfaith whenever we attempt to solve our problems or satisfy our desires apart from God's directives (Num. 20:12).

For Eve, the turn toward unfaith came when she listened to the voice of the serpent. Acting like a knowledgeable informant, he told her that God had not given them the whole story and that He had even lied to them about the prospect of death. By encouraging her to transfer her trust from God to himself, the serpent helped institute a rebellion that overturned the order of creation. God had ordained that people would serve as His vice-regents, exercising authority over the rest of creation. When they followed the counsel of the serpent, they put the creature over the Creator, and the order of creation was flipped upside down (Rom. 1:25). The turn toward unfaith thus constitutes a turn toward idolatry.

One of my sons used to have a red nylon race car driver's outfit that he liked to wear. It had sewn-on patches advertising high-performance auto parts up and down both sleeves, elastic around the wrists and ankles, a long zipper down the front, and a velcro collar—very cool! Depending on his mood, that outfit turned my little guy into an astronaut, a superhero, or the winner of the Daytona 500. One day he was trying to put it on by himself, and he seemed to be having some trouble. "Would you like some help?" I asked.

"No!" he answered. "I can do it by myself!"

Not quite convinced of his abilities but willing to let him try, I went into the other room and sat down to read. After about five minutes I heard him coming. Thump, thump. "Daddy!" Thump, thump. "Dad!" He hopped down the hall toward my study, and then just stood there and whimpered. He had one leg in a sleeve and the other in a pant leg, one arm in a pant leg and the other in a sleeve, and the suit was so twisted behind his back that he looked as if he was wrapped up in a little red straitjacket. "Daddy, I need some help."

When we chase after the false gods of unfaith, we get just as tangled up in the futility of our efforts. We try to look capable, self-assured, and confident, and we might even be able to convince ourselves that everything is fine, but we've got it all backward. Reinhold Niebuhr put it this way: "Man is mortal. That is his fate. Man pretends not to be mortal. That is his sin."[2]

The appropriate response to the serpent's temptation would have been faithful obedience to God. By responding with unfaith and disobedience, Adam and Eve placed perceived self-interest ahead of God's plan. That response was an act of pride, the very essence of sin.

A Matter of Pride

"Your eyes will be opened, and you will be like God" (Gen. 3:5). When Eve accepted those words from the serpent, pride was born in the human heart. Pride works hand-in-hand with unfaith, contributing the self-interest that makes unbelief seem reasonable. Ted Peters described pride as that "self-exaltation that results from centering our attention on ourselves when pursuing our own pleasures rather than the long-range purposes of God. Pride essentially refuses to allow God to be God. It tries to co-opt divinity for itself."[3] Further, pride produces "the belief that the world is made up of winners and losers and that we must always be the winners."[4]

It is difficult to imagine those who were made a little lower than God (Ps. 8:5) coming to believe they deserved a more elevated status, but Eve was tempted to become godlike (Gen. 3:5), and she and Adam were seduced by the prospect of knowledge and power. When they succumbed to that temptation, they became a part of Satan's cosmic mutiny against the Creator, seeking a promotion for themselves even if it cost God a share of His throne (Rom. 16:20; Rev. 12:9).

Newspapers offer daily examples of the pride of power, especially in political leaders who gain personal glory through public service. Their motives are not entirely selfish, but even the purest intentions are tainted by pride. With apparent reference to Winston Churchill, Niebuhr wrote, "The love of God and the love of self are curiously intermingled in actual life. The worship of God and the worship of self confront us in a multitude of different compounds. There is a taint of sin in our highest endeavors. How shall we judge the great statesman who gives a nation its victorious courage by articulating its only partly conscious and implicit resources of fortitude; and who mixes the most obvious forms of personal and collective pride and arrogance with this heroic fortitude? If he had been a more timid man, a more cautious soul, he would not have sinned so greatly but neither would he have wrought so nobly."[5]

Unfortunately one could say the same thing about many church leaders, who claim to be "just serving the Lord" but who inwardly live for the praise of their congregations. Likewise we can all think of philanthropists who display their power by making a show of their unselfishness. These people do many wonderful deeds, but their works are inevitably mixed with pride.

Eve heard that the forbidden fruit would open her eyes, making her like God in her knowledge of good and evil (Gen. 3:5). She then saw that the tree "was desirable to make one wise" (3:6), so she took and ate, seeking both power and knowledge. Perhaps it would be better to say that she sought power through knowledge. The wisdom offered by the tree would bring her to God's level.

Those who work in an academic environment can certainly understand how learning yields influence. Prizefighters size one another up by "the tale of the tape," but the scholarly pecking order is based on degrees earned, schools attended, and works produced. A similar situation also exists beyond the academic world. Throughout history and in all cultures, knowledge has brought power. After Joseph and Daniel interpreted their rulers' dreams, they were given tremendous authority to govern, for they had demonstrated unusual understanding (41:39–40; Dan. 2:48). Likewise, because

Solomon was gifted with wisdom in order to rule the people with justice (2 Chron. 1:11–12), even the kings of other lands came to honor him, for he surpassed them all in wisdom and in riches (9:22–23). In the modern workplace advanced training brings promotions and job security. Knowledge brings power, and Eve seized the opportunity to have the same kind of knowledge as God.

Pride of knowledge, like all forms of pride, fails to recognize one's limitations. It boldly assumes a final understanding and seeks no further instruction. It may be seen in the professor who quits reading new material or the young student who dogmatically lectures his peers. When reality calls for humility and a teachable spirit, pride of knowledge tolerates neither. It refuses to stop and ask directions when lost on the road, and it doesn't even consult a map.

Some of those examples, the last in particular, may strike some readers as more typically male than female. Indeed, some have argued that pride is primarily a male phenomenon, suggesting that women are more likely to sin by hiding their desires than by asserting them. However, hiding is a natural expression of self-interest on the part of those who lack the power to defend their concerns more vigorously. If pride consists essentially of self-interest, then even self-protection can be seen as an expression of pride.

The pervasiveness of pride may be seen most clearly in our final category, the pride of virtue. Those who feel they no longer exalt themselves through power and knowledge may be guilty of overestimating their goodness. It was with good reason that Paul said, "Let him who thinks he stands take heed lest he fall" (1 Cor. 10:12). Those who think they have finally attained humility have probably just lost it.

A church in my hometown used to advertise in the newspaper's religion section every Saturday. The ad carried a picture of the church's founder, along with a quotation: "Have not sinned or been sick for twenty-two years." She updated the claim every January—"Have not sinned or been sick for twenty-three years"—but as far as I could tell, she sinned every Saturday. She had fallen into the pride of virtue.

We can see this form of pride in the embarrassment we feel when caught doing something wrong or foolish. One night while working at a gym, just before my well-publicized departure to attend seminary, I lost my temper in an argument with one of the members. It did not last long, but when I stopped yelling, I looked around to see every person in the room staring at me. One family was standing in the doorway, having just arrived with a going-away gift for me! The two little children looked scared. I wished I could turn back time and have all those words back, but I couldn't. I started a long round of apologies by asking the forgiveness of the fellow I had berated, and by the time I got over to my friends in the doorway things seemed pretty much back to normal. Still, I was crushed. Those folks had thought I was such a nice guy, and what did they think now? I felt bad about compromising my testimony, but I was more concerned about my own reputation. My pride of virtue had been wounded. Frederica Mathewes-Green described the feeling well. "'Oh, no,' Embarrassment whispers. 'People will think . . .' People are going to think I'm such a fool. Well, the truth is I *am* a fool. I just did the stupid thing in question, didn't I? What do I need, a certificate? And the fact that I'm a fool isn't exactly classified information. God certainly knows it, and the devil does too (and relies on it). It's a pretty good bet that everyone who knows me knows it as well. Apparently the only person left out of this information loop is me."[6]

One night in class I was describing the connection between pride and racism (a topic addressed later in this book). One student raised an objection, and he went on to describe his own success in cross-cultural ministry to reinforce his point. After class he met me in the parking lot with something of a confession. "I've been thinking," he said, "and it seems to me the way I was talking about myself in class demonstrated the same sort of pride you were describing."

"That's a very good observation," I replied. "I think you're probably right. And you're probably proud of yourself for noticing that, aren't you?" His laugh told me I was right, but that we were still friends, so I continued. "And you know what? I'm pretty proud of the fact that I caught you!"

Pride so pervades our character that even our best works are tainted. That's why models of sanctification that claim sinless perfection have to limit their definition of sin to conscious, willful disobedience. If our self-centered pride is sinful, then we all continue to fall short of God's standard, even when we think we are doing pretty well.

The opposite of pride is, of course, humility, and the appropriate response to the serpent's temptation, rather than prideful rebellion, would have been humble obedience to God (Eph. 4:2; Phil. 2:3; James 4:6–10; 1 Pet. 5:5–6). What we are starting to see, however, is that just as faith works hand-in-hand with contentment, pride works hand in hand with concupiscence.

Desiring the Forbidden

After hearing the words of the serpent, Eve gazed at the tree and its fruit. She saw that "the tree was good for food, and that it was a delight to the eyes" (Gen. 3:6). Its appearance pleased her, though it probably did not look very different from the other trees in the garden. With their leaves glistening from the watering mist and their branches heavy with succulent fruit, lawful trees surrounded the forbidden one on all sides as Eve stood talking with the serpent. But she wanted the one she couldn't have. In place of the contentment that would follow from faith in God's goodness, she was demonstrating concupiscence—the desire to possess more than she had been given. Humility would have encouraged the acceptance of God's provision. Since pride says we deserve better, it produces lust, covetousness, and greed.

In the early fifth century Augustine, bishop of Hippo, North Africa, provided a classic example of this principle when he wrote about his own sin with a fruit tree. He stole pears as a child, not to satisfy his hunger, nor to profit from their sale, but simply because they were forbidden, for that made them desirable.[7] In the same way, Paul said his covetousness was awakened by the law against coveting (Rom. 7:7–8). It apparently worked like a "Wet paint" sign that causes us to touch and see for ourselves. When something is forbidden, it poses a challenge to our pride.

The major problem with concupiscence is that it cannot be satisfied. Eve's interest in the tree came not from the uniqueness of the tree, but from the pride planted in her heart by the tempter. In the same way, our lust comes not from the object of our desire, but from within (James 1:14). If it came from the things we seek, their acquisition would resolve the problem. Since it comes from within ourselves, obtaining the things we desire just makes us want more.

One can see that principle in the desire for sex. Genesis 3 gives us little reason to believe the temptation had anything to do with copulation. They recognized their nakedness after eating the fruit (3:7), but they had been naked and unashamed since the Creation (2:25), and lovemaking had likely been a part of their experience already. However, theologians and commentators have frequently understood the fall of humanity as a surrender to sexual desire, an interpretation best explained by the prominence of sensuality in our own experience. Almost everyone knows what it is to experience sexual lust, however, and it illustrates well the insatiability of concupiscent desire. Ted Peters wrote, "The flame of passion ignited by the presence of someone sexually desirable seems to burn and consume the soul with bodily desire. . . . Like a grass fire, concupiscence burns field after field, and there is no hope that it will be extinguished until all fuel is consumed. Long before the fuel is consumed, of course, the consumer is extinguished."[8]

When we pursue what is forbidden, we follow Eve's example of unfaith, persuading ourselves that there will be no consequences to our wrong actions. The serpent's lie—"You surely shall not die!" (3:4)—is repeated in innumerable ways every minute of the day. "It'll be okay." "This won't hurt you." "Nobody will know." "Go ahead! They can't see you." In Proverbs 7, a young man goes to the house of his lover under the cover of darkness (7:9), and she assures him they will be alone (7:19). It sounds safe, and it looks as if there will be nothing but pleasure ahead, so they walk cheerfully into the trap like birds into a snare.

There are consequences for taking what is forbidden. Adam and Eve discovered that when they ate the fruit, they were filled with shame. They understood good and evil, and they knew what they had done was not good. Instead of demonstrating faith by acting in humble obedience and being content with a paradise full of fruit trees, they revealed unfaith, acting in prideful disobedience and pursuing what God had forbidden. But that was not all. They knew they were wrong, and once they had sinned, they sought to cover it up.

Self-Justification and Blame

Just as we don't know how carefully Adam repeated God's command-ment to his wife, we don't know how closely he stood by her during the temptation. After eating the fruit herself, "she gave also to her husband with her, and he ate" (Gen. 3:6). He may have been with her the whole time, or he may have simply been in the vicinity. Either way, the text does not attempt to assign blame to just one of them. They were both respon-sible for their actions, but you wouldn't know it from the way they reacted.

After eating the fruit, Adam and Eve were suddenly ashamed of their nakedness, so they hid from each other by covering themselves with fig leaves (3:7), and then hid from God in the cover of the Garden (3:8). They quickly discovered there is not much point in playing hide-and-seek with God. He called the man out from his hiding place and confronted him regarding his disobedience. "Have you eaten from the tree of which I commanded you not to eat?" (3:11). Then the real cover-up began. Adam said, "The woman whom Thou gavest to be with me, she gave me from the tree, and I ate" (3:12).

Adam's answer reminds me of an incident in our home several years ago. Somebody had apparently gotten into a little trouble in the kids' bath-room. He evidently had stepped in something that should never have been on the floor, and now it was on the floor, the sink, and the walls. Judging from the appearance of the washcloth and two handtowels I found wad-ded up in the corner, the problem must have spread when the irresponsible party was making an effort to clean it up. At some point he abandoned the job, concluding that it was either clean or futile, but it looked as if we still needed a couple of bottles of Lysol. I stepped out into the hall and called for some assistance. "Boys!!! Get in here!!!" They arrived on the double—three of the most innocent faces you ever saw in your life. It was time for a little conversation.

"Who did this?"

"Not me."

"Not me."

"Not me."

"Oh, come on! How do you think this happened?"

"I don't know."

"I didn't do it."

"Wow! Who did that?"

"That's what we're trying to figure out. Obviously somebody did it. Any ideas?"

"Becky!"

"Becky did it!"

"Yeah, Becky did it!"

At the time, Becky was three months old. She couldn't say anything to defend herself, but I'm sure she didn't do it! It has been said that there is nothing so creative as the human mind when it is engaged in self-justification. And it starts early.

Protecting his own interests at the expense of everyone else's, Adam attempted to remove the blame from himself by placing it on his wife. He even blamed God—"the woman whom *Thou* gavest to be with me" (3:12).

Self-justification almost always involves the transfer of blame to others. As in the children's rhyme about stealing cookies, sometimes the only way to avoid condemnation is to accuse someone else. "Who, me? Couldn't be! *Susie* stole the cookies from the cookie jar!" That makes it Susie's turn to find the culprit! When Adam passed the blame to Eve, it was her turn either to accept the guilt or to pass it to someone else. "Then the LORD God said to the woman, 'What is this you have done?' And the woman said, 'The serpent deceived me, and I ate' " (3:13).

The serpent was not given a chance to say anything, but Adam and Eve had already said enough. He blamed her, she blamed the serpent, and they both implicated God (after all, He had created both the woman and the serpent, and He hadn't prevented them from meeting). In their pride Adam and Eve attempted to justify their own actions instead of responding with humble confession. By passing the blame, ultimately even to Him, they dug themselves deeper into sin and rebellion. "Adam and Eve have learned to draw the line between good and evil, and they immediately try to place themselves on the good side of the line, even if this means placing God on the evil side."[9]

Some have suggested that the postmodern plea for universal tolerance demonstrates an unwillingness to draw any lines at all. When individuals stop short of condemning the Holocaust because they don't want to assume unchanging standards of right and wrong, it sounds as if the effect of the fruit has worn off—Adam's descendants no longer know good and evil. However, that conclusion would misunderstand postmodern tolerance. It is not so much that individuals have learned to stop blaming and no longer practice self-justification. Rather, their habits of self-justification have become so individualized and entrenched that they call for tolerance in order to avoid being blamed. The essential message is not "I respect what you're doing," but "Get out of my face and leave me alone." And that message is usually aimed at those who seek to enforce standards, as God did in the Garden. In the name of tolerance, He would have been the one asked to leave. Making God the scapegoat, we follow in the footsteps of Adam.

Self-justification comes naturally to those who fear their deeds being exposed, but at least such persons know in their hearts that they are guilty. The situation is much more serious when we believe our own lies. "If we say that we have no sin, we are deceiving ourselves, and the truth is not in us. . . . If we say that we have not sinned, we make Him a liar, and His word is not in us" (1 John 1:8, 10).

A few years ago a man in my Sunday school class refused to speak to his wife for a week. She asked him questions and tried to get him to sit and talk about their problems, but he acted as if she was not in the room. He spoke cheerfully to friends in her presence, but he would not acknowledge her at all, even in front of other people. I eventually got wind of the problem, so I called him up and asked for an explanation. He launched into a long tirade about all the things she had done wrong, but I stopped him after a couple of minutes and said, "Time out. What about you? Are you in any way part of the problem?" There was silence on the other end of the phone as he thought about the question, and he finally responded, "No, not that I can see."

Self-justification and blame make it easier to see a speck in someone else's eye than a log in one's own (Matt. 7:1–5). The disturbing reality is that what we see as our most virtuous moments may actually be some of our most sinful. Speck removal can easily reinforce our selfish pride, and moral crusades that are not accompanied by confession turn too easily into grand displays of self-justification (see Gal. 6:1–4).

The same pattern may be seen in the devil-made-me-do-it attitude so prevalent in popular Christian books on spiritual warfare. They trace sinful thoughts and behaviors to indwelling demons, maintaining that deliverance from the demons will allow one's true self to shine forth. They frequently imply that the demons have been passively acquired through physical objects, inheritance, or curses. Put simply, they justify blaming demons for their sinful behavior and by blaming others for the pressure of the demons.[10] As Alexander Solzhenitsyn has written, the real explanation for evil is far more disturbing. "If only it were all so simple! If only there were evil people somewhere insidiously committing evil deeds, and it were necessary only to separate them from the rest of us and destroy them. But the line dividing good and evil cuts through the heart of every human being. And who is willing to destroy a piece of his own heart?"[11]

Self-justification not only expresses self-deception; it also constitutes a prideful denial of the central doctrine of Christianity—justification by faith. If we are already righteous, we have no need of "the righteousness which comes from God on the basis of faith" (Phil. 3:9); if we have no sin, we have no need for forgiveness. In that case Christ died for no reason (Gal. 2:21). Niebuhr made this point powerfully. "Luther rightly insisted that the unwillingness of the sinner to be regarded as a sinner was the final form of sin. The final proof that man no longer knows God is that he does not know his own sin. The sinner who justifies himself does not know God as judge and does not need God as Saviour."[12]

Instead of responding to the temptation by trusting God enough to obey Him, Adam and Eve demonstrated unfaith. In place of humility they acted in pride; instead of contentment they embraced desire. Even after all that, we might expect to see them confess their sins and repent, but Genesis records no such thing. Instead, we see them making one last stand in the Garden, attempting to justify themselves before the sovereign God. They were so eager to prove themselves right that they were willing to imply that even God was wrong. It is difficult to imagine anything more futile, for "all things are open and laid bare to the eyes of Him with whom we have to do" (Heb. 4:13). In self-justification we deceive only ourselves.

When Blame Turns Cruel

Our desire for justice is usually driven more by self-interest than by godliness. We give little thought to injustices far from home, but if we (or those we love) have been unfairly injured by others, we often look forward to the day when they will get what is coming to them. This desire for retribution is grounded on the pattern of self-justification and blame. We see ourselves as good, so what happened to us must not have been fair. Someone must be held responsible for this unjust act, and if the authorities refuse to execute judgment, perhaps we should do it ourselves. That kind of thinking forms a thoroughfare from pride to cruelty, and it led Cain to the first murder.

Cain and his brother Abel each brought an offering to the Lord. Abel, the keeper of flocks, sacrificed an animal, while Cain, the farmer, brought some grain (Gen. 4:3–4). We don't know how much God had revealed to them about the nature and purpose of sacrifices, nor do we know what was expected of each man. We do know that the Lord was not pleased with Cain's offering, but He was satisfied with Abel's (4:4–5). Cain apparently felt slighted, expressing anger at being treated unfairly. God urged him to do right, but he decided to kill his brother instead. The motive is not entirely clear. Either Cain blamed Abel for the inadequacy of his own offering or he blamed God and decided to take his anger out on the Lord's apparent favorite. Either way, Cain thought his offering should have been acceptable (self-justification), and he went a step beyond blame to cruelty.

Chapter 11 discusses the nature of societal violence more thoroughly, but we need to recognize that self-righteous cruelty can be expressed at both individual and group levels. We see it in hate crimes against homosexuals and minorities, in racist acts of lynching and ethnic cleansing, and in marriages where blame turns to fury. The *Dallas Morning News* recently told about a young Indian woman who was horribly abused on her wedding night by her drunken husband and his friends because her family did not provide what he considered an adequate dowry. In another story suicide bombers attacked a crowded Israeli market in what they regarded as an act of holy war. People do things that are just plain evil, but they don't think of themselves as evil people. They see themselves as good, and they see their actions as righteous, and that assessment is part of the problem.

If this pattern is accurate, then one of our most common sins, self-justification, is just a half-step away from cruelty. That may be hard for us to imagine, because we think of ourselves as too virtuous to mistreat others. But our perception of virtue leads us too near the brink. "Let him who thinks he stands take heed lest he fall" (1 Cor. 10:12).

The ultimate form of cruelty may be blasphemy, not murder. Peters has argued that blasphemy consists of stealing the symbols that normally bring hope to the oppressed. When the sacrament is desecrated, it becomes a symbol not of hope but of despair. When the Scriptures are used to deny the humanity of particular ethnic groups, their hope of redemption is taken away. Instead of loving God and loving their neighbor, blasphemers show a hatred for both, identifying God with evil and drowning out the message of salvation.[13] Their rebellion appears to be complete.

Implications

From above, the slide from unfaith to cruelty looks like an elegant spiral staircase. Each step is made of finished hardwood, and white spindles support its smooth, graceful railing. You start to descend with pleasure, but your confidence is somewhat shaken by the fact that each step feels slightly narrower than the one before. The rail is apparently just for show, for it proves inadequate to support your weight, so you concentrate on your steps and move downward a bit more gingerly. By the time you lose sight of the upper landing, only your heels will fit on the treads, and you decide you might have to turn around if the next step is not any bigger. But the next step is not there. For just a moment you are in free fall, then bouncing and sliding between the spindles and the waxed floor of the slide, which continues to spiral downward with no end in sight.

Unbelief does not *inherently* lead one to cruelty, for some pause while still on the steps. However, unbelief does *naturally* lead one toward cruelty, and unchecked pride accelerates the descent. Cornelius Plantinga Jr. described sin's progression well when he wrote, "A fuller statement of [William James's] great law of returns would go something like this: sow a thought, reap a deed; sow a deed, reap another deed; sow some deeds, and reap a habit; sow some habits, and reap a character; sow a character, and reap two thoughts."[14] There is no way to reverse the cycle apart from divine grace.

The condition of humanity is not encouraging if viewed realistically. But an accurate understanding of sin will prevent us from being easily disillusioned, and it will point us toward workable solutions instead of idealistic dreams. Barry Goldwater, the Republican nominee for President in 1964, described the human situation quite well.

> We have conjured up all manner of devils responsible for our present discontent. It is the unchecked bureaucracy in government, it is the selfishness of multinational corporate giants, it is the failure of the schools to teach and the students to learn, it is overpopulation, it is wasteful extravagance, it is squandering our national resources, it is racism, it is capitalism, it is our material affluence, or if we want a convenient foreign devil, we can say it is communism. But when we scrape away the varnish of wealth, education, class, ethnic origin, parochial loyalties, we discover that however much we've changed the shape of man's physical environment, man himself is still sinful, vain, greedy, ambitious, lustful, self-centered, unrepentant, and requiring of restraint.[15]

If that is true, then our society's problems will not be solved through political elections, Olympic games, special concerts, or moralistic calls to just get along. Our perspective on individual morality may itself be immoral, and our need for forgiveness and grace is more profound than we could ever imagine.

PUTTING DOWN THE REBELLION

After listening to Adam blame Eve and Eve blame the serpent, God interrupted the pattern and spoke before the serpent could blame anybody else. "Because you have done this," he said to the serpent, "cursed are you more than all cattle, and more than every beast of the field; on your belly shall you go, and dust shall you eat all the days of your life" (Gen. 3:14).

The serpent had been the most crafty of animals (3:1), but now he was the most cursed. Readers have long wondered if the serpent had legs up until this moment, but the physical form of the serpent is of little significance. The point is that he will be humbled by forever occupying the lowliest of positions (Isa. 65:25). This was an appropriate punishment for the one who had just attempted, by winning the allegiance of God's vice-regents, to seize the highest throne.

God also said that He would "put enmity" between the serpent and the woman, and between his seed and her seed. "He shall bruise you on the head, and you shall bruise him on the heel" (Gen. 3:15). Some have understood the "seed of the woman" here as a reference to Christ and His virgin birth, suggesting that women do not normally have "seed" according to ancient usage. However, "seed" usually refers to offspring, not semen, and the descendants of women are described as their seed several times in Genesis (4:25; 16:10; 24:60). There may be some reference to Christ here as the consummate Man or the promised Descendant, especially since the New Testament more clearly identifies the serpent with Satan and speaks of him being crushed underfoot (Rom. 16:20; Rev. 12:9). However, the more immediate point seems to be that there would be continuing alienation between people and animals as a consequence of the Fall. Future generations are described as the woman's seed because Genesis 3 is highlighting the need for a properly ordered relationship between the serpent and the woman.

As we have already seen, God placed people over the rest of creation as His vice-regents. That established an ontological difference between people and God and between people and animals. That is, we do not have the same nature or essence as other creatures, nor do we possess the divine nature of God. The woman was brought to the man to receive a name after he had already named the animals (2:18–23). The name he gave her was derived from his own, demonstrating their shared essence, but the fact that he gave her a name at all probably reveals an ordering of their relationship even before the Fall. They were partners, but their roles were not necessarily identical, and Adam's naming of his wife suggests he was in a position of responsible authority over her. If that is the case, the original order of creation might be outlined in the following way:

God

Man/Woman

Animals

In the temptation the serpent approached the woman, who gave fruit to the man, who joined them both in rebelling against God. That pattern effectively reversed the order of creation as it had been established.

Animals (Serpent)

Woman/Man

God

When God addressed each individual regarding the consequences of his or her sin, He progressively reestablished the original creation order while speaking of the discontent that would characterize each relationship. The seed of the woman would be over that of the serpent, but there would be enmity between them (3:15). The man would rule over the woman, but there would be rivalry in their relationship (3:16). God would rule over them both, but they would be banished from the Garden (3:23). They would continue to rule over the ground, but their gardening would be an ongoing struggle (3:18–19). Order was restored and the rebellion put down, but the world is not what it was nor what it will be. There is now alienation and conflict in each relationship.

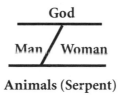

Animals (Serpent)

By focusing on the seed of the woman, God emphasized that the serpent will not again usurp her authority or that of her descendants. However, they will have a contentious relationship indefinitely.

Consequences for Eve and Her Marriage

When He turned to address the woman, God spoke directly to her relationship with the man. He said, "I will greatly multiply your pain in childbirth, in pain you shall bring forth children; yet your desire shall be for your husband, and he shall rule over you" (Gen. 3:16). The reference to childbirth may be a response to Eve's desire to be like God. In the ancient near East, goddesses were sometimes thought to give birth painlessly after several days of pregnancy. But by contrast, Eve was not destined to be a goddess in a heavenly pantheon. Rather than disappear, her pain would increase.

Further, Eve's "desire" would be for her husband. The meaning of this statement has been much disputed, in part because the word *desire* is used only two other times in the Old Testament—in Genesis 4:7 and Song of Solomon 7:10. The structure and vocabulary of the original Hebrew statement in Genesis 4:7 is almost identical to that of 3:16. There sin is described as an animal lying in wait for Cain, building a lair right outside his door. Its "desire" was for him, but instead God directed Cain to "rule over" or "master" it. Raymond Ortlund paraphrased this verse and applied it to 3:16 in the following way: "To paraphrase and amplify the sense: 'Sin has a desire, Cain. It wants to control you. But you must not allow sin to have its way with you. You must rule over it.' How does this parallel statement illuminate the interpretation of 3:16? Most importantly, it clarifies the meaning of the woman's 'desire.' Just as sin's desire is to have its way with Cain, God gives the woman up to a desire to have her way with her husband. Because she usurped his headship in the temptation, God hands her over to the misery of competition with her rightful head."[16]

Song of Solomon 7:10 uses the word quite differently, apparently describing sexual desire ("I am my beloved's, and his desire is for me"). Following this example, Mary Stewart Van Leeuwen has argued that "the woman is being warned that she will experience an unreciprocated longing for intimacy with the man."[17] She will long for the kind of relationship they had before the Fall, but he will rule over her instead.

These are obviously very different interpretations, but Ortlund seems closer to the truth than Van Leeuwen. Genesis 4:7 is a much nearer, more significant parallel than Song of Solomon 7:10, and his interpretation aligns more appropriately with the concept outlined above regarding the creation order. God restored the original order by His statements to the serpent, the woman, and the man, but each relationship would be characterized by strife as a consequence of sin. The woman would experience rivalry in place of contentment in her marriage, perhaps in part because of the inevitable self-centeredness of her husband's "rule," but also because of her own pride of power. One of the problems with Van Leeuwen's interpretation (which, like Ortlund's, is widely held) is that the woman bears virtually no responsibility for her lack of contentment. She wants only the purity of the past, while her brutish husband slides alone into depravity. I'm more inclined to see it as a team effort.

While we are on this subject, we need to pursue an important related point. I have argued that the pronouncements of Genesis 3:14–19 restored a pretemptation order to all human relationships. God reestablished His own sovereignty over humanity, Adam's leadership in the world's only marriage, and humanity's dominion over creation. However, He did not restore those relationships to a prefallen condition. That restoration is reserved for salvation in the future, the new creation established by Christ.

Recognizing that pattern, some have argued that God's establishment of the church on the Day of Pentecost constitutes "women's liberation day"—the reversal of the curse and the beginning of a new egalitarianism both in marriage and in the leadership of God's people. It is fitting that we seek to reduce the consequences of the Fall. We affirm the application of environmentally appropriate techniques to keep weeds from our farms; we encourage the use of anesthesia to ease the pain of childbirth; we value premarital counseling that reduces the potential strife between a husband and wife; and we look forward to a day when such inadequate means of dealing with our fallen world will no longer be needed (Rev. 21:4; 22:3). However, since we seek to overturn not the original creation but the curse, we should not regard egalitarianism (fully interchangeable roles in the marriage relationship or in the church) as the ideal. Instead, our goal should be that the husband demonstrates such selfless, loving leadership that his wife trusts him and joyfully follows his guidance (Eph. 5:22–25). Since a relationship between equal partners with distinctive roles seems to have been a part of the Edenic ideal, those who have been redeemed within the church should seek to enjoy such a relationship without the pain stemming from abuse or rivalry.

Consequences for Adam and His Labor

After addressing the serpent and the woman, God turned to the man. Whatever chores had been required in the cultivation of the garden, Adam's work was about to get significantly more difficult. "Cursed is the ground because of you; in toil you shall eat of it all the days of your life. Both thorns and thistles it shall grow for you; and you shall eat the plants of the field; by the sweat of your face you shall eat bread, till you return to the ground, because from it you were taken; for you are dust, and to dust you shall return" (Gen. 3:17–19).

We have some wonderful friends who live on a hilltop in rural West Virginia. I wrote portions of this book on their back porch, which overlooks miles of tree-covered mountains, a handful of distant farms, and a gentle river in the valley below. Other than the infrequent rattle of a pickup on the dirt road out front, civilization's only intrusion is the faint sound of an occasional airliner thirty-five thousand feet overhead. When the strawberries are ripe and the fellowship is sweet, that back porch feels a little like Eden, especially after a busy year in Dallas.

Most of their nine-acre "backyard" is either cleared or forested, but my friends have one area that provides a vivid reminder of Genesis 3. Just beyond that lovely porch, on the other side of the children's play area, the hillside drops sharply toward the forest below. That steep slope, which seems to catch every stray baseball and Frisbee, is a one-acre patch of horticultural mayhem. Completely covered with thornbushes, short honey locust trees, and weeds, it needs to be cut back on occasion just to keep it from taking over. I got out there one summer with a machete, trying to maintain my balance on the hillside while whacking away at the locust trees with their two-inch thorns. With my back to the beautiful vista of the distant mountains, I had little interest in the wonder of creation. I was too preoccupied with the curse.

Jobs like that would not be so bad if they needed to be done only once, but I discovered on a return trip several months later that the hillside was once again overgrown. Every locust tree I had cut down had sprouted at least five thorny shoots, each already about four feet tall. I wonder if Adam knew it would be like this.

Destined to beat back thorns and thistles in order to cultivate the plants of the field, Adam would have to obtain food by the sweat of his brow (3:19). The perspiration that dripped from his skin came as a consequence of his quest for independence, and it provided an ongoing reminder of the need to live in faithful dependence on God. That lesson may lie behind Luke's reference to sweat in another garden, Gethsemane. In His most excruciating moment of submission to the will of the Father, Jesus' sweat fell to the ground like drops of blood (Luke 22:44). He was identifying with fallen humanity, but His sweat showed dependence, not rebellion.

God's final pronouncement to Adam was that His initial warning would in fact be fulfilled. Adam and Eve had believed the serpent when he said, "You surely shall not die" (Gen. 3:4), but now God told Adam that he would not live forever. He had been taken from the dust, and he would return to it (3:19). Ever since they had been formed from dust and animated by the breath of God (2:7), physical survival had depended on His life-giving presence. That presence was about to come to an end because of sin, and they would surely die. Later God made a similar statement about the human race: "My Spirit shall not abide[18] in man forever, because he also is flesh; nevertheless his days shall be one hundred and twenty years" (6:3).

God would bring death not only through the withdrawal of His life-giving Spirit, but also by His separation of Adam and Eve from the tree of life. After His pronouncements against the serpent, the woman, and the man, God said to His heavenly court, "Behold, the man has become like one of Us, knowing good and evil; and now, lest he stretch out his hand, and take also from the tree of life, and eat, and live forever" (3:22). Then God sent them out of Eden. Life comes from God alone, so the tree of life would not have rendered Adam and Eve independently immortal through a single serving of its fruit. As in the eternal state, when the tree of life will provide new fruit each month for the continuous "healing of the nations"

(Rev. 22:2), the tree in the Garden of Eden likely functioned as a sign of Adam and Eve's continual dependence on God for life. They would have been expected to demonstrate that dependence by eating from it regularly, but now they had chosen the other tree, the one demonstrating independence, and as a result they lost access to the one associated with life.

That understanding helps us address an ongoing question about human immortality. Were people created immortal, becoming mortal only through the Fall, or were they created mortal, becoming immortal only in the resurrection? If by "immortal" we mean people have the innate capacity to live forever, neither position is correct. God alone possesses immortality (1 Tim. 6:16), so our eternal life is never innate; it is only derived. God sustains us in life. Adam and Eve were capable of dying from the moment they were created, but they might also have lived forever. It all depended on the life-giving work of God, which He conditioned on human obedience. When they ate the forbidden fruit, death became a reality.

Implications

The curses of Genesis 3 explain the major struggles of life in the ancient Near East. The words to the woman reflect tensions within the home and the realities of childbearing. The words to the man give lasting perspective to work, sweat, weeds, and death in an agrarian society.

The gender-relatedness of these pronouncements should not cause us to stumble. Women have always done more than their share of pulling weeds, and men should be as concerned as their wives about the affairs of their homes. The point is that, regardless of sex, we see ourselves and our struggles more vividly here than we would like to admit. We still demonstrate unfaith, pride, desire, self-justification, and cruelty. We still reap sin's consequences in the home, the workplace, and the cemetery.

8

The Effect of Sin on Human Nature

AFTER THEY HAD BEEN DRIVEN OUT of the Garden, Adam and Eve found that the only road back was blocked by the flashing sword and the cherubim. They had not hesitated to challenge the authority of God when it took the form of a verbal threat, but the sword would prove more effective than the commandment. Self-interest now told them to stay where they were. That way they could at least stay alive, although life here was certainly different. There would be no more easy cultivation of the fruit trees, as the ground felt hard beneath their feet and their clothes snagged on the wild brush. Better to tear garments than one's flesh, and neither of them wanted to go naked, but those clothes still felt odd next to their skin. That wasn't so bad; they would grow used to the clothing. But the loneliness was something different. Standing together to the east of Eden, each felt alone—betrayed by the other, alienated from God, and confused about how it had all come apart so quickly. Neither they nor their descendants would ever be comfortable with that.

The children were all born outside of Eden. Cain came first (Gen. 4:1), then Abel (4:2), Seth (4:25), and other sons and daughters (5:4), who married and had children of their own.[1] None of them ever saw the tree of life or had a chance to taste or reject the forbidden fruit. At the same time, none of them enjoyed marriage relationships without some degree of rivalry or resentment, and they inevitably ate bread produced

161

by the sweat of their brow. Born into a fallen world, they knew only the curse, never Eden. Still they knew this was not the way life was supposed to be. When Noah was born, his father Lamech hoped that somehow the boy would bring relief "from the toil of our hands arising from the ground which the LORD has cursed" (5:29).

Adam and Eve had sinned alone, but they were not the only ones locked out of the Garden. Cut off from the tree of life, they and their descendants were all destined to die. That fact is underscored in Genesis 5, which contains the Bible's first genealogical record. Many other Scripture passages record family histories, but this is the only one with the repeated phrase "and he died" after each name listed. Adam lived 930 years, "and he died" (5:5). Seth lived 912 years, "and he died" (5:8). Enosh lived 905 years, "and he died" (5:11). Kenan, Mahalalel, Jared, Methuselah, Lamech—every one of them died. Other than Enoch, whom God "took" (5:24), every one of Adam's descendants experienced death the same way he had. Each one followed Adam from dust to dust, apparently sharing the consequences of his disobedience.

That may not seem entirely fair to us. We might think it would have been better for the angels to have run a nursery school for Adam's children back in the Garden, giving each of them a chance to grow, mature, and take their own turn with the serpent. There would be two different civilizations—one consisting of those who had not yet disobeyed and the other of those who had, with buses departing Eden each evening for those who failed the test. But God did not orchestrate things this way. As the patriarch of the human family, Adam made choices that continue to affect his descendants. We have all made additional choices ourselves, for which we are held responsible (as Cain was for his rejection of God's warning and his murder of Abel; 4:7–12), but we continue as members of Adam's family. Born and raised outside of Eden, we live out the penalty of his disobedience as if it were our own.

SPIRITUAL DEATH AND
THE INHERITANCE OF ADAM'S GUILT

Dead in Trespasses and Sins

In Ephesians 2:1 Paul began a review of his readers' salvation by reminding them that they had been dead in trespasses and sins before experiencing new life in Christ. Since they were obviously alive physically during that time, commentators often describe this as "spiritual death." That expression does not mean that one's "spirit" has ceased to exist, for that would constitute the annihilation of the individual. To be spiritually dead is to be alienated from God, to have no vital relationship with Him.

We have already seen that the Jewish view of life encompassed more than just physical existence. It also included blessing in the land of promise in fellowship with God. Those who lacked that kind of existence (like Israel in the Exile) lacked life in its fullness. Since Gentiles, like deceased persons (Ps. 88:4–5), were estranged from the worshiping community and alienated from God's life-giving Spirit, it was not uncommon for later rabbis to describe them as "dead." That description accords well with Paul's comments about his readers' preconversion condition. As those who were spiritually dead, they had been "separate from Christ, excluded from the commonwealth of Israel . . . strangers to the covenants of promise, having no hope and without God in the world" (Eph. 2:12). "Excluded from the life of God" (4:18), they were cut off from communion with Him, isolated by their sinfulness (Col. 2:13).

We who have been born outside of Eden have been born into that condition. Held back from the tree of life, we are estranged from God's presence from the very beginning. We can see that condition in the experience of Adam's immediate descendants, but also in Paul's statements in Romans 5:12–19.

His lengthy comparison between Adam and Christ began with an emphasis on the mediation of Christ in the first part of the chapter. "We have peace with God *through our Lord Jesus Christ*" (5:1). He is the One "*through whom* we have obtained our introduction by faith into this grace in which we stand" (5:2). He "*died for*" us when we were ungodly sinners (5:6, 8). We have been "justified *by His blood*" and "shall be saved from the wrath of God *through Him*" (5:9). "We were reconciled to God *through the death of His Son*" and "shall be saved *by His life*" (5:10). We now "exult in God *through our Lord Jesus Christ*," who, as the Mediator of our salvation is the One "*through whom* we have now received the reconciliation" (5:11). These statements reveal the apostle's major focus at this point in his letter. Describing the work of Christ on our behalf, Paul used the Cross as a conclusive proof for the doctrine of justification by faith.

An Examination of Romans 5

To clarify the mediatorial effect of the Cross, Paul compared it to the sin of Adam, which brought sin into the world. He did not intend to bypass the role of the serpent, whom he apparently identified with Satan (16:20), but to highlight sin's entrance into human experience and its resulting effect on the cosmos (8:19–21). "Through one man sin entered into the world, and death through sin" (5:12). Adam opened the door to sin as an invited guest, but the guest brought along a companion—death. God had warned Adam that death would follow sin, and humanity's banishment from the tree of life fulfilled His word.

Paul continued, "so death spread to all men, because all sinned." This portion of the verse has occasioned much discussion. We have no problem affirming that all people die, but what did Paul mean when he linked death to sin—"death spread to all men because all sinned"? Some believe that his statement refers to the independent choices of individuals. In other words, all people choose to sin of their own free will, and we all die as a result. However, that view runs into two major problems. First, what about infants and mentally handicapped persons who die without making moral choices? How did death spread to them if they have not sinned? Second, how would this position do justice to the rest of Paul's argument? In verses 15–19 he made several statements describing the universal consequences of Adam's sin. "By the transgression of the one the many died" (5:15). "The judgment arose from one transgression, resulting in condemnation" (5:16). "By the transgression of the one, death reigned through the one" (5:17). "Through one transgression there resulted condemnation to all men" (5:18). "Through the one man's disobedience the many were made sinners" (5:19). According to these verses Adam's sin brought death, judgment, and condemnation to all his descendants. Since we experience these things as a consequence of his sin, not ours, there must be some special relationship between us and Adam.

The passage also suggests an explanation for the death of those who never had the chance to make their own moral choices. They died not because of their sin, but because of Adam's. Paul seems to say as much in verses 13 and 14: "for until the Law sin was in the world; but sin is not imputed when there is no law. Nevertheless death reigned from Adam until Moses, even over those who had not sinned in the likeness of Adam's offense, who is a type of Him who was to come." People who lived before the Mosaic Law clearly committed sin ("until the Law sin was in the world"). Two of the Bible's most familiar acts of judgment—the Flood and the destruction of Sodom and Gomorrah—occurred during this period. However, apart from the clearly defined boundaries that would be marked out by the Law, not everyone's sin was evident ("sin is not imputed when there is no law").[2] The Law would eventually reveal sin to be sin and make everyone's failure apparent (3:19–20; 7:7–13), but from Adam to Moses the boundaries were not always so clear. As Paul said earlier in this same letter, "Where there is no law, neither is there violation" (4:15). Still, even those who were comparatively righteous died during this period. "Death reigned from Adam to Moses, even over those who had not sinned in the likeness of Adam's offense" (5:14). Adam had transgressed an explicit commandment, and so would the recipients of the Law. Between them, however, lived people who had no stated commandment to transgress, no clear boundary to cross. But they still died. Moral men, virtuous women, newborn babies—they all died. Why? Paul's words in 5:15 offer an explanation. "By the transgression of the one the many died." Their death shows their guilty standing for a sin committed—in Adam.

Implications

In debates concerning the precise nature of the relationship between us and Adam, two positions have emerged—realism and federalism. Although we have already used the label *realism* with regard to our use of science and our hopes for moral behavior in society, we now employ it again because of its common use in theological discussions of sin. In this context, realism is the belief that all persons *really* sinned along with Adam. As Berkouwer stated, "The hallmark of realism is the conviction that all men are 'co-sinners' with *Adam* in the fullest meaning of that word."[3] John Murray described it more explicitly: "In brief, the position is that human nature in its unindividualized unity existed in its entirety in Adam, that, when Adam sinned, not only did he sin but also the common nature which existed in its unity in him, and that, since each person who comes into the world is an individualization of this one human nature, each person as an 'individualized portion' of that common nature is both culpable and punishable for the sin committed by that unity."[4]

Realists insist that we can be held accountable only for what we have actually done, and they often see a model for our relationship to Adam in the biblical argument that Levi paid tithes to Melchizedek while in the loins of Abraham (Heb. 7:10). Some have understood this "seminal" connection quite literally, maintaining that sin is passed from one generation to another through the seed of the parents.

Federalists are not as confident that the consolidation of human nature in Adam resulted in universal culpability, nor do they believe that we must have been "in" Adam to share the guilt for his sin. If we are guilty because we were in Adam's loins, they ask, does that mean we are also guilty of every sin the rest of our ancestors committed? Why would Adam's sin be highlighted if that were the case? Federalists believe there must be an explanation for Adam's uniqueness that goes beyond the fact that he was the first man, so they say Adam represents us as our covenantal or "federal" head. In this view, his guilt is imputed to us on the basis of his representation of humanity. Some defend this through the concept of "corporate solidarity," in which one member of a group essentially stands for all others. That concept has probably been overstated by some adherents, but it is true that the decisions of kings and patriarchs in the ancient Near East largely determined the fate of their people (Josh. 7:24; 2 Sam. 24:15–17). As king of the earth and patriarch of the human race, Adam failed on behalf of us all.

A "softer" version of federalism maintains that Adam's sin was imputed to us through the mediation of our own choices. In other words, we share in Adam's guilt because each of us has repeated his rebellion. As we might expect, this concept of "mediate imputation" encounters some difficulty in Romans 5, where we have already witnessed Paul's emphasis on the single transgression of Adam. That is why so many federalists hold to "immediate imputation," the idea that Adam's guilt is imputed directly to us, independently of our own sin.

Paul's comparison between Adam and Christ favors federalism over realism, and immediate over mediate imputation. Death spread to all persons not because all sinned in Adam, but because Adam sinned as our representative. We are justified through the work of Christ, not because we were "in Christ" in some seminal or realistic way, but because He functioned as our representative, dying for us and rising again as the Head of a new humanity. Further, our justification does not depend on our own righteous deeds (Rom. 3:28; 4:4–5; Eph. 2:8–9), or even our own determinative choice of Him (Rom. 8:29–30; 9:11–22), so it is best to say that the benefits of salvation are not mediated through our works in any sense. The choices of both representatives, Adam and Christ, are immediately imputed to those under their headship.

Many find the idea of inherited guilt very offensive. It seems to hold people responsible for something in which they had no part, and that arrangement does not seem fair. S. Lewis Johnson Jr. answers this charge by appealing to the imputation of righteousness in Christ. "Since we have fallen in a representative, it is much easier to see why we may be restored through a representative. In the wise and infinite mercy of God there has come a Second Man, a Last Adam. On the principle of representation, he may stand for us. Since he has stood his probation for us victoriously, we may rise in the same manner in which we fell. We fell through no personal fault of our own; we rise through no personal merit of our own. When a father strikes oil, the children get rich. And we have hit a gusher in the Last Adam! I must say that I like representation."[5]

Few people object to representation when it brings so obvious a benefit, but many still believe the principle is unfair when the consequences are negative. They often argue that the Lord explicitly denied inherited guilt when He spoke the following words through Ezekiel: "What do you mean by using this proverb concerning the land of Israel saying, 'The fathers eat the sour grapes, but the children's teeth are set on edge'? As I live . . . you are surely not going to use this proverb in Israel any more. Behold, all souls are Mine, the soul of the father as well as the soul of the son is Mine. The soul who sins will die" (Ezek. 18:2–4).

Jeremiah also prophesied against the "sour grapes" proverb, writing, "In those days they will not say again, 'The fathers have eaten sour grapes, and the children's teeth are set on edge.' But everyone will die for his own iniquity; each man who eats the sour grapes, his teeth will be set on edge" (Jer. 31:29–30). Maintaining that these texts emphasize personal responsibility while ruling out inherited guilt, Smith wrote, "Augustine's doctrine that all human beings are made guilty (and the similar doctrine of others since) because of Adam's sin is simply unbiblical. Ezekiel disposes of such a concept."[6] This objection is more damaging to federalism than to realism, since the latter claims that every individual actually ate the sour grapes in Adam. However, the broader context of these prophecies demonstrates that they are not inconsistent with either model of original sin.

While warning of impending exile, the prophets had to endure scorn, ridicule, and excuses from their skeptical audience. The proverb about sour grapes was apparently one of the more popular excuses. Expressing self-justification and blame, the people claimed that it was unfair to punish them, innocent as they were, for the sins of their fathers. God told Jeremiah, "Now it will come about when you tell this people all these words that they will say to you, 'For what reason has the LORD declared all this great calamity against us? And what is our iniquity, or what is our sin which we have committed against the LORD our God?'" (Jer. 16:10). God then instructed the prophet to tell them judgment was coming not only for their fathers' sin, but also for their own. "Then you are to say to them, 'It is because your forefathers have forsaken Me,' declares the LORD, 'and have followed other gods and served them and bowed down to them; but Me they have forsaken and have not kept My law. You too have done evil, even more than your forefathers; for behold, you are each one walking according to the stubbornness of his own evil heart, without listening to Me. So I will hurl you out of this land into the land which you have not known, neither you nor your fathers; and there you will serve other gods day and night, for I shall grant you no favor'" (16:11–13).

The Exile *was* connected to the sin of their fathers, but the present generation was guilty as well. God did not allow them to justify their own sin by blaming others. In the same way, God told the nation through Ezekiel that they had no right to accuse Him of being unfair in His punishment. "But the house of Israel says, 'The way of the Lord is not right.' Are My ways not right, O house of Israel? Is it not your ways that are not right?" (Ezek. 18:29).

The slogan about the sour grapes had become a statement of self-justification and blame. The people of Israel used it to deny their own sin, to blame their ancestors for whatever judgment was to come their way, and to accuse God of injustice. In that context Jeremiah and Ezekiel had an important message to deliver. Those who were about to experience exile could not excuse themselves by blaming earlier generations, for they were just as sinful as their fathers.

That message does not challenge our interpretation of Romans 5, but rather enhances it. Our tendency toward self-justification makes it especially tempting to blame Adam for God's judgment, just as those in Ezekiel's generation blamed their fathers, but Paul did not leave room for that excuse. As Berkouwer concluded, "Our confession of original sin may not function and cannot function as a means of *excusing ourselves* or of *hiding behind another man's guilt*."[7] We do share a corporate responsibility, as did Israel, but we also have our own personal guilt. Our own choices continually reinvest the dividend of guilt imputed from Adam, and the interest is compounded daily.

Many hear about the authoritative representation of kings and patriarchs and ask, "Who made him king over me? I ought to rebel! Why must I suffer the consequences of his folly?" In the case of Adam, the objection encounters two major obstacles. First, if God made him king of the earth and patriarch of humanity, then to challenge that system is to challenge the One who designed it. Second, though we might say that we would like to overthrow Adam's headship, the continuing sinfulness of our choices demonstrates that we are more comfortable with his leadership than we confess.

SPIRITUAL DEATH AND
THE DOCTRINE OF TOTAL DEPRAVITY

In chapter 4 we briefly considered the effect of the Fall on humanity's being created in the image of God. The image has been defaced but not erased, tarnished but not destroyed, as humanity has exchanged the glory of God for idolatry (Rom. 1:22–23). We retain the capacity to demonstrate God's likeness (even though it is not fully realized), the ability to make moral decisions (even if we make them wrongly), and the potential to reflect the glory of God physically (even if it doesn't look that way now). We were created to reign over the earth as God's vice-regents, but through sin we have surrendered our allegiance to another authority, Satan. Therefore, in spite of the fact that all things were subjected to people (Ps. 8), we do not presently see all things subjected to us (Heb. 2:8).

Because of the Fall, all human existence is today only a shadow of what it was supposed to be. No one fully manifests the image of God. No one is clothed with God's glory the way Adam was. No one stands over creation the way he did. No one demonstrates God's likeness the way he could. Other than the last Adam, Jesus, no one has done any of those things adequately since the day Adam fell. Instead, we find ourselves born as fallen people into a fallen world. We have inherited depravity.

Not everyone sees it that way. Those who deny the historicity of the Fall typically deny the fallenness of human nature as well, frequently maintaining that all people are born essentially good, or at least morally neutral. While their optimism may be tempered by experience, such persons usually believe that we have the ability, through education and will power, to transform human relations and society. We may never create a new Eden, they say, but we could come close.

Christians are not usually quite that cheerful about human nature, and not just because we believe in the Fall. We also believe in salvation by grace through faith. If people can be truly obedient to God or see genuine moral progress in society apart from Christ, what is the place of the gospel? What is the need for grace?

Our beliefs about human nature and the role of grace determine the course of our theology like the rudder on a sailboat. An errant turn here and we shall run aground, endangering the gospel itself. The issue of human ability shapes our expectations for individual morality, social reformation, and spiritual regeneration. It affects the methods we employ in evangelism, discipleship, preaching, and teaching, and it establishes a pattern for our worship as we come to appreciate the matchless grace of our Savior.

The Pelagian Controversy

Pelagius, an ascetic monk from the British Isles, was a popular Christian leader in Rome at the end of the fourth century. He was a gifted individual. Trained in both law and theology, and fluent in Latin and Greek, Pelagius developed a strong following among Roman aristocrats, many of whom dedicated themselves to the ascetic life under his supervision. That life, as understood by Pelagius, was made possible by the grace of God, who gives everyone the natural capacity to follow His will. Someone wishing to please the Lord needs only to exercise that capacity for obedience in will and behavior. He wrote, "We do either good or evil only by our own will; since we always remain capable of both, we are always free to do either."[8] Though he believed Christians should be better persons after being cleansed by the blood of Christ and regenerated, Pelagius maintained that all persons are capable of holy behavior. They may have developed habits of sin that are later difficult to break, but the fault lies not with their nature or with God's standard, but only with their will, which can direct them to either obedience or sin. Pelagius supported his view in the following way. "No one knows the extent of our power better than the one who gave us our strength. No one understands what we can do better than the one who endowed us with the capacity for virtue. The just one did not choose to command the impossible; nor did the loving one plan to condemn a person for what he could not avoid."[9]

Such statements met with wide approval in Pelagius's day, and some modern readers may also be perfectly comfortable with his position, which sounds like some recent defenses of free will. His contemporary Augustine, however, recognized some problems.

Augustine regarded the Fall as a watershed in human history. Pelagius apparently didn't see it that way, and that was bound to produce some disagreements. Augustine was not as well trained as Pelagius, and he may not have had as charismatic a personality or as striking an appearance. However, as anyone reading his *Confessions* can see, Augustine knew the grace of God, and from his own experience he knew the weakness of human nature. He saw neither of these concepts in the teachings of Pelagius.

From Augustine's perspective, Pelagius did not properly acknowledge the role of God's grace in obedience. It was not sufficient, Augustine argued, to say that God provides us with examples of faithfulness, insight into His commandments, or a neutral capacity to make decisions. Citing Paul's statement that God is at work in us "both to will and to work for His good pleasure" (Phil. 2:13), Augustine said that God must act to produce good works in us if they are to be performed at all. Otherwise, we will not desire to do as we should nor act as we should. Pelagius's error, he said, was in believing that our will and our capacity to act "are so stable, strong, and self-sufficient that they do not need God's aid. Thus he believes that God does not help us to will, that he does not help us to act, that he helps us only to be able to will and to act."[10] Augustine's own perspective is evident in the following statement. "My entire hope is in your very great mercy. Grant what you command, and command what you will. You require continence. A certain writer has said: 'As I knew that no one can be continent except God grants it, and this very thing is a part of wisdom, to know whose gift this is.' . . . He loves you less who together with you loves something which he does not love for your sake. O love, you ever burn and are never extinguished. O charity, my God, set me on fire. You command continence; grant what you command, and command what you will."[11]

Augustine's view was plain. Left to ourselves, we will not obey. "Command what you will"—Lord, tell me to do whatever You wish. But "grant what you command"—unless You move me to do what You have commanded, I simply will not do it.

That selection from Augustine's *Confessions* reportedly enraged Pelagius, who saw it as an example of the passivity he sought to condemn. Why would God have to grant us the ability to obey if He has already created us according to His own plan? Did He not know what He was doing when He created us, or perhaps when He gave us commandments? Pelagius believed God had been gracious in giving us laws and helping us understand them. Augustine agreed, but said God was even more gracious in helping us obey them. Apart from that grace, we would transgress His commands, and the Law would result only in condemnation. As Augustine wrote, the Law "diagnoses illness but does not cure."[12]

At the heart of their debate lay a simple disagreement about human nature and the Fall. Pelagius believed that people had been created neutral and could choose to obey or disobey. Augustine believed that because people are fallen, they are no longer neutral. Fallen people, he argued, have a bent toward evil, and they will perform evil unless moved by God to do good. He wrote, "Since [the saints] will not actually persevere unless they both can and will, in the abundance of [God's] grace he gives them both the capacity and the will to persevere. Their wills are so inflamed by the Holy Spirit that they are able because they so will, and they so will because God causes them to will."[13]

Augustine's model of human nature is obviously connected to a much larger question—the relationship between divine sovereignty and human responsibility in salvation. The implications for salvation are what make this issue so important. Are all persons capable of choosing salvation? Or are our hearts so hardened by sin that we will not choose God unless He first chooses us and then moves us to embrace the gospel? Augustine strongly believed the latter, so he thought that Pelagius's emphasis on human ability constituted a denial of the grace of God, even a denial of the gospel itself.

According to Augustine, "the grace Pelagius acknowledges is God's showing and revealing what we ought to do, not his giving and helping us to do it."[14] Augustine responded to this teaching by citing biblical texts that describe God's work in salvation, arguing that God influences the will of selected individuals, making them willing to embrace the gospel. For example, he observed that John 6:45 reads, "Everyone who has heard and learned from the Father comes to Me." Then he commented, "If this grace only helped our capacity, the Lord would have said, 'Everyone who has heard and learned from the Father can come to me.' This, however, is not what he said, but instead, 'Everyone who has heard and learned from the Father comes to me.' . . . Yet it does not follow that a person who can come actually does come unless he wills and accomplishes it. Everyone, however, who learns from the Father not only can come, but actually does come. Here, the actualization of the capacity, the movement of the will, and the achievement of the operation are found together."[15]

We are drifting rather quickly into issues better treated in a volume on salvation, but Augustine treats all these doctrines as implications of his view of sin. If the Fall has left us unwilling to come to Christ, then God must make us willing if we are to be saved. Not everyone comes; only those come whom God graciously draws to Himself, whom He has chosen for salvation before they even existed to somehow merit the choice. If He so moves our will, we inevitably embrace the gospel. Moreover, we continue to persevere in the faith only because God continually enables us to do so, completing the work He set out to accomplish. "We whom God is pleased to aid more fully through Jesus Christ our Lord receive not only the assistance necessary to be able to persevere if we so will, but the kind of help which also makes us will it. This grace of God not only makes us able to do what we will in receiving and steadfastly retaining good, but it actually makes us will to do what we can."[16]

Here we see concepts that have been taught and debated throughout the history of the church. Irresistible grace, the perseverance of the saints, and unconditional election, three of the doctrines that became definitive for what would later be called Calvinism, can all be found in Augustine's writings against Pelagius. We will not consider those teachings in any detail, but we do need to take some time with a fourth "Calvinistic" doctrine, the one that served as the focal point of the Pelagian controversy and held the rest of these ideas together—the concept of total depravity. J. Patout Burns summarized that belief as it was taught by Augustine:

> In [a] fallen condition, asserted Augustine, the human person lacks the resources to love and choose the good which he can still recognize through the natural light of reason, the revelation of the commandments, the teaching and example of Christ. In the absence of the grace of charity, he is morally and religiously impotent, incapable of moving toward salvation. Although he may struggle against the power of concupiscence and restrain his fleshly appetites, he only overcomes one passion by another or by the fear of punishment rooted in self-love. Without the grace of Christ, a person's freedom of choice is in servitude to sin, selfishly choosing among evils."[17]

Siding with Augustine one year after his death, the Third Ecumenical Council at Ephesus condemned Pelagius in 431. Their assessment has been repeated by almost every major council, creed, and confession ever since, so no self-respecting Christian theologian would ever want to be known as a Pelagian. However, not everyone agreed with Augustine either, and for sixteen hundred years, various moderating positions have been suggested. That makes it all the more necessary that we examine the issue of depravity from a biblical perspective. Are we born morally neutral, or with an overwhelming tendency toward evil? How has the Fall affected our ability to make moral choices, to reason rightly, or to desire what is good?

The Fallen State of Humanity

Early in Jesus' ministry, when He was in Jerusalem for the Passover, many people were believing in Him because of the signs He performed. "But Jesus, on His part, was not entrusting Himself to them, for He knew all men, and because He did not need anyone to bear witness concerning man for He Himself knew what was in man" (John 2:24–25). John did not go any further to explain what makes all people untrustworthy, but we might speculate that it is a heart that prefers personal glory to God's (5:44).

Many Roman Catholics, following Augustine, have argued that baptism overcomes original sin by infusing sanctifying grace, the grace of God by which an individual manifests personal righteousness. Some have relied on that doctrine to say that the primary effect of original sin itself must be the *absence* of sanctifying grace.[18] However, our sinful state consists of more than just alienation from God or the privation of His grace. We also have a natural tendency toward evil. After all, we not only fail to perform good works, sins of omission; we also actively pursue rebellious deeds, sins of commission. Left to our own devices, we sin. Jesus knew "what was in man," not just what was lacking.

Still, immediately after reporting Christ's negative assessment about human nature, John presented the story of Nicodemus, who heard Jesus say that "unless one is born again, he cannot see the kingdom of God" (3:3). To be born again, or born of the Spirit (3:5–8) is to be regenerated by the indwelling of the Holy Spirit (7:37–39; Titus 3:5–6). John set up an interesting tension by placing these two accounts together. Jesus "knew what was in man"—an untrustworthy heart. But He focused on what was not in man—the Spirit.

The solution makes good sense in light of biblical theology. The spiritual death that resulted from Adam's sin might be described most clearly as alienation from the Spirit of God. His absence brings death, but His presence through the gospel brings eternal life and ethical transformation (Rom. 8:11–14; Gal. 5:22–25; see also Ezek. 36:27). That ethical transformation is demanded by our natural tendency to sin, a predisposition that God counters in the elect as He re-creates them through the inbreathing of His Spirit. We will see that pattern repeatedly as we examine several verses that treat the presence of the Spirit as the solution to human depravity.

According to 2 Corinthians 4:4, unbelievers have had their minds blinded by Satan, "the god of this world." As a result, they cannot come to an accurate assessment of the gospel. For believers, however, the situation is different. "For God, who said, 'Light shall shine out of darkness,' is the One who has shone in our hearts to give the light of the knowledge of the glory of God in the face of Christ" (4:6). He has taken the initiative to remove the blindness, enabling us to see and embrace the gospel. As a result, "we all, with unveiled face beholding as in a mirror the glory of the Lord, are being transformed into the same image from glory to glory, just as from the Lord, the Spirit" (3:18).

We see the same pattern in Paul's first letter to the Corinthians. People do not naturally embrace the message of the Cross, but instead regard it as absurd (1 Cor. 1:18). "A natural man does not accept the things of the Spirit of God; for they are foolishness to him, and he cannot understand them, because they are spiritually appraised" (2:14). The context reveals that "the things of the Spirit of God" are the essential features of Paul's gospel preaching, and here he explains why people do not accept the message. They think it is foolish and they can't understand it. They might be able to repeat the tenets of the gospel, but they do not recognize that it is true. They just don't get it. Why not? Because the message is "spiritually appraised." Apart from the Spirit, they do not come to an accurate understanding. Without His appraisal, it looks foolish.

In Ephesians 4:17–19 Paul wrote, "This I say therefore, and affirm together with the Lord, that you walk no longer just as the Gentiles also walk, in the futility of their mind, being darkened in their understanding, excluded from the life of God, because of the ignorance that is in them, because of the hardness of their heart; and they, having become callous, have given themselves over to sensuality, for the practice of every kind of impurity with greediness."

Some may see this generalized statement about the condition and behavior of Gentiles as an example of Jewish bigotry, but Paul, apostle to the Gentiles, was addressing a largely Gentile church and encouraging them not to fall back into their former manner of life. This is not prejudice, nor is it hyperbole. It is Paul's perception of those with unbelieving minds. They are hardhearted, ignorant of the truth, and spiritually dead. By contrast, Paul reminded the Ephesian believers that they had been given life through the gospel (2:4–6), and he prayed that God would grant them strength and a deep knowledge of His grace through the Spirit (3:14–19). Again, if not for the Holy Spirit, they would be just as depraved as their neighbors.

Romans 1:18–32 contains a similar indictment, one in which Paul used the present tense. They *"suppress* the truth," and are "*being filled* with all unrighteousness." This rebellion is not just a matter of historical record; it is ongoing. People are *now* suppressing the truth that is evident in the creation, and they are *now* filled with every imaginable evil.

Paul included all humanity in this description. The vice list was meant not to be selective, but inclusive; these are the sorts of things sinful people do. If anyone thinks he has been left off the list, he is mistaken, for arrogance and boasting show up along with all the rest! To drive that point home, Paul opened his next paragraph by writing, "Therefore you are without excuse, every man of you who passes judgment, for in that you judge another, you condemn yourself; for you who judge practice the same things" (2:1). He then addressed the Jewish members of his audience more specifically, recognizing that they may have thought chapter 1 was only about the Gentiles. He wrapped up his case in 3:9–12 by writing the following: "What then? Are we better than they? Not at all; for we have already charged that both Jews and Greeks are all under sin; as it is written, "There is none righteous, not even one; there is none who understands, there is none who seeks for God; all have turned aside, together they have become useless; there is none who does good, there is not even one.""

For someone attempting to go the way of Pelagius, this passage of Scripture would not be very encouraging. God's grace in bringing us to salvation must go beyond His gracious gift of the Law, for Paul argued that the Law offers no way out. It only reveals our sinfulness. The problem is not one of clarity, but one of willingness. Natural revelation should have made God's presence obvious (1:19–20), and every person's conscience bears witness of universal standards (2:15), but the Law went much further than that. It provided "the embodiment of knowledge and of the truth" (2:20). Paul's point is that all people know what they should do, but nobody does it. We may naturally know moral standards, but we don't naturally pursue moral behavior. Our utter failure demonstrates that salvation can only be by grace. If it hinges on our obedience or our own natural willingness to seek after the Lord, it simply won't happen. "There is none who does good, there is not even one" (3:12).

This bleak conclusion about the condition of the human race provided the foundation for Paul's emphasis on justification by faith, which he explained in Romans 4–5. Christ died for us when we were helpless, ungodly sinners (5:6, 8). We were God's enemies, alienated from God through the fall of Adam, guilty of our own sinful actions, and more inclined to rebel than to obey, but "we were reconciled to God through the death of His Son" (5:10). On our own, we did not seek after the Lord, and we might have even been described as "haters of God" (1:30). But "the love of God has been poured out within our hearts through the Holy Spirit who was given to us" (5:5), and He has enabled us to "exult in God through our Lord Jesus Christ, through whom we have now received the reconciliation" (5:11). That change of heart may not be quite what the psalmist had in mind, but his words still fit: "He put a new song in my mouth, a song of praise to our God" (Ps. 40:3). That song wasn't in our hearts before, and we didn't write it. We praise the Lord as an expression of His grace.

Grace has always made some people a little uncomfortable. A newspaper columnist recently referred to eternal security as "the doctrine of slack." Paul anticipated that response from some of his readers. "What shall we say then? Are we to continue in sin that grace might increase?" (6:1). That question set up a lengthy discussion in which the apostle told his readers why they should faithfully obey God. It would take us beyond our subject to examine the entire argument, in which Paul essentially reminded believers that they no longer owed any allegiance to sin, but are newly accountable to God, who has reconciled us to Himself in Christ.[19] However, we do need to ponder Paul's comments here about the condition of individuals apart from Christ.

"You were slaves of sin" (6:17), Paul wrote, and "you presented your [bodily] members as slaves to impurity and to lawlessness, resulting in further lawlessness" (6:19). To be a slave of sin is to follow its lead continually. Now, since believers have been "freed from sin and enslaved to God," Paul said, "Do not let sin reign in your mortal body that you should obey its lusts" (6:12). It should no longer govern our behavior as it did when one act of disobedience led to another, when we were on that slide toward radical evil.

Paul provided an extended illustration of sin's mastery over an unbeliever in Romans 7. Many interpreters read his words and conclude that Paul must have been describing his own present experience. After all, he wrote in the first person, used the present tense, and spoke of wanting to do good. However, several factors suggest that he was describing a typical unbeliever's experience (perhaps his own).

First, we need to recognize the structure of Paul's argument. We see from 8:9 that Paul would never describe believers as being "in the flesh." That verse reads, "You are not in the flesh but in the Spirit, if indeed the Spirit of God dwells in you. But if anyone does not have the Spirit of Christ, he does not belong to Him." Believers, all of whom belong to Christ, are all indwelt by the Spirit of God. Those not indwelt by the Spirit—unbelievers—are all "in the flesh." That sheds considerable light on Paul's introductory comment in 7:5: "While we were in the flesh, the sinful passions, which were aroused by the Law, were at work in the members of our body to bear fruit for death." That statement, which reflects back on preconversion "in-the-flesh" experiences, provides a preview of what follows in the rest of the chapter. In verses 7–11 Paul described the manner in which sinful passions were aroused by the Law, and in verses 11–23 he discussed the way in which those passions were at work in the members of his body to bear fruit for death. Thus verse 5, which describes the experience of one "in the flesh," nicely previews the rest of chapter 7. Verse 6 then previews chapter 8: "But now we have been released from the Law, having died to that by which we were bound, so that we serve in newness of the Spirit and not in oldness of the letter." Chapter 8 opens with the idea that we have been freed from sin and death at conversion, and it describes in detail our service to God through the Spirit. If 7:5–6 provides a preview of the rest of

Paul's argument, as they seem to do, then most of chapter 7 is describing a preconversion experience.

Second, Paul's statements about being "sold into bondage to sin" (7:14) and being made "a prisoner of the law of sin which is in my members" (7:23) more appropriately describe the experience of an unbeliever. Many of us read Romans 7 and identify with the struggle it details, but the fact that we see ourselves here does not mean Paul wrote these words to describe believers. It may simply be that our experience is alarmingly similar to that of an unbeliever attempting to fulfill the Law. Since Paul had just said that believers are "no longer slaves to sin" (6:6), are "freed from sin and enslaved to God" (6:22), and are "released from the Law" (7:6), it would be surprising to see him immediately describe himself as sold into bondage to sin.

But why did he write in the first person, using the present tense? Paul apparently regarded himself as a representative Israelite, identifying with his people so thoroughly that he put himself "in their shoes" with his writing. He used the same technique in 3:7: "But if through my lie the truth of God abounded to His glory, why am I also still being judged as a sinner?" Paul did not believe he was still subject to judgment any more than he believed he was still a slave of sin, but he identified with those who remained in his former condition and vividly recalled the experience.

If Romans 7 does describe the preconversion experience of someone who wished to fulfill the Law, it gives us a more complete picture of human depravity, one that provides balance to the passages discussed earlier. Unbelievers can, in some sense, have a "zeal for God," but it is inevitably misdirected. Paul wrote of unsaved Jews, "For I bear them witness that they have a zeal for God, but not in accordance with knowledge. For not knowing about God's righteousness, and seeking to establish their own, they did not subject themselves to the righteousness of God" (10:2–3). Such a person may take great comfort, even delight, in the Law while refusing to subject himself or herself to the One to whom it points (John 5:46). One may have an inner agreement with the Law and a desire to obey it, but if that zeal is misguided, or the stated desire for obedience is not reflected in the decisions of one's heart, the whole effort is futile. If written from that perspective, as seems to be the case, Romans 7 may be more an autobiography than an

"Everyman" account. Paul himself had faithfully studied the Law and zealously kept the commandments, considering himself a defender of the faith and a righteous man (Phil. 3:5–6). But on the Damascus Road he found himself on the wrong side. As a persecutor of the church, he stood opposed to Christ (Acts 9:4). That is the sort of person A. W. Pink had in mind when writing about the moral unbeliever.

> If all men alike are totally depraved, then how is it that some lead less vicious lives than others? In examining this question it is necessary to revert to our definition of terms, and bear in mind that total depravity does not consist in what a man *does*, but what he *is* in himself. It also consists in a man's relation and attitude *to God*. Because particular persons are not swearers, morally unclean, drunkards or thieves, they are very apt to imagine they are far from being wholly corrupt; in fact, they consider themselves good and respectable people. These are described in Proverbs 30:12: "There is a generation that are pure in their own eyes, and yet is not washed from their filthiness." However irreproachable may be the walk of the natural man, his nature is polluted and his heart thoroughly defiled. And the very fact that he is quite unaware of his vileness is sad proof of the binding power of indwelling sin.[20]

Indwelling sin twists the motives of apparently good acts and consistently produces a selfish bent toward evil. Several biblical passages regard it as a universal problem, one that begins at birth. "Foolishness is bound up in the heart of a child" (Prov. 22:15). "The intent of man's heart is evil from his youth" (Gen. 8:21). "Behold, I was brought forth in iniquity, and in sin my mother conceived me" (Ps. 51:5). "The wicked are estranged from the womb; those who speak lies go astray from birth" (58:3). We "were by nature children of wrath" (Eph. 2:3). People may become enslaved to particular sins by practice, but they are enslaved to sin itself by nature.

The Bondage of the Will

In Romans 8 Paul described the freedom experienced by those who are in Christ. "There is therefore now no condemnation for those who are in

Christ Jesus. For the law of the Spirit of life in Christ Jesus has set you free from the law of sin and of death" (8:1–2). Christ delivered us from the penalty of sin, so there is no more condemnation. He has fulfilled the requirements of the Law on our behalf, so it no longer declares us guilty (8:3–4; 10:4). His death, resurrection, and exaltation resulted in the sending of the life-giving Holy Spirit, who transforms (indeed, re-creates) us, delivering us from the power of sin.

This continues the pattern we have seen in other passages. People have a natural bent toward evil, but God counters it with the gift of His Spirit. Here Paul described unbelievers as those who "walk according to the flesh" and "set their minds on the things of the flesh." Believers, however, "walk according to the Spirit" and "set their minds on the things of the Spirit" (8:4–5). The "mind set on the flesh" yields death, but the "mind set on the Spirit" yields life and peace. "The mind set on the flesh is hostile toward God; for it does not subject itself to the law of God, for it is not even able to do so; and those who are in the flesh cannot please God" (8:7–8). By contrast, those who are in the Spirit "are putting to death the deeds of the body" (8:13), and are "being led by the Spirit of God" (8:14).

The changed lifestyle experienced by believers is attributed to the Spirit. It is "by the Spirit" that Christians are "putting to death the deeds of the body (8:13)," and it is the Spirit who enables us to call God "Abba! Father!" (8:15). Those "in the flesh," devoid of the Spirit, cannot subject themselves to God's law or know Him as Father. Martin Luther wrote, "The elect, who fear God, will be reformed by the Holy Spirit; the rest will perish unreformed."[21]

But if unbelievers cannot truly reform themselves, if they are unable to subject themselves to God's Law, how can they still be liable for their sin? John Taylor, an eighteenth-century English clergyman, stated the problem this way: "If we come into the World infected and *depraved* with sinful Dispositions, then Sin must be *natural* to us; and if *natural,* then *necessary;* and if *necessary,* then no Sin."[22] Sin is natural to those born outside of Eden, and that does make it inevitable. However, sin is inevitable because our depraved wills desire it, not because we have been compelled to choose it. Within the constraints of our humanity, we are free to do what we desire. Our problem lies in the fact that we apparently do not really desire to do good; otherwise we would do it. We would rather sin. As Luther wrote, "A man without the Spirit of God does not do evil against his will, under pressure, as though he were taken by the scruff of the neck and dragged into it, like a thief . . . being dragged off against his will to punishment; but he does it spontaneously and voluntarily."[23] Reflecting that perspective, Jonathan Edwards answered Taylor by saying that sin may be "morally necessary" in that morally depraved people will certainly choose it, but it is not "naturally necessary," for nothing outside of oneself compels anyone to choose sin.[24] People are not forced to do it; they want to do it. And for that reason they are responsible.

Edwards reinforced the point by distinguishing between natural and moral inability. We're naturally unable to fly by simply flapping our arms. We couldn't get airborne even if we chose to try. Unbelievers are naturally able to obey God, for His commands are not impossible for humans to follow, but they are morally unable to obey Him, because their twisted wills do not allow them to submit to His authority. We cannot be blamed for natural inability, but we are responsible for moral inability. Sam Storms suggests the following example: "If it is placed upon a person as a duty to give money to the poor and yet, through no fault of his own, he has no money to give, he is not blameworthy for not giving. He labors under a *natural inability*. But if he has the money and does not *want* to give, he labors under a *moral inability*, namely, a lack of the required disposition and inclination of heart, and thus is to be blamed."[25]

When we sin, we have nobody to blame but ourselves. We sin because we choose to do so. However, as slaves of sin, we will not choose to do righteousness unless God intervenes. Apart from Him, we will continue to choose sin. Augustine said, in a statement later quoted by John Calvin, "To will is of nature, but to will aright is of grace."[26] In the same way, Luther argued that the unbeliever's willingness to sin "is something which he cannot in his own strength eliminate, restrain, or alter."[27] The will is in bondage to sin, and it will not be released except through the outside intervention of the Spirit of God. Luther stated, "Let all the 'free-will' in the world do all it can with all its strength; it will never give rise to a single instance of ability to avoid being hardened if God does not give the Spirit, or of meriting mercy if it is left to its own strength."[28]

Like the concept of inherited guilt, this perspective on what Luther called "the bondage of the will" does not set very well with many modern-day readers, who would prefer a stronger emphasis on human freedom. We must remember, however, that people are always free to do what they *choose* to do, within the constraints of their nature and their circumstances. I am not free to fly unassisted, for that would violate human nature. Nor am I free to walk on the moon, for I am constrained to earth by my circumstances. Here in my home, however, I am free to get out of my chair and walk wherever I wish. It is humanly possible for anyone to worship God, and one can worship in any setting, so there are no outward constraints preventing anyone from adoring the Savior. However, the inward constraint of a heart that is "more deceitful than all else and is desperately sick" (Jer. 17:9) prevents unbelievers from genuine worship. We are free to do what we *wish*, but because our choices demonstrate the orientation of our hearts, when left to ourselves *we will inevitably choose evil.*

The concept of depravity helps explain why unbelievers continue to sin, but why does sin remain such a problem for Christians? Indwelt by the Holy Spirit, we have the capacity to conduct ourselves in a way that is pleasing to God. Why do we continue to fail?

The Christian's Struggle with Indwelling Sin

We have seen that Adam's sin left all humanity in a state of spiritual death. We have also seen that those who are thus alienated from God will not produce works of righteousness on their own, for they follow the desires of their sinful hearts and continually rebel against God. That self-centered orientation is overcome by the Spirit of God, who brings enlightenment to those who had been blinded in unbelief, life to those who were spiritually dead, and the love of God to those who had been His enemies. His presence enables believers to obey as they "put to death the deeds of the body" (Rom. 8:13) and are conformed to the image of Christ (2 Cor. 3:18).

However, all these operations are progressive. The elect are enlightened enough through the Spirit's effectual calling that they embrace the gospel (Acts 16:14; Rom. 8:30),[29] but He continues to provide insight into the love of Christ, enabling us to grow in our devotion to Him (Eph.

3:14–19; Phil. 1:9–11). When we finally see Him, we will know as we are known (1 Cor. 13:12). In the same way, we have been made alive in Christ (Eph. 2:5), but we still look forward to the resurrection (Rom. 8:11, 23). While we wait, we find that suffering and obedience progressively manifest His life in us (2 Cor. 3:11–12, 16). Paul's references to putting to death the deeds of the body (Rom. 8:13), being led by the Spirit of God (8:14), and becoming conformed to Christ's image (2 Cor. 3:18) are all in the present tense, describing ongoing action. We are *being* changed, and the Spirit's presence in us constitutes the firstfruits, not the fullness, of the life to come (Rom. 8:23).

That incomplete conformity to the image of Christ means that even Christians continue to demonstrate the consequences of Adam's sin. All people share in Adam's guilt, for he sinned as our appointed representative. That guilt, along with the guilt of our own sins, has been forgiven for those of us who are in Christ. Everyone experiences alienation from God as a consequence of the Fall, but that too has been overcome for believers. We have been reconciled to God and indwelt by the Spirit. However, as already noted, guilt and alienation are not our only problems. We are also born with a natural bent toward evil. Apparently that leaning has been countered, but not yet fully corrected.

God promised a "new heart" as part of the New Covenant (Ezek. 36:26), and some Christians think they have already received it in its fullness. Believing that to be the case, they attribute a believer's sinful actions to something other than his true self—old habits, poor instruction, or even demonic oppression. However, we have already seen that there is no "real me" other than the one that thinks and acts day after day. I am being changed by the presence of the Spirit, but I am not becoming the real me, nor is the real me revealing his true colors. Instead, the real me has an inconsistent heart, and my choices evidence both a God-given love for the Savior and a continuing love for myself. We as Christians must continually "put on a heart of compassion, humility, gentleness, and patience" (Col. 3:12) and be transformed by the renewing of our minds (Rom. 12:2). The re-creation work of the Spirit has begun, but it is not yet complete.

Many Christians locate sin in a particular "part" of their being, which they label the "flesh," attempting to follow Paul's usage of the term in

Galatians 5. I prefer not to describe indwelling sin in that way, because Paul's primary point in contrasting the flesh and the Spirit is more complex. In Philippians, Paul wrote that he did not want to "place confidence in the flesh" but to glory in Christ instead (Phil. 3:3). He then described how he might have trusted in the flesh. "If anyone else has a mind to put confidence in the flesh, I far more: circumcised the eighth day, of the nation of Israel, of the tribe of Benjamin, a Hebrew of Hebrews; as to the Law, a Pharisee; as to zeal, a persecutor of the church; as to the righteousness which is in the Law, found blameless" (3:4–6). Some of Paul's Jewish opponents believed one usually entered into a right relationship with God by being born into the covenant as a descendant of Abraham, and they thought one maintained that relationship by obeying the Law.[30] Circumcision served as the sign of both membership in the covenant and conformity to the Law. The apostle described trust in that system as trust "in the flesh." He had once followed that pattern, trusting in his inheritance and his zeal for the Law, but it had left him opposed to Christ, and he forsook it "in view of the surpassing value of knowing Christ Jesus my Lord" (3:8).

Paul feared that the Galatians were going the opposite direction. His opponents wanted the Gentile converts there to be circumcised, demonstrating their adoption of the Mosaic Law and their desire to keep it. Paul was convinced that such action would constitute an abandonment of the gospel (Gal. 5:2–4). He told his readers he was confident they would not really do that (5:10), but he had no such confidence in the false teachers. "They desire to have you circumcised that they may boast in your flesh" (6:13). Paul knew that circumcision itself did not really matter (5:6; 6:15), but it mattered greatly when it symbolized a different gospel. Believers, he argued, were not under the Law and had no need for the symbol.

In that context Paul argued that the flesh and the Spirit are opposed to one another as competing ways of salvation. He highlighted their incompatibility by personifying the flesh as having "desires" that oppose those of the Spirit (5:17). The flesh could never bring salvation, because righteousness does not come through the Law (2:21). The Law simply shows people where they are guilty, thus helping to prepare them for the gospel of Christ (3:21–24). Those who pursue righteousness through the Law will end up in rebellion, pursuing the same kinds of sins as the Gentiles (e.g., idolatry), and they will not inherit the kingdom of God (5:19–21). By contrast, those who find salvation by genuinely embracing the gospel will actually fulfill the intent of God's Law as they walk by the Spirit (5:22–23).

In Galatians, Paul used the term "flesh" to describe a Spirit-less attempt at righteousness (represented most prominently by circumcision), and in Romans 8:9 he described unbelievers as "in the flesh." His use of the term in these other contexts helps explain why Paul could say in Romans 7:18 that "nothing good dwells in me, that is, in my flesh." Apart from the Spirit, unbelievers are, so to speak, nothing more than unanimated, dead flesh. Nothing is good about that condition. They experience only depravity and service to sin (7:25).

This perspective on the struggle between the flesh and the Spirit argues that sin is not located in a particular part of us known as the flesh. The physical connotations of the term should always have rendered that view suspect. After all, how could "flesh" denote something essentially immaterial? But when those physical connotations were retained, the term was occasionally used to support an unbiblical dualism in which the body, the physical flesh, is inherently evil. Such efforts to locate sin in a single aspect of our being seem inappropriate. We are fallen, and are being redeemed, as whole and complex persons. That reality suggests the first major implication of this discussion on depravity. We continue to sin, but we cannot blame our struggle on a particular part of ourselves, nor can we blame it on others. To do so would be to avoid full responsibility for our behavior, and that avoidance would only compound the problem.

IMPLICATIONS

Some believers respond to their continuing struggle with sinful desires by punishing or cursing themselves. For example, a thirteenth-century Franciscan, Giacomino di Verona, wrote, "In a very dirty and vile workroom you were made out of slime, so foul and so wretched that my lips cannot bring themselves to tell you about it. But if you have a bit of sense, you will know that the fragile body in which you lived, where you were tormented eight months and more, was made of rotting and corrupt ex-crement. . . . Other creatures have some use; meat and bone, wool and leather; but you, stinking man, you are worse than dung: from you, man, comes only pus."[31]

A "pious" French woman a few centuries later continually afflicted her body in order to remind herself of her depravity. Jean Delumeau re-counted her story: "This woman engaged in extended discipline, wore studded belts, burned herself with candles, let molten wax drip all over her body, wrapped herself in nettles, extracted her own healthy teeth, walked with pebbles in her shoes, and ate filth. At one point she put her lips and tongue on a hideous lump of spit."[32]

That attitude is not biblical. The New Testament expects us to be less preoccupied with ourselves and more oriented toward serving one an-other in the name of Christ. Further, Christ loved us and died for us even in the midst of our depravity, and He is now transforming us, producing good in us by the work of the Spirit. The doctrine of depravity should not drive us toward self-loathing, but toward confession, compassion, faith-fulness, and prayer.

Confession

We have no one to blame for our sin other than ourselves. We sin because we choose to sin, not because we are forced into it by the Devil or any other external power. As Berkouwer put it, "We may never trace back our guilt to causes other than *our guilt*."[33] As a result, our first response to the doctrine of depravity ought to be confession. In that act we acknowledge our sinfulness before God, embracing His free offer of forgiveness in Christ. Forsaking any attempt to justify ourselves or blame others, we admit that we are without excuse and humbly ask for mercy. "If we say that we have no sin, we are deceiving ourselves, and the truth is not in us. If we confess our sins, He is faithful and righteous to forgive us our sins and to cleanse us from all unrighteousness" (1 John 1:8–9).

This habit ought to be particularly characteristic of believers. Since we are always liable to sin, always prone to wander, we must acknowledge our weakness. Still, having been enabled by the Spirit to act differently, we are no longer constrained by the dictates of our old master, and we must acknowledge our power. Knowing our weakness, we should never be surprised at our own potential for evil. Knowing our power, we should always be scandalized by our performance of evil. We are expected to be people who obey God (1 John 2:4). When we continue to sin, we must admit that we are fully responsible.

Compassion

Most of us are relatively forgiving toward those who share our own struggles. Unfortunately our attitude in such cases may be a form of self-justification as we tell ourselves that the sin in view is really not so bad. To avoid the danger of denying our guilt, we must acknowledge the serious-ness of our own sin in confession before attempting to correct or encourage others. Only those who have confessed their own sins and have experi-enced forgiveness are prepared to forgive others and lead them to grace in Christ. On the other hand, if we remain revengeful or condemning, it means that we probably have not yet come to an understanding of our own sinfulness and forgiveness. As the master told the unforgiving slave in Jesus' parable, "You wicked slave, I forgave you all that debt because you entreated me. Should you not also have had mercy on your fellow slave, even as I had mercy on you?" (Matt. 18:32–33). In the same way, Paul wrote, "Accept one another, just as Christ also accepted us to the glory of God" (Rom. 15:7).

Faithfulness

When a car's front end is out of alignment, the driver has to maintain a firm hand on the wheel to keep the car from drifting into another lane. That often takes a conscious effort, especially on long trips, when boredom makes it easy to relax one's grip. In our incessant inclination to sin, our hearts are out of alignment, and they will stay that way until we are glori-fied with Christ. The problem remains with us; it won't be fixed by a quick visit to some spiritual mechanic. Therefore, if we are to stay on course for a lifetime, we must keep a steady hand on the habits and relationships that encourage us toward righteousness. Even more, we must continually rely on the Spirit of God, who enables us to live holy lives. Such reliance finds expression in continual prayer and faithful obedience. By contrast, an independent spirit leads to prayerlessness and hardness of heart.

Prayer

The doctrine of human depravity gives us realistic expectations both of ourselves and of others. We expect unbelievers to act like unbelievers. We do not expect them to be kind or loving, and we do not place much faith in social reforms that demand unselfish behavior on a widespread scale. As Niebuhr wrote, "A just society is not going to be built by a little more education and a few more sermons on love."[34] It will come only through the transforming grace of God. We recognize that even believers will frequently act according to their own interests, and any good that is produced through us will come through the work of the Holy Spirit.

Therefore we must pray. We must ask God to do what only He can do. Persuasive sermons, passionate appeals, and endless books will accomplish good only if they are so used by the Spirit of God. Without His intervention, such endeavors will yield nothing more than hardness of heart in those who hear. This doctrine has a direct impact on our approach to evangelism. Preachers who believe conversion is their responsibility have historically employed more high-pressure tactics than those who think the job belongs to God. The Spirit has graciously worked through a variety of approaches, but evangelists should never take personal credit for the faith of others. All glory goes to God, who alone brings change to the human heart. We acknowledge that fact when we pray.

The Universal Need for Salvation

This chapter has argued that everyone enters this life in a state of spiritual death. Already bearing the consequences of Adam's sin, they quickly compound the problem with their own rebellious choices. As a result, everyone has a need for salvation.

Further, because of the sinfulness of our hearts, we tend to run from

God rather than to Him. We cannot produce works of righteousness apart from His Spirit, for we act in accordance with our own desires, and our desires are evil. Even if we could fulfill God's Law, we could never overcome the guilt already incurred by our sinful acts in the past. As a result, we cannot save ourselves.

Everyone has a need for salvation, but we cannot save ourselves. But, "while we were still helpless, at the right time Christ died for the ungodly" (Rom. 5:6).

To God alone be glory!

Evil and the Essence of Sin

"**B**Y THE WAY, a Bulgarian I met lately in Moscow," Ivan went on, seeming not to hear his brother's words, "told me about the crimes committed by Turks and Circassians in all parts of Bulgaria through fear of a general rising of the Slavs. They burn villages, murder, rape women and children, they nail their prisoners to the fences by the ears, leave them so till morning, and in the morning they hang them—all sorts of things you can't imagine. People talk sometimes of bestial cruelty, but that's a great injustice and insult to the beast; a beast can never be so cruel as a man, so artistically cruel. The tiger only tears and gnaws, that's all he can do. He would never think of nailing people by the ears, even if he were able to do it. These Turks took a pleasure in torturing children, too; cutting the unborn child from the mother's womb, and tossing babies up in the air and catching them on the points of their bayonets before their mother's eyes. Doing it before the mother's eyes was what gave zest to the amusement. Here is another scene that I thought very interesting. Imagine a trembling mother with her baby in her arms, a circle of invading Turks around her. They've planned a diversion; they pet the baby, laugh to make it laugh. They succeed, the baby laughs. At that moment a Turk points a pistol four inches from the baby's face. The baby laughs with glee, holds out its little hands to the pistol, and he pulls the trigger in the baby's face and blows out its brains. Artistic, wasn't it? By the way, Turks are particularly fond of sweet things, they say."

"Brother, what are you driving at?" asked Alyosha.

"I think if the devil doesn't exist, but man has created him, he has created him in his own image and likeness."

"Just as he did God, then?" observed Alyosha.

"It's wonderful how you can turn words, as Polonius says in *Hamlet*," laughed Ivan. "You turn my words against me. Well, I am glad. Yours must be a fine God, if man created Him in his image and likeness."[1]

Fyodor Dostoevsky used horrifying images of human depravity to raise questions about the nature and existence of God. Unfortunately the experiences are not uncommon, and the questions are not unique. Throughout human history, people have abused, tortured, betrayed, and murdered one another, and all too often the victims are helpless children. What kind of God would allow such agony? Why do the heavens so often remain silent while people suffer?

ADDRESSING THE PROBLEM OF EVIL

In light of our previous chapter, we recognize that no one is truly innocent. Adam's sin has brought condemnation on us all, even the little children described by Dostoevsky. However, we don't suffer equally, and that inequity is the problem. When we refer to the question of "innocent" suffering, we mean that these individuals don't deserve to be singled out for such affliction. When Dostoevsky's "Turks" laugh and go free after shattering the lives of those who meant no harm, we recognize blatant injustice. We confess that all are guilty, but heinous acts have gone unpunished while the least guilty have experienced the most pain, and we scream that life just isn't fair. To say anything else, to imply that the infants suffer because of their sinfulness, would justify the cruelty of those wielding the bayonets. That defense would offer a sinful lie to obscure a sinful deed, treating murder as an act of justice when the Bible sees it as an act of rebellion. Further, it would suggest that all is fair in the world when we know injustice is rampant. The Holocaust, Stalin's purges,

Cambodia's killing fields, ethnic cleansing—one cannot consider such atrocities without asking, Where is the justice? Where is the intervention of an all-powerful God? Why does He allow these things to continue?

Asaph's Answer

As long as people have suffered, they have asked those very questions. Asaph asked them in Psalm 73, and he was fortunate enough to receive an answer, though an incomplete one. The psalm begins with an affirmation of faith: "Surely God is good to Israel, to those who are pure in heart!" (73:1). That He *is* good is one of the most basic principles in biblical theology (Pss. 25:8; 34:8). But our experience can cause us to question that goodness. Asaph continued, "But as for me, my feet came close to stumbling; my steps had almost slipped. For I was envious of the arrogant, as I saw the prosperity of the wicked" (73:2–3). These people mock and oppress the righteous (73:8), rebel against God (73:9), and don't believe they will ever be punished (73:11). It certainly does not appear as though they are being punished now. They live in comfort and abundance (73:4), and "they are not in trouble as other men; nor are they plagued like mankind" (73:5).

To the psalmist, God did not seem fair. He had attempted to live right-eously, but the wicked seemed to have the greater reward. "Surely in vain I have kept my heart pure, and washed my hands in innocence; for I have been stricken all day long, and chastened every morning" (73:13–14). Asaph knew there was something wrong with this perspective, but he couldn't resolve the problem. "When I pondered to understand this, it was troublesome in my sight" (73:16). Surely God is good to the pure in heart (73:1), but sometimes that statement of faith was hard for the psalm-ist to believe.

It was especially hard for him to believe when he contemplated his own experience. However, as his meditation progressed, Asaph was granted a glimpse of the future, and he realized that justice really was coming. In the sanctuary of God he "perceived their end" (73:17). "Surely Thou dost set them in slippery places; Thou dost cast them down to destruction. How they are destroyed in a moment! They are utterly swept away by sudden terrors!" (73:18–19). The wicked would receive the judgment due them, and the righteous would be exonerated. "Nevertheless I am continually with Thee; Thou hast taken hold of my right hand. With Thy counsel Thou wilt guide me, and afterward receive me to glory" (73:23–24).

Even though God's final justice was put off to the future, Asaph realized that the righteous could also experience God's goodness in the present. That goodness may not have satisfied the psalmist's expectations for a life of ease, but intimacy with God provided a more than adequate reward, especially compared to the fate of the wicked. "Whom have I in heaven but Thee? And besides Thee, I desire nothing on earth. My flesh and my heart may fail, but God is the strength of my heart and my portion forever. For, behold, those who are far from Thee will perish; Thou hast destroyed all those who are unfaithful to Thee. But as for me, the nearness of God is my good; I have made the Lord GOD my refuge, that I may tell of all Thy works" (73:25–28).

Asaph's resolution to the problem of injustice is eschatological. Justice will come, but not yet. Peter came to a similar conclusion. Responding to those who questioned whether God would ever judge the world, he wrote, "The Lord is not slow about His promise, as some count slowness, but is patient toward you, not wishing for any to perish but for all to come to repentance" (2 Pet. 3:9). The day of judgment will surely arrive (3:10), but the fact that it has not come yet demonstrates neither indifference nor inability on the part of the Judge. It demonstrates His patience.

The Possibility of Immediate Justice

That insight provides an initial response to the classic problem of evil. Philosopher David Hume stated the ancient question plainly. "Is [God] willing to prevent evil, but not able? then he is impotent. Is he able, but not willing? then he is malevolent. Is he both able and willing? whence then is evil?"[2] In other words, an all-powerful God could prevent evil, and an all-loving God would prevent evil. However, since evil acts continue to take place, God is apparently either not all-powerful or not all-loving.[3] Asaph's eschatological perspective affirms the assumption that an all-powerful, all-loving God can be expected to destroy evil, but it does not agree with Hume that such a God should be expected to prevent all evil in the present. God's justice will be fully manifested in the future, but until then He exercises patience. In the terms used by Hume, God is both able and willing to prevent evil, but He has chosen not to do it yet. Hume thought that kind of choice must be malevolent, but Peter said it was a sign of God's mercy.

If the continuing presence of evil in the world seems more malevolent than merciful, simply consider the alternative. Do we really want immediate justice? D. A. Carson answered that question bluntly.

> Suppose, for argument's sake, that God gave instant gratification for every good deed, every kind thought, every true word; and an instant jolt of pain for every malicious deed, every dirty thought, and every false word. Suppose the pleasure and pain were in strict proportion to the measure of goodness or badness God saw in us. What kind of world would result? . . . Such a system of enforced and ruthlessly "just" discipline would not change our hearts. We would be smouldering with resentment. Our obedience would be external and apathetic; our hearts and devotion would not be won over. The jolts might initially gain protestations of repentance, but they would not command our allegiance. And since God examines the heart, he would be constantly administering the jolts. The world would become a searing pain; the world would become hell. Do you really want nothing but totally effective, instantaneous justice? Then go to hell.[4]

We really *don't* want instantaneous justice (unless perhaps we and our friends can be excluded), and that admission may help us accept God's merciful hesitation. He withholds judgment not because He is unconcerned or preoccupied with trivial matters. He waits because He is merciful.

Evil and the Sovereignty of God

The image of God "waiting" assumes His ability to bring justice at any time. Not everyone agrees with that assumption. Committed more to the goodness of God than to His omnipotence, many contemporary theologians have argued that God would like to prevent evil, but for one reason or another He cannot. If He is constrained by the limitations of His nature, then

Hume was right—God is impotent, or at least not all-powerful. More commonly, it has been suggested that He is constrained by the dictates of His own prior choices. For example, if He has chosen to create a world in which humans have absolute freedom, then He cannot intervene in such a way as to violate that freedom. He cannot overturn the natural consequences of free human acts without contradicting His design for the world.

Many have found that last argument appealing, because it seems to excuse God for some of the horrendous evil in our world without compromising His omnipotence. God is all-powerful, but His purposes call for a world in which people are free. The evil we experience is not by His choice, but ours.

Unfortunately this argument goes too far. The world described in the Bible is not one in which God cannot overturn the free choices of people, but one in which people cannot overturn the free choices of God. "Our God is in the heavens; He does whatever He pleases" (Ps. 115:3). "Whatever the Lord pleases, He does, in heaven and in earth, in the seas and in all deeps" (135:6). "For His dominion is an everlasting dominion, and His kingdom endures from generation to generation. And all the inhabitants of the earth are accounted as nothing, but He does according to His will in the host of heaven and among the inhabitants of earth; and no one can ward off His hand or say to Him, 'What hast Thou done?'" (Dan. 4:34–35).

When a child reaches for something forbidden, a parent might grab her little hand and say, "No, no! Don't touch!" According to Daniel, nobody can say that to God. His actions are unchallenged, limited only by His nature and His will. If He were to be constrained by our choices, wouldn't we be the ones in charge?

Further, if God cannot intervene in human affairs because He is committed to the preservation of human freedom, then how can we explain His acts of deliverance? The angel of the Lord killed 185,000 Assyrians in one night (2 Kings 19:35). Was their freedom preserved? What about Pharaoh and his army? Did God tell Israel they would have to live with oppression because He couldn't overturn Pharaoh's decisions? The arguments some apologists have used to explain God's apparent silence in the modern era would also demand His inactivity in the past. It may be convenient to say that God could not stop the Holocaust, but if that were true He could never have been the God of the Exodus.

Several years ago some of my colleagues and I were asked to spend a day ministering to a grieving church. Eight of their high schoolers had been headed to a retreat center in the church van when they were hit broadside by a gravel truck. Most of them were killed, along with their driver, a delightful seminary student who had skipped my class that day so she could take the kids to camp. If God has any power at all, He could have prevented that collision. He could have caused the van to stall or the driver to take a different route. He could have dispatched angels to set up a roadblock or slow the gravel truck with a flat tire. But He chose not to.

There must have been some purpose behind His choice, but we do not know what it was. Standing before those grieving families, I would have loved to have known the mind of God, to have been able to explain why there was no angelic roadblock that summer afternoon. But God has not chosen to give us that information. Some church members have since testified that a number of young people came to Christ shortly after the loss of their friends, but it would be presumptuous of me to say that their conversion was the reason for their friends' suffering. Even if I could offer that kind of explanation for the van accident, how could I possibly explain the recent slaughter of several hundred villagers in Algeria? The fact is that we really don't know. We know that God is in charge; we know that He is good; and we trust His purposes even though they are frequently hidden from us. "Therefore, let those also who suffer according to the will of God entrust their souls to a faithful Creator in doing what is right" (1 Pet. 4:19).

I have always found it interesting that God never told Job why he had suffered so much. When God finally spoke at the end of the book, He did not justify Himself by describing Satan's schemes, nor did He accuse Job of disobedience. He simply reminded Job who was in charge—and who wasn't. "Where were you when I laid the foundation of the earth? Tell Me, if you have understanding" (Job 38:4). As Carson wrote, "He does not respond to the 'whys' of Job's suffering, nor does he challenge Job's defense of his own integrity. The reason he calls Job on the carpet is not because of Job's justification of himself, but because of Job's willingness to condemn God in order to justify himself. In other words, God does not here 'answer' Job's questions about the problem of evil and suffering, *but he makes it unambiguously clear what answers are not acceptable in God's universe.*"[5]

Specifically, it will not do to accuse God of evil intentions or malevolent acts. He is sovereign, but not blameworthy, for He is righteous in all His deeds (Ps. 11:7; Dan. 9:14). He oversees all things in accord with His will, but He is not the source, the cause, or the author of sin. Those statements may seem inconsistent to some readers, but they have provided the boundaries for orthodox discussion about the problem of evil throughout church history, and we should always choose tension, or even inconsistency, over blasphemy. We operate within the following parameters: God in His power is always capable of intervening in human affairs, but even when He does not intervene, and even when He does not explain Himself, we trust that His purposes are good, while confessing our own responsibility for sin.

The Hidden Purposes of God

One of Anne Rice's best-selling novels, *Memnoch the Devil,* describes an effort by the Devil to recruit the vampire Lestat as his prince.[6] Seduced by the invitation, Lestat accompanied the evil one, calling himself Memnoch, on first a trip to heaven, then a trip through history, and finally a trip to hell. Along the way, the boundaries got very blurry. Much of the story was told by the Devil, and Lestat never really determined whether he was telling the truth. The author herself never answered that question, but it really doesn't matter. Enough criticisms were leveled against Christianity along the way that readers are left with the impression that God isn't all that good and the Devil isn't all that bad.

Rice's Lestat described himself as totally evil, so much so that he questioned God's existence. If God exists, he thought, surely He would strike dead so villainous a creature as himself. Lestat saw his own continuing existence as an argument against the existence of God. Working within the same set of assumptions about what God could be expected to do if

200

He were all-powerful and all-loving, Memnoch argued that God is not loving at all. God has not been paying attention to the realities of human suffering because He simply does not care and cannot understand.

Christians generally appeal to the Incarnation as a demonstration that God understands human suffering, and there is plenty of biblical support for that idea. "For since He Himself was tempted in that which He has suffered, He is able to come to the aid of those who are tempted" (Heb. 2:18). "For you have been called for this purpose, since Christ also suffered for you, leaving you an example for you to follow in His steps" (1 Pet. 2:21). However, Memnoch argued that the Incarnation did not aid God's understanding at all. Jesus always knew that His sufferings would be temporary and that He would be returning to glory. He never had to experience the despair of meaningless suffering, so He could never understand the realities of human existence. In the end, Lestat refused to serve either God or the Devil. Evil as he was, he regarded himself as more virtuous than either of them.

The novel is skillfully crafted, and even Lestat is left with unanswered questions in the end. Was Memnoch telling the truth? Did God ever present His own side of the story? Was Lestat's vision of heaven just another one of Memnoch's lies? Did Lestat unwittingly fulfill the Devil's wishes by striving to be independent? However the reader is expected to answer these questions, we need to be prepared to respond to Memnoch's accusation. Doesn't even the Incarnation enable Jesus to understand human suffering?

It is true that Jesus knew His sufferings would be temporary and that He would soon be restored to glory. However, it is not true that our own sufferings are utterly pointless and absurd. A high view of the providence of God affirms that all things ultimately have purpose, even evil acts which appear to be completely senseless. Jesus' sufferings serve as a model for us, not simply because He experienced pain, but because He experienced hope in the midst of the pain. Consider the exhortation of Hebrews 12:1–3: "Therefore, since we have so great a cloud of witnesses surrounding us, let us also lay aside every encumbrance, and the sin which so easily entangles us, and let us run with endurance the race that is set before us, fixing our eyes on Jesus, the author and perfecter of faith, who for the joy set before Him endured the cross, despising the shame, and has sat down at the right hand of the throne of God. For consider Him who has endured such hostility by sinners against Himself, so that you may not grow weary and lose heart."

Jesus endured the cross "for the joy set before Him," and we are to endure suffering from the same perspective. "All discipline for the moment seems not to be joyful, but sorrowful; yet to those who have been trained by it, afterwards it yields the peaceful fruit of righteousness" (12:11). Paul wrote, "Therefore we do not lose heart, but though our outer man is decaying, yet our inner man is being renewed day by day. For momentary, light affliction is producing for us an eternal weight of glory far beyond all comparison, while we look not at the things which are seen, but at the things which are not seen; for the things which are seen are temporal, but the things which are not seen are eternal"(2 Cor. 4:16–18). Our suffering is not pointless and eternal, but purposeful and temporary.

However, that assurance does not always enable us to rest comfortably with our afflictions. We can sometimes guess at God's purposes when persecution yields holiness or when a difficult experience helps bring someone to faith in Christ. However, we must admit that any sense of divine purpose is often completely obscured. Try as we might to see beyond the veil, evil experiences frequently seem completely senseless. In such circumstances we continue to trust in the goodness and providence of God, and we look to the pattern of the Cross.

When Jesus became an innocent sufferer Himself, crucified for our sins, God seemed utterly absent, perhaps more so than in any other event we can imagine. Jesus' followers watched helplessly as He cried out, "My God, my God, why hast Thou forsaken me?" (Matt. 27:46). Some held out hope for a miraculous deliverance, but nothing happened. At least, nothing happened that they could see. At the time it seemed as though God had been shut out from the situation. But we know in retrospect that at that moment He had deliberately excluded Himself. Taking our sin upon Himself, Jesus was more directly identified with humanity and more engaged with human misery than at any time in history. The resurrection demonstrated that God had indeed been at work, even when He seemed most absent. That prompted Alister McGrath to write, "Experience cannot be allowed to have the final word—it must be judged and shown up as deceptive and misleading. The theology of the cross draws our attention to the sheer unreliability of experience as a guide to the presence and activity of God. God *is* active and present in his world, quite independently of whether we experience him as being so. Experience declared that God was absent from Calvary, only to have its verdict humiliatingly overturned on the third day."[7]

The Danger of a Nice Explanation

We must be careful, however, to balance all these arguments with a caveat. No matter how we address the problem of evil, we must never grow comfortable with its presence. We have said that the all-loving and all-powerful God shows patience while delaying His inevitable judgment of evil, and we trust that He has benevolent and holy purposes even when they remain obscure to us. But that argument must never cause us to regard evil itself as an expression of God's goodness. Sin is an intruder, not a member of the household, and the danger of all theodicies, answers to the problem of evil, is that they make us comfortable with the stranger in our midst. Voltaire highlighted that error in *Candide* through Pangloss, the metaphysician who consistently described this as "the best of all possible worlds." Pangloss was a rather pathetic figure whose beliefs seemed naively optimistic to everyone but himself. Those who offer complete and confident theodicies today are in danger of joining him.

Evil was not present in God's original creation, when He "saw all that He had made, and behold, it was very good" (Gen. 1:31). However, somewhere between that moment and Eve's temptation, evil arrived on the scene. (Actually, it may be more appropriate to say that some part of the goodness departed. Theologians have long viewed evil not as a thing, for God created all things, and all that He made was good. Evil is instead described as the absence, or privation, of good.) Following the evil guidance of the serpent, Adam and Eve brought sin into human experience.

We have discussed the relationship between Adam's sin and our own in some detail already, and one of the dangers of that discussion, like the debate concerning the problem of evil, is that we may assign blame to others while overlooking our own responsibility. That tendency is why, when considering the question of sin's origin, Berkouwer wrote, "This question is illegitimate for the simple reason that a logical explanation assigns a sensibleness to that which is intrinsically nonsensical, a rationality to that which is irrational, and a certain order to that which is disorderly. In that light it is obvious why Scripture makes no effort at all to explain the origin of sin in terms of its component parts. There is no allusion to an impenetrable darkness or an unfortunate gap in our knowledge. There is only the *confession of our guilt.* In the act of confession we do not, and we cannot, yearn for an 'explanation' of our sins. We recognize our sin as our *very own.*"[8]

"We try to find some sense in the senseless, some reason in the irrational, and some legitimacy in the illegitimacy of sin,"[9] but we must resist that temptation. Sin cannot be seen as something good, and our sinful acts cannot be blamed on someone else.

We may not be able to resolve fully the problem of evil, and we may not be able to explain the origin of sin, but we can see the boundaries that must be maintained when addressing these issues. We share in Adam's guilt, but we cannot blame him for our sin. God is sovereign, and He exercises His providential control over all things, but we cannot blame Him either. God permits injustice to continue, but He neither causes it nor delights in it.

The Challenge to Shalom

Sin occurs in a world still ruled by the sovereign God, who "works all things after the counsel of His will" (Eph. 1:11), but sin itself is senseless. It defies explanation. It is futile rebellion against the good purposes of God. Evil is an intruder, and we must never be so satisfied with our theodicies that we grow comfortable in its company. Nicholas Wolterstorff, a Christian philosopher whose son was killed in a mountain-climbing accident, expressed this understanding well.

Someone said to Claire, "I hope you're learning to live at peace with Eric's death." Peace, shalom, salaam. Shalom is the fullness of life in all dimensions. Shalom is dwelling in justice and delight with God, with neighbor, with oneself, in nature. Death is shalom's mortal enemy. Death is demonic. We cannot live at peace with death.

When the writer of *Revelation* spoke of the coming of the day of shalom, he did not say that on that day we would live at peace with death. He said that on that day "There will be no more death or mourning or crying or pain, for the old order of things has passed away."

I shall try to keep the wound from healing, in recognition of our living still in the old order of things. I shall try to keep it from healing, in solidarity with those who sit beside me on humanity's mourning bench.[10]

We must not cauterize that wound by pretending that our responses to the problem of evil have fully resolved it. Again, we can do little more than identify the necessary boundaries of the conversation. God is loving, not malevolent. He is sovereign, but not the author or cause of sin. We cannot blame anyone but ourselves for our sin, which has no acceptable motive and remains incomprehensible (Rom. 6:2). Sin cannot be explained by attributing it to some outside power or fate, and it should not be regarded as an understandable part of the world. It has entered by human invitation, but sin remains a trespasser, an invader seeking the destruction of shalom.

Cornelius Plantinga Jr. described shalom as the ideal of the biblical prophets: " The webbing together of God, humans, and all creation in justice, fulfillment, and delight is what the Hebrew prophets call *shalom*. We call it peace, but it means far more than mere peace of mind or a cease-fire between enemies. In the Bible, shalom means *universal flourishing, wholeness, and delight*—a rich state of affairs in which natural needs are satisfied and natural gifts fruitfully employed, a state of affairs that inspires joyful wonder as its Creator and Savior opens doors and welcomes the creatures in whom he delights. Shalom, in other words, is the way things ought to be."[11]

By contrast, sin sweeps in and attacks that ideal like the army of Chaldeans described in Habakkuk 1:6–11.

That fierce and impetuous people who march throughout the earth to seize dwelling places which are not theirs. They are dreaded and feared.

Their justice and authority originate with themselves. Their horses are swifter than leopards and keener than wolves in the evening. Their horsemen come galloping, their horsemen come from afar; they fly like an eagle swooping down to devour. All of them come for violence. Their horde of faces moves forward. They collect captives like sand. They mock at kings, and rulers are a laughing matter to them. They laugh at every fortress, and heap up rubble to capture it. Then they will sweep through like the wind and pass on. But they will be held guilty, they whose strength is their god.

As in Habakkuk's prophecy, God will one day judge the marauding army. Sin will be removed and shalom restored. But this is not that day. For now, we follow the example of Habakkuk himself, who never made peace with the invading army, but still trusted in the Lord. He wrote, "I heard and my inward parts trembled, at the sound my lips quivered. Decay enters my bones, and in my place I tremble. Because I must wait quietly for the day of distress, for the people to arise who will invade us. Though the fig tree should not blossom, and there be no fruit on the vines, though the yield of the olive should fail, and the fields produce no food, though the flock should be cut off from the fold, and there be no cattle in the stalls [in other words, though there be no shalom], yet I will exult in the LORD, I will rejoice in the God of my salvation. The Lord GOD is my strength, and He has made my feet like hinds feet, and makes me walk on my high places" (3:16–19). With quiet resignation, the prophet accepted the fact that God must know what He is doing. That knowledge did not necessarily bring a smile to his face, but it enabled him to face the day.

We are not supposed to live at peace with sin and evil, but we are supposed to live at peace with God. We continue to trust in His goodness, His sovereignty, and His mercy, and we continue to confess our own responsibility for sin.

THE ESSENCE OF SIN

Sin's character as a violation of shalom can be seen in the biblical language used to describe it. The Bible employs what one scholar called "a mournfully numerous group of words" to speak of sin,[12] but they all point to its common essence as prideful rebellion. The Hebrew word *ḥaṭṭaʾt* denotes an offense committed against another person, a violation of agreed-on standards for the relationship.[13] It has frequently been described as an archery term referring to one's failure to hit the target, but the best evidence suggests that it never had that concrete meaning, and the few texts that seem to use it that way (like Judg. 20:16) are probably metaphorical. Subjects committed *ḥaṭṭaʾt* against their kings through rebellion (1 Sam. 24:11), and kings committed *ḥaṭṭaʾt* against the people through oppression and injustice (19:4). It refers to the offenses of brother against brother (Gen. 50:17) and servant against master (31:36), but far more commonly *ḥaṭṭaʾt* describes one's transgression against God (Exod. 32:30; 1 Sam. 15:24). *Ḥaṭṭaʾt* is inevitably an act of rebellion against the Creator.

The Hebrew term *pešaʿ* refers to actions that breach relationships between persons or nations. When directed against other people, *pešaʿ* often constitutes cruelty. When directed against one's rulers, it constitutes revolt. Amos condemned most of the nations surrounding Israel for committing *pešaʿ* against their neighbors (Amos 1:3–2:2). They were guilty of what we might call "crimes against humanity." He then condemned Judah for revolt. They had rejected the law of the LORD, committing *pešaʿ* against Him by refusing to keep His statutes (2:4). As with *ḥaṭṭaʾt*, God is the most common object of *pešaʿ*. We commit transgression against one another, but the Bible places much more emphasis on our transgression against God.

Similarly the New Testament employs the Greek words *hamartia*, *paraptōma*, and *parabasis* to speak of offense or transgression. They can denote actions that injure other persons, but they usually refer to our sin against God. Beyond these, the New Testament also speaks of ungodliness (*asebeia*), disobedience (*parakoē*), lawlessness (*anomia*), and unrighteousness (*adikia*)—terms that emphasize the violation of a divine standard.

In every case sin is portrayed as a violation of the ideal. It injures proper relationships or is described negatively as law*less*ness, *dis*obedience, *im*piety, love*less*ness, *un*belief, *dis*trust, *un*righteousness, *un*thankfulness, *wrong*doing, or faith*less*ness. It is a *fall* from a right standing, an *un*natural descent into *darkness* from light. As Daniel Doriani wrote, "Sin opposes

God's law and his created beings. Sin hates rather than loves, it doubts or contradicts rather than trusts and affirms, it harms and abuses rather than helps and respects."[14] Its purposes are determined negatively in opposition to the will of God, prompting Berkouwer to write, "Evil has no thesis in itself but only antithesis."[15] It is contra, always against what is good.

If the Law can be summarized in the commands to love God and one's neighbor (Mark 12:28–31; Rom. 13:10), then sin can be described as that which is contrary to those commands. It is prideful rebellion against God instead of loving submission. It is the selfish pursuit of our own interests above those of others, an orientation directly opposed to divine expectations. Ironically, sin employs even the love command to its own end. We hear "love your neighbor as yourself" and we determine to love ourselves first so we can love our neighbors more intelligently. But the command assumes that we are already committed to our own interests, and it directs us to serve one another instead of ourselves. To use that command to justify narcissism misses the point entirely, but that is what sin does.

Some theologians have described sin as a defect in passion, a twistedness in desires that might otherwise be good. The desire for food and drink is a good thing—we need it if we are to survive. Likewise, we rightly seek clothing, shelter, and protection from our enemies, "for your heavenly Father knows that you need all these things" (Matt. 6:32). However, when such things occupy so much of our attention that they usurp God's role as the Supreme Good, we participate in an insurrection against His purposes. Sin takes even that which is good and twists it into rebellion.

Sin is always directed against God. More than just a natural deficiency, it consists of active opposition to God and His commands. Even sinful actions that injure other individuals are more fundamentally acts of rebellion against God. David committed adultery with Bathsheba and had her husband killed, but in his confession he said to the Lord, "Against Thee, Thee only, I have sinned, and done what is evil in Thy sight" (Ps. 51:4). The exploitation and abuse of people opposes the God who created them. Failure to love another person constitutes a failure to love Him.

We oppose God in the name of self-interest, so pride has often been identified as the essence of sin. Sinful pride causes us to exalt ourselves rather than God. We rebel against His will by pursuing our own, we defend that rebellion through self-justification, and we seek independent freedom when He calls us to dependent faith. Sin is *against* the purposes of God and the interests of other people, supporting only the twisted interests of self.

THE RELATIVE SEVERITY OF SINS

As an affront to the authority and character of the Creator God and a violation of shalom, every transgression, every ungodly thought, and every rebellious inclination deserves to be punished. "For whoever keeps the whole law and yet stumbles in one point, he has become guilty of all" (James 2:10). One cannot remain innocent after committing even a single offense, for that act requires that the offender be named among the guilty.

Still, apparently some actions will be judged more severely than others. James wrote, "Let not many of you become teachers, my brethren, knowing that as such we shall incur a stricter judgment" (3:1). And Jesus said to Pilate, "He who delivered Me up to you has the greater sin" (John 19:11). Evidently those who squander their greater access to divine revelation will be judged more severely than those with less exposure to the truth. While denouncing unrepentant cities, Jesus said, "Woe to you, Chorazin! Woe to you, Bethsaida! For if the miracles had occurred in Tyre and Sidon which occurred in you, they would have repented long ago in sackcloth and ashes. Nevertheless I say to you, it shall be more tolerable for Tyre and Sidon in the day of judgment, than for you. And you, Capernaum, will not be exalted to heaven, will you? You shall descend to Hades; for if the miracles had occurred in Sodom which occurred in you, it would have remained to this day. Nevertheless I say to you that it shall be more tolerable for the land of Sodom in the day of judgment, than for you" (Matt. 11:21–24).

When someone sins in ignorance, his behavior seems more understandable, indeed, more forgivable, than that of someone who knows better and sins on purpose. Children learn that lesson at an early age. When confronted by the tears of a bullied little brother, they cry, "I didn't mean to hurt him!" Asked about the muddy trail across the living room, they say, "I didn't know that would happen!" One of our favorite stories (in retrospect!) comes from the time our oldest son tried to drive the car. My wife was arriving home with all the kids, and she got out to open the garage door. Just as she unlocked it, she heard the Suburban drop into gear, and she could only watch in horror as Steve rammed it right into the garage. After determining that everyone was okay, Julie was madder than the kids had ever seen her, and five-year-old Danny couldn't understand why. "Mom," he said, "you never told us we couldn't drive the car."

Most judges are more strict with those who obviously understand the illegality of their actions, and rightly so. However, as any law-enforcement officer will affirm, ignorance of the law is no excuse. Paul said he had "acted ignorantly in unbelief" while persecuting the church (1 Tim. 1:13), but he still regarded himself as the foremost of sinners during that period (1:15). The Hebrew Scriptures employed a special term for "sins committed in ignorance"—$š^egāgâ$. It could refer to the unintentional violation of a known law ("I didn't mean to hurt him!") or the ignorant violation of an unknown law ("You never told us not to drive the car."), but it was still a violation, and the guilty parties were still guilty. The Mosaic Law prescribed a variety of offerings for sins committed in ignorance (Lev. 4:2–3, 22, 27; Num. 15:22–29), because those who violated God's commands, regardless of the circumstances, still needed to be forgiven.

Although any violation of shalom is a serious matter, it is even more serious when it occurs purposefully. Numbers 15:30 condemns the sin committed with a high hand, one that constitutes the willful, deliberate disobedience of God's commands. Someone who takes a life in ignorance has no excuse, but one who does the same thing knowingly and with malice aforethought has committed a greater sin. That person has compounded manslaughter with cruelty and hardness of heart, resulting in premeditated murder. It is willful disobedience, a "high-handed" sin, and the anticipated judgment will be more severe. The serious nature of willful disobedience helps explain Paul's great concern about young believers whose consciences were being violated by the behavior of others. If they thought it was sinful to eat certain foods, he said, then they should not be encouraged to violate their consciences. Even though the foods themselves were not forbidden, it would be wrong to eat them if one had to harden one's heart in order to do so. If we perceive something as an act of rebellion and proceed to commit it, an act of rebellion it becomes (Rom. 14:13–23).

Roman Catholicism has used this principle to distinguish between "mortal" and "venial" sins. A mortal sin is one "whose object is grave matter and which is also committed with full knowledge and deliberate consent."[16] "Grave matter is specified by the Ten Commandments," but some (murder, for example) are thought to be more serious than others.[17] "Sin committed through malice, by deliberate choice of evil, is the gravest."[18] One who violates grave standards "without full knowledge or without complete consent" is guilty of only a venial sin, just like someone who committed a lesser offense.[19] Such venial sins must still be taken seriously. Like innumerable droplets gathered into a flood, the collective weight of "lesser" sins increases with their number until it presents a grave danger. This gradation of sins rightly places more emphasis on the heart of the sinner than on particular acts, but the division of all sins into two major categories is probably too neat and clean. More problematically, this classification of sins is directly connected to the Roman Catholic system of penance, which involves priestly mediators and introduces unnecessary doubts about the security of salvation.

Isolated from such formal categories, many Protestants tend to determine the severity of various sins for themselves. Unfortunately such efforts usually demonstrate a significant degree of self-justification; our own sins are regarded as less grievous than those of others. I addressed a congregation one Sunday morning on the church's response to homosexuality, emphasizing the need for grace in light of the fact that every one of us has qualified for Paul's vice lists in one category or another (Rom. 1:28–32; 1 Cor. 6:9–11; Gal. 5:19–21; 1 Tim. 1:9–10). The apostle's purpose, I said, was not to highlight particular evils and single out certain persons for condemnation, but to reject summarily all kinds of evils and to include all persons in the need for salvation.

A gentleman approached me after the service and asked, "Don't you believe that some sins are worse than others?" I agreed with that point and mentioned some of the Scriptures discussed above. "Then don't you agree," he said, "that homosexuality is the worst of the lot?"

"No," I said. "That distinction belongs to blasphemy against the Spirit of God."

"Oh yeah, okay. Well, wouldn't you say that homosexuality is second only to that one?"

"No. Offhand, I'd have to say that acts of cruelty like murder and torture are a lot worse than homosexuality."

He was not comfortable with that answer either, in part because he thought Romans 1 placed homosexual practices at the very bottom of the slide into radical evil. However, Paul's vice list continues for several more verses after the mention of homosexuality, and any ranking of sins would place more emphasis on transgressions that are far more common than homosexuality. Paul mentioned unrighteousness, wickedness, greed, malice, envy, murder, strife, deceit, gossip, slander, hatred toward God, insolence, arrogance, and many other sins before concluding with this line: "and, although they know the ordinance of God, that those who practice such things are worthy of death, they not only do the same, but also give hearty approval to those who practice them" (1:32).

What, then, if anything, is at the bottom of the slide? Willful, informed disobedience. And immediately before that, in the previous verse, we find those who are "unloving" and "unmerciful." Once again, our own self-justification brings us closer to the bottom than we like to think.

But we should not have been surprised. The attitudes or actions the Bible treats as most serious are those that epitomize sin's essence as prideful rebellion against God. The cruel mistreatment of those made in His image does that, as does any self-righteous denial of our sinfulness. We have seen that self-justification constitutes a rejection of the church's fundamental confession—justification by faith. Those who declare themselves righteous see no need for forgiveness, no need for the Cross, no need for a Savior. When that attitude becomes permanent, it crosses a final line. It becomes the unpardonable sin.

"Therefore I say to you, any sin and blasphemy shall be forgiven men, but blasphemy against the Spirit shall not be forgiven. And whoever shall speak a word against the Son of Man, it shall be forgiven him; but whoever shall speak against the Holy Spirit, it shall not be forgiven him, either in this age, or in the age to come." These words of Jesus in Matthew 12:31–32 present a challenge when compared to the gospel's familiar promise of forgiveness for all who believe in Christ. When the apostles extended that promise "for you and your children, and for all who are far off" (Acts 2:39), should they have added an aside—"that is, unless you've spoken a word against the Spirit?" Many young believers fear that they may have committed this sin in the past. Are they really forgiven, or might they have committed something that the blood of Christ will never cover?

In Matthew 12, those whom Jesus warned of blasphemy had just attributed His miraculous works to Satan. "This man casts out demons only by Beelzebul the ruler of the demons" (Matt. 12:24). Jesus had actually performed those works by the power of the Spirit in fulfillment of Isaiah's prophecy (12:18–21 [Isa. 42:1–3]; Matt. 8:14–17 [Isa. 53:4]; Matt. 11:4–6 [Isa. 35:5]), so we can say that the Spirit had predicted it through the prophet and performed it through the Son. Those who witnessed those events should have understood what was happening, and many did. "All the multitudes were amazed, and began to say, 'This man cannot be the Son of David, can he?'" (Matt. 12:23). The Pharisees came to a radically different conclusion, and their contention that Jesus was demonized constituted a rejection of both the Spirit's testimony through the Scriptures and His testimony through the works of Jesus. They evaluated what the Spirit had so obviously produced and they decided to attribute it to Satan.

Some have argued that these circumstances are unrepeatable in our own day, for we do not have the visible works of Jesus to assess alongside the Spirit's prophetic witness. However, we do have the apostolic testimony about Jesus in the New Testament, and we have been urged to believe in Him on the basis of their words (John 20:30–31). In our day, blasphemy against the Spirit may well be displayed by those who carefully examine the words and works of Jesus through the Spirit-inspired testimony of the apostles, assess His relationship to the prophetic hope, and then definitively reject Him. That seems to match the description of those bound for judgment in Hebrews 10:26–29, who have received "the knowledge of the truth," but continue to sin willfully as they "trample under foot the Son of God," "regard as unclean the blood of the covenant," and "insult the Spirit of grace." This is the informed, premeditated, and final rejection of Christ.

Jesus said that blasphemy against the Son would be forgiven, but blasphemy against the Spirit would not. The difference between the two is difficult to understand, but it probably relates to the knowledge accompanying one's rejection of the gospel. If blasphemy against the Spirit includes a determined abandonment of His testimony concerning Jesus, then blasphemy against Christ must not be as well informed. Paul's example is probably instructive. He described himself as having been a "blasphemer," but said that he "acted ignorantly in unbelief" (1 Tim. 1:13). Paul had rejected Christ before his conversion, but he did not know any better. Obviously his ignorance did not excuse his sin, but it did mean his self-righteous rejection of the gospel was still open to correction. His hardness of heart had not yet become permanent.

If the unpardonable sin, blasphemy against the Spirit, consists of an informed and final rejection of the gospel, those who now trust in Christ have apparently never committed it. They would not believe in Him now if their earlier blasphemies had been educated and permanent. Further, since they would have continued to regard the gospel message as foolish apart from the Spirit's initiative and enlightenment, those who trust that message now need not question their election or the forgivability of their sins. The promise of eternal life is extended without reservation to all who believe, whom the Lord has in fact already called to Himself (Acts 2:39; 13:48).

At the bottom of the slide into radical evil, blasphemy against the Holy Spirit epitomizes sin's common essence as prideful rebellion. It violates shalom while consciously and willfully opposing God. This final rejection of Christ is ultimately an individual matter, but we recognize that the blasphemy described in Matthew 12 was committed by a group. Such actions consist of more than just the sum of individual choices. Those personal choices are multiplied through the power of the group, which then performs more evil than any of its members might have imagined. That is the subject of our next chapter.

Life in an Immoral Society

THE SKY IS OFTEN STILL DARK when I take my place in line on the interstate each morning. At that hour the traffic has not yet frozen up, so even some drivers who aren't solo skip the carpool lane, and we all stream toward the city a little faster than the speed limit. I usually recognize a couple of the cars from other mornings—the red Stealth with the crease in the right rear fender, the old Datsun plastered with bumper stickers. I have no idea who the drivers are or where they are headed. I only know that we have shared this stretch of road more than once before.

I experience the same kind of low-level camaraderie on the mornings I run with my dog through a nearby park. Enough people keep up the same routine that I see several familiar faces every time we run. We exchange greetings as we pass, and we might call out something about the weather, but I don't know any of their names. I only know that they like to exercise in the park.

The anonymity of our daily routines helps explain a story that recently appeared in our local newspaper. An elderly woman died of natural causes while at home in her nice suburban neighborhood, but her body was not discovered until over a year later. Her neighbors could tell that no one was keeping up the lawn, but they didn't know who lived (or died) in the house, and they never took the time to find out. She apparently had no friends who noticed her absence, and her family was so fragmented that they had grown accustomed to long periods of silence. Local commentators expressed shock at this sad story, not understanding how a community could fail to notice the death of one of its members. Had they been talking about the kind of community in which individuals are bound together by common ideals and the pledge of mutual support, their surprise would have been justified. However, the old widow did not live in that type of community. She lived in a city.

People are not motivated to live in cities by common ideals, but by self-interest. That is, cities do not possess aims that *transcend* the concerns of its residents, only those that *reflect* the concerns of its residents. Dallas Seminary, where I teach, seeks to train godly servant-leaders for the body of Christ. That greater purpose overrides whatever individual interests my coworkers and I may possess, demanding that we set our personal concerns aside in the service of our corporate goal. That common, transcendent ideal forms the basis for the seminary community. Those who cannot support it have to leave.

The city where I live also asks me to set aside some of my individual preferences, but its request is not driven by transcendent ideals. Cities derive their goals from the interests of those establishing them. In a dictatorship those aims are determined by the autocratic ruler and in a democracy by the city's residents. My city maintains a local government because we residents desire the establishment of laws, a police department because we want those laws enforced, and a fire department because we want our lives and property protected.

Even in less democratic settings, however, people live in cities not because they wish to contribute something to others, but because they wish those others to contribute something to them. The city provides shelter from the hostile forces of nature and protection from potential enemies. It makes available goods and services which cannot be found elsewhere, and it offers the possibility of human companionship. In spite of the memorable words of John F. Kennedy, I live here not because of what I can do for the city, but because of what the city can do for me.

However, since the city's aims are determined by the collective self-interests of its residents, an ironic tension develops. People value the city because of what it offers to them, and the city values them because of what they offer to it. Individuals are punished if they injure the common good, but they may also earn wide acclaim for aiding it, even if they are primarily motivated by a selfish desire for that kind of attention. Those thought to contribute little may be regarded as a burden, and the city may even wish to eliminate that encumbrance. In that setting we should not be surprised that the death of a secluded old woman would go unnoticed. Her passing was unknown because her presence was unappreciated in a city driven by collective self-interest.

Judging from our own experience, it should come as no surprise that biblical theology often portrays the city as a stronghold of rebels. Those who gather together for self-preservation while sharing little more in common than pride and desire won't come very close to any biblical ideals. We have seen that God's creative pattern called for men and women to work together as His representatives, establishing families as the most basic social unit. However, the first family dissolved into self-justification and blame as Adam and Eve refused to accept responsibility for their own sin (Gen. 3:12–16), and Cain found it easier to remove Abel from the picture than to admit his own failure. One might say that Cain preferred to work alone, so he killed his brother (4:5–8). At the same time, he was pleased to associate with those who would serve his own desires, for, after being banished from the presence of the Lord in the land (4:14, 16), Cain built himself a city (4:17).

God had told Cain he would live out his days as a fugitive, a wanderer on the earth (4:12), and Cain's immediate establishment of the city apparently constituted a rebellious rejection of that divine edict. At the same time, we recognize that he was probably also motivated by fear. Hearing that he was to be banished, Cain had told the Lord that the punishment was too severe, for "it will come about that whoever finds me will kill me" (4:14). God promised sevenfold vengeance against anyone taking his life (4:15), but Cain apparently did not think that pronouncement was sufficient. By building a city, he sought to protect himself within a fortress.

Inside those walls Cain headed a technologically advanced civilization characterized by violence and cruelty. His descendants developed various tools and musical instruments, but their orientation was summed up by Lamech, who said to his wives, "I have killed a man for wounding me; and a boy for striking me; if Cain is avenged sevenfold, then Lamech seventy-sevenfold" (4:23–24). He apparently believed that he was better able to defend himself than God had been able to defend Cain.[1] By contrast, the community that grew up from the line of Cain's brother Seth responded with humility to life's temporal character. Seth named his first-born "Enosh," meaning "mortal," and they began to call on the name of the Lord (4:26).

Genesis 4 provides the history of Cain's civilization, culminating in the words of Lamech. Genesis 5 does the same for Seth's family. That genealogy also culminates in a descendant named Lamech, and, like his counterpart in chapter 4, he is the only one in the record who speaks. The Lamech from the city of Cain boasted that he could protect himself better than God protected Cain. But the Lamech who rose up among Seth's descendants expressed hope not in personal retribution, but in redemption from the curse. At the birth of his son, Noah, Lamech said, "This one shall give us rest from our work and from the toil of our hands arising from the ground which the Lord has cursed" (5:29).

Cain's civilization later experienced judgment in the Flood, but other rebellious cities were built by the descendants of Noah. Nimrod was known as a great hunter or warrior (10:9), and he established a kingdom for himself by constructing a number of cities, apparently including both Babylon and Nineveh (10:9–11).[2] These great cities became strongholds for Israel's most powerful enemies, and their names function as symbols of rebellion against God throughout biblical history (Isa. 47; Nah. 1–3; Rev. 16:19; 18:21).

With Babylon, that rebellious pattern started early. "And they said, 'Come, let us build for ourselves a city, and a tower whose top will reach into heaven, and let us make for ourselves a name; lest we be scattered abroad over the face of the whole earth' " (Gen. 11:4). Just as Genesis 1 countered the popular creation traditions of the ancient Near East, chapter 11 rejects some of the local beliefs about civilization and power. The tower of Babel was likely one of several great ziggurats, which the Babylonians built as man-made mountain sanctuaries for the worship of their gods. They named their city *Babili*, "the gate of god," and, in a display of power, they tried to build this ziggurat to heaven. It must have been very impressive, but when the true God came to see it, He had to "go down" (11:5, 7). He halted the construction by confusing the speech of the workers, causing them to do the very thing they were trying to avoid—scatter across the land (11:4, 9). God's judgment created a nice play on words. The city's name sounded like the Hebrew word for confusion, and that is precisely what resulted. They thought they were building *Babili*, "the gate of god," but their efforts led to nothing more than *Babel*, "confusion."

Babylon and Nineveh demonstrate the antithesis of God's ideal for human society. Rather than pooling their gifts, sharing their labors, and working together as God's vice-regents, Nimrod and his descendants established alliances through which they defended their own interests and pursued violence. Their cities honored pagan deities while regarding the true God as unnecessary and irrelevant.

The judgment against Babel showed that God thought it better that people have no community than one that encouraged ongoing rebellion. However, He immediately took steps toward the establishment of a new community, a nation that would represent His purposes in the world. He chose Abraham to be the leader of this new people, assuring him that He would make his name famous and mold his descendants into a great nation (12:2). As God pursued this plan, He continued to bring occasional judgment against the rebellious cities (19:24–25; Deut. 3:4–6; Isa. 13), but He showcased Jerusalem as the holy and faithful city, the center of His activity. Sadly, Jerusalem also rebelled, for God's own people aligned themselves with their insubordinate neighbors (Ezek. 5:5–17).

With a heavy dose of irony, God used the notoriously evil cities of Nineveh and Babylon to judge Jerusalem (Ps. 137; Hab. 1). With that judgment He also gave the promise of final deliverance, characterized as a new creation. God's salvific work would restore His purposes through a righteous remnant, established forever as a new community in the Lord (Ezek. 36:23–36) and marked by the presence of the Spirit (37:14; Isa. 44:3–4; Joel 2:28–29). That community began on the Day of Pentecost (Acts 2:1–5). When the followers of Jesus spoke in tongues by the Spirit, the same God who once scattered Nimrod's people through the confusion of language used the gift of language to unite His people as a multinational and multiethnic "city of God" in this world. That new community—the church—will one day issue into the full manifestation of His kingdom, in which Christ will reign over all the nations and their cities from the glory of a restored Jerusalem (Rev. 20–21).

Human communities, then, are not inherently evil, for they ultimately constitute an important part of God's ideal. However, by bringing together thousands of individuals who are intent on survival and the protection of their own interests, cities generally function as centers of rebellion against God. Like Lamech, modern city dwellers believe they must be aggressive about their own protection. Further, like Nimrod and his peers, they celebrate other deities and glory in their own accomplishments while neglecting the grandeur of God. Our cities protect us from the natural world, but they also cut us off from its beauty, encouraging us to forget the presence of the Creator as we follow our anonymous routines. As one of my students wrote, "In the city, nature becomes contrived and ornamental. We see it in parks, as we are saluted by an army of trees planted at careful attention along the sidewalk. It is calculated and contained—stripped down—no longer capable of provoking our wonder."[3] With nature subjugated, we feel safe behind our fortress walls, especially if we have plenty of insurance against what the policies call "acts of God."

The first city was founded when Cain sought protection from outside attack, but the greatest threat to shalom in the city comes from within the walls. The city operates under the collective self-interest of *sinners*, and that has profound social repercussions.

Individual Sin and Society

Driven by selfish desire, individuals succumb to temptation because they expect to enjoy the fruit of their decision. In that sense temptation is both seductive and deceptive. It seduces by promising pleasure and deceives by concealing pain. Solomon compared it to a baited trap (Prov. 7:23), one which promises a good meal but conceals the snare. I've never gone hunting, and I haven't caught a fish in about twenty years, but my friends who do that sort of thing are always figuring out new ways to attract and deceive their prey. Hunters wear camouflage clothing and hide in carefully prepared blinds while using decoys and bird calls to lure the quarry. They deceive the hunted into seeing himself as the hunter, not springing the trap and revealing the truth until escape is impossible.

We are familiar enough with our own temptations to recognize that pattern, so we often try to encourage ourselves toward perseverance by posting reminders of concealed consequences. Antismoking campaigns publicize personal health risks, and dieters tape pictures of pigs to their refrigerators with sayings like, "A moment on the lips, a lifetime on the hips." Even then, however, the appeal is typically directed toward self-interest. You will be happier if you do not smoke. You will be more popular if you do not overeat. That kind of motivation is certainly realistic, and it may be appropriate in situations like these, but it neglects the fact that we are not the only ones affected by our choices.

Because we find ourselves in relationships with other people, our behavior always affects those around us. Even the most private sins help shape a person's character, and that character determines what he or she brings to the family or to the wider community. Further, since the essence of sin is pride, it may be described as a commitment to one's own interests over those of God and neighbor, and the failure to love one's neighbor can bring disastrous consequences to society. We may be the only ones to nibble the bait, but our friends and families end up sharing the hook.

Sportscasters often say that a good basketball player makes the other players on his team better. He leads by example, directs traffic on the court, draws defenders away from his teammates, passes the ball at appropriate moments, and helps everyone function as a team. Sin can be just as influential, but it makes others worse, not better. It encourages disobedience by its example, misdirects friends through foolish counsel, and sets up others for failure in pursuit of personal gain. In basketball terms, sin hogs the ball, then dribbles it out of bounds.

Naturally avoiding any admission of our sinfulness, we inevitably interpret our irresponsible treatment of others as a virtue. For example, when we are commanded to love our neighbor as ourselves (Mark 12:31), we insist on learning to love ourselves thoroughly before addressing the needs of our neighbor. Justifying self-interest through the love command calls for remarkable creativity, but we find a way! In our self-centeredness we inevitably value personal freedom over community responsibility, even in our churches, where "individual soul freedom" often negates any sense of corporate accountability. In short, sin has resulted in a selfish turn for a social creature, and our communities reflect it.

Collective Sin and the Individual

Kings and patriarchs in the ancient Near East often made decisions that determined the fate of their people. Adam represented all humanity when he sinned in the Garden (Rom. 5:12), and Achan's sin was initially credited to all Israel ("Israel has sinned," Josh. 7:11). Achan was later singled out, but the transgression was still considered so severe that his entire family was stoned along with him, cutting off his line forever (7:24–25). Later in Israel's history, idolatrous leaders drew God's wrath against the whole nation by leading them away from the Lord (2 Kings 13:2–3). In these and many similar cases, we see that individual sin can produce serious corporate consequences.

When nations are judged, every citizen usually suffers. God "rescued righteous Lot" and his family from the judgment poured out against Sodom (2 Pet. 2:7; Gen. 19:16), and Rahab was delivered along with her family from the destruction of Jericho (Josh. 6:23–25), but such individualized treatment seems to have been more the exception than the rule. When other cities experienced judgment, their entire populations were wiped out (Deut. 3:6; Josh. 8:24–26).

Such devastation cannot be explained simply by appealing to the sinful actions of their leaders. The kings and patriarchs did sin, and their individual decisions did have corporate consequences, but the communities themselves had also collectively rebelled against God. They established their own power through the violent oppression of other peoples (Amos 1:3, 6, 9, 11, 13). They rejected the Law of God and pursued other deities (2:4; Jer. 10:1–25). They oppressed the poor (Amos 2:6–7; 4:1; 5:12) while living extravagantly in luxurious homes (6:4–7). They demonstrated arrogance in the belief that their cities were secure and invulnerable (6:1–3; Jer. 48:42; Obad. 1:3). Their public officials demanded bribes and their personal friends betrayed confidences (Mic. 7:3, 5–6). They refused prophetic correction while pursuing their own lusts, believing they would surely escape judgment (Jer. 5:7–13). They were sinful individuals who compounded their guilt through sinful communities.

A community built on self-interest typically demonstrates the same kinds of sin as an individual. Instead of dependent obedience, the city acts in unfaith by seeking to establish itself as a powerful entity. It reveals pride by boasting in its own security or virtue, while imposing its cultural standards on other groups of people. It desires the territories or resources belonging to foreign nations, a collective form of concupiscence, and it pursues those things through cruelty and violence. Like individuals, nations often get caught up in cycles of self-justification and blame, attempting to identify their purposes as God's own, while demonizing their international rivals. It is difficult for individuals to recognize these collective expressions of sin from within the community, and it is equally difficult to avoid them. The community both honors and justifies each personal contribution to the collective cause, and it treats resistance to that cause as an act of betrayal.

This happens not only with nations but with all human communities. Racial, economic, and political groups demonstrate the same dynamic, as do businesses, schools, and the associations that comprise them. Anytime we affiliate with people who share our particular purposes, we tend to join them in forwarding and defending those purposes. Any prejudices or sins that are common to the group will be reinforced, not challenged, and any values that are foreign to it are likely to be rejected.

The values of a community are often expressed in particular social structures. On a national level our retail and healthcare industries demonstrate our collective commitment to consumerism and vitality, while our educational and political systems reveal our desire for training and order. Such social structures reflect our collective interests, sometimes even enforcing those interests against other nations or groups. That observation raises the possibility that the structures themselves express the collective sin of our community. Many theologians have described this pattern as "structural sin," implying that the prejudices of a particular group live on in the social systems they have created. Henry Fairlie outlined it well.

A society is not only the individuals who compose it. It has its own life, in its laws and institutions, customs and values, and through them it is able to impose on us. It can incite us to do what we ought not to do, and lull us into not doing what we ought to do. We may be ultimately responsible as individuals, since we could change our societies if we wished, but that they are capable of sinning on their own, even in our name, without our direct participation or approval, is beyond any question. If we neglect the poor, it is not only because each of us is avaricious, not even only because those who manage the economy may be particularly avaricious, but because the economic system itself is founded on Avarice.[4]

This is not the place to debate the relative merits of particular economic systems, especially when we are not in a position to effect any changes. However, we do need to confront our collective prejudices, particularly when they contribute to our justification of sinful attitudes or actions.

SOCIAL EXPRESSIONS OF THE SEVEN DEADLY SINS

One could examine the topic of social sin from many different perspectives, but I have chosen to consider it through a lens more commonly directed toward individuals.[5] First enumerated many centuries ago as vices that were especially damaging to monks, the Seven Deadly Sins are just as common in modern corporations as they were in medieval cloisters. They demonstrate the common tendencies of fallen human nature, both individually and corporately.

Pride

Pride is the essence of sin and the central failing of every individual, but *group* pride is the most destructive impulse in human history. It starts wars, racial conflicts, and "crimes against humanity," and then pins the blame on the other side. Group pride results in self-justification and cruelty on a global scale.

Group pride abides in every community, and it begins innocently enough, as individual self-interest expands to include our families and friends. The closer someone is to us, the more we care about his or her health and well-being. We are most committed to ourselves and our families, somewhat less committed to our friends, and significantly less committed to our acquaintances. Group pride has a good result when it encourages us to love one another, but it quickly turns evil when it encourages us to love *only* one another. We usually have little concern for those we have never met, especially if they live far away and we do not have much in common. For example, when a hurricane recently struck Mexico, many Mexican-Americans quickly organized relief efforts while other groups barely noticed. Both the negligent and the merciful demonstrated group pride, offering to love their neighbor only when he was their brother.

Group pride encourages every community to defend its interests by defending those who share them. Just as we usually act more humanely toward those perceived as "family" than toward those outside, we tend to involve ourselves in issues of justice only when the injustice strikes close to home. As Reinhold Niebuhr wrote shortly after the bombing of Pearl Harbor and the subsequent declaration of war by the United States, "We could not agree upon our responsibilities to the victims of aggression until we had been joined to them, not by moral act but by historical fate."[6] Niebuhr's comment may have been cynical, but it was true. All nations inevitably portray their actions as moral, but they are always self-serving, and they are not drawn into wars unless they have something at stake in the conflict.

That realization is still disconcerting, but it is easier to accept today than it would have been a hundred years ago. As they approached the twentieth century, liberal Protestants were remarkably utopian. With their hopes buoyed by technological advances, a strong economy, and the Darwinist notion of continual development, they believed humanity was making wonderful progress. Anticipating that people would become increasingly moral, they gave their leading periodical a name that reflected their expectations—*The Christian Century.*

But it was not to be. Instead, we now live in what many have called "the post-Christian era." There are many reasons why this did not turn out to be the Christian century, but one of them is the Western world's inability to reconcile its optimistic theology with the experience of economic depression, two world wars, repeated genocide, and weapons of mass destruction. It is difficult to believe in the goodness of human nature after witnessing depravity in technicolor.

Niebuhr was one of the first modern theologians to recognize what the experiences of this century have revealed about human nature. His *Moral Man and Immoral Society,* published in 1932, rejected social-gospel liberalism by arguing that the liberals failed to understand the collective pride of groups or nations.[7] Niebuhr believed that liberal "moralists" would never produce lasting reform because they were naive about human nature. They "seemed to believe that the only reason men had not followed the love commandment in the vast collective relations of mankind was because no one had called their attention to the necessity."[8] He himself was far more pessimistic. Individuals may at times yield to moral arguments, but groups (and therefore society as a whole) will not.

If our secretary of state attempted to hand over the state of Montana to Canada, receiving nothing in return, she would undoubtedly be fired, and she might be tried for treason. We expect our representatives to preserve our nation's interests, not to engage in international philanthropy out of the goodness of their hearts. If we believe an action helps us, we are for it. If it hurts us, we are against it. That is why Niebuhr wrote, "As individuals, men believe that they ought to love and serve each other and establish justice between each other. As racial, economic and national groups they take for themselves, whatever their power can command."[9]

Because our world is filled with so many different groups and communities, each pursuing its own interests, "a just society is not going to be built by a little more education and a few more sermons on love."[10] Individual persons might be motivated by such things, but groups do not respond to rational, moral, or emotional arguments. They respond only to power. That power does not need to be violent, indeed, it should not be, but it does need to create an incentive for the group to cooperate. Nations sign peace treaties because they believe the terms of the treaty will be more advantageous than the continuation of war. The whites in South Africa did not give up apartheid because they were nice people. They gave it up because they were outnumbered at home and their policies were opposed by protest and economic pressure from the rest of the world.

All groups pursue their own desires, conceding some of their aims only when other groups have sufficient power to hold them in check. Without that kind of restraint, injustice becomes inevitable as the powerful impose their will on the weak. As a result, the most just societies are those that maintain a healthy balance of power, while the most unjust are those in which one group has the capacity to dominate the others.

Some people are surely more virtuous than others, and leaders will guide their communities toward different standards of behavior, but injustice does not result primarily from the *wrong* group's domination of the others. It results from *any* group's domination of the others. Failure to recognize that fact has been one of the great mistakes of contemporary liberation theologians. They do not realize that today's oppressed could be tomorrow's oppressors. The selfishness of the dominant community may be most obvious at the present time, but that is because they are in a position to follow their hearts most freely. Given the opportunity, those who have been exploited will just as easily exploit their neighbors, and more so if their desires are mixed with vengeance.

The desire for revenge comes easily to those caught up in self-justification and blame, and those tendencies follow just as naturally from collective pride as they do from the pride of individuals. Nations and groups routinely believe their own purposes are just, perhaps even inspired by God, and they see their enemies as evil and demonic. As Cornelius Plantinga Jr. wrote (also quoting James Burtchaell), "Despite centuries of war, no one has ever [broken the peace]. Nobody has ever fired a first shot. All strikes are claimed to be counterstrikes. All shots are return fire. 'For the allies, WWII began at the Polish border in 1939; for the Germans, hostilities dated back to Versailles. Your military operation is an attack; mine is a retaliation.' "[11]

Of course, retaliation never simply evens the score. It invariably strikes an extra blow to regain the upper hand. It escalates the violence to such a degree that participants are shocked by the cruelty of their own behavior. For example, consider the atrocities committed by both Hutus and Tutsis in central Africa or the bloody conflict between former neighbors in the Balkans. Regarding the latter, Miroslav Volf wrote the following.

It does not seem that anybody is in control. Of course, the big and strategic moves that started the conflict and that keep it going are made in the centers of intellectual, political, and military power. But there is too much will for brutality even among the common people. Once the conflict started it seemed to trigger an uncontrollable chain reaction. These were decent people, helpful neighbors. They did not, strictly speaking, *choose* to plunder and burn, rape and torture—or secretly enjoy these things. A dormant beast in them was awakened from its uneasy slumber. And not only in them: the motives of those who set to fight against the brutal aggressors were self-defense and justice, but the beast in others enraged the beast in them. And so the moral barriers holding it in check were broken and the beast went after revenge. In resisting evil, people were trapped by it.[12]

It may not happen until that violent cycle brings at least one of the combatants to the brink of annihilation, but the shooting will eventually cease. The vengeful beast, on the other hand, does not die. Nurtured by group pride, it returns to hibernation, where it waits for another day.

Collective self-interest causes even Christians to get caught up in the agendas of their secular communities. Consider the following four examples. First, theologians have discussed the criteria for a "just war" since the time of Augustine, but they have almost always concluded that the causes of their own governments are just. Adolf von Harnack helped draft public statements for the Kaiser explaining Germany's role in the First World War, while American liberals and fundamentalists engaged in a bitter dispute about which of them were more patriotic.

Second, apparently more committed to the preservation of Southern culture than they were to biblical ethics, many nineteenth-century American theologians prepared extensive arguments in defense of slavery.[13] For the next century many white conservatives persisted in opposing civil rights, sometimes describing it as a threat to the southern way of life. Even now, Bible-believing Christians continue to divide along racial lines as they address issues like welfare and affirmative action.

Third, in the mid-nineteenth century, Americans appealed to their civil religion to justify the doctrine of manifest destiny. They believed that God had ordained their domination of North America, and they sought to remove other peoples and cultures from the territories they claimed as their own. As Daisy Machado wrote, "It was a belief that the God of the New Israel taking shape on the North American continent had no use for red and brown people."[14]

Fourth, during the recent tribal conflicts in central Africa, many pastors, not adequately grounded in the faith, placed their tribal affiliation ahead of their allegiance to Christ. Some went so far as to assist in the massacre of rival tribesmen within their churches. One of my students was targeted for assassination by other "believers" in that region when he continued to preach forgiveness and reconciliation in the name of Jesus.

Unless something can be done to change the human heart, group pride presents an intractable problem. Even Niebuhr and the other "realists," who helped explain the basis for ethnic strife and international conflict, foresaw no genuine solution.[15] Inherently selfish, people look out for their own interests ahead of everyone else's. The problem is complicated by the fact that each individual participates simultaneously in several different communities, sharing beliefs and concerns with each of them. For example, I have some stake in the collective self-interest of United States citizens, but I also share narrower concerns with other residents of Texas and other homeowners on my street. I value many of the same things as do other middle-income parents, and I no doubt carry certain assumptions and prejudices that are common among white American men.

However, as a Christian, I should identify more closely with the body of Christ than with any other group, and it is in the church that we see a solution to the problem of group pride (Col. 3:8–15).

God has designed the church as a community in which the conflicts caused by group pride are overcome by the work of the Spirit. It is a "new humanity" which calls believers to leave behind the ethnic divisions of our former way of life, a new family consisting of both Jews and Gentiles (Eph. 2:14–18). Brought by Christ into this new community and empowered by the Spirit to overcome sin, we are expected to live differently than those in the old city.

Pride is the most central of the Seven Deadly Sins, the one Fairlie called "the keystone of the arch,"[16] but we don't have to search very long in an immoral society before we find the others as well. When "every inclina-tion of the thoughts of their hearts" is "only evil continually" (Gen. 6:5, NRSV), every form of rebellion will show up sooner or later.

Envy

When I was a seminary student, I worked on a paint crew along with several other students. We painted all kinds of homes, from cheap apart-ments to multimillion-dollar condominiums, and we became good friends as we talked about sports and theology, while scraping and sanding or spreading the paint. One fall afternoon, after spending all day painting the shutters of a beautiful mansion in north Dallas, we sat down for a break on the upstairs porch. With our ladders on the east side of the house early in the morning, we had admired the homeowner's cars—a classic T-bird convertible, a Mercedes sedan, a Corvette, a new Seville, and a cus-tom truck. When we moved to the north side around lunchtime, we had been able to see the flower gardens and the greenhouse. Now, resting on a porch that was twice the size of my apartment, we looked out over the swimming pool and about three acres of the backyard. No one said any-thing as we gaped at the surroundings, but the immediate lesson was obvious. None of us would ever come close to owning a house like this. We couldn't afford even one of the cars. We could barely afford the cars we had, which smelled like paint thinner and needed body work. It was a nice day and we were in a lovely spot, but we were starting to get de-pressed. Hoping to put a moral on the story, I turned to one of my coworkers and said, "But are they really happy?" His reply was immedi-ate: "It sure looks like it!"

That was not the first time my friends and I had fallen into the sin of envy, nor would it be the last. Envy is not quite the same as covetousness, which simply wishes to possess particular people or objects. Envy wants to trade places with those who possess those things. The man who covets a car may be content to have one just like his neighbor's, but the man who envies his neighbor wants to have *his* car. If covetousness whines, "Me too," then envy whispers, "Better me than you."

The flip-side of envy is conceit. Envy looks at another person's privileges and says, "Better me than you," but conceit looks at one's own privileges and says, "Better me than others." Both envy and conceit are driven by pride. We believe we are more deserving and more talented than other people, and that belief produces the conceit through which we justify our own possessions. It also produces envy, which asks how others could possibly have acquired the objects that we who are more talented still lack. Since they appear to have grabbed the brass ring, we attribute their success either to luck or to choices that we could have made just as easily as they. The green eyes of envy look forward to the day when our rival's luck will change, but they also look back with regret at the road not taken.

"If I had gone on to medical school, I'd be living in a house like that, too."

"I followed my conscience, and look where it got me. I could have been the one to get that promotion."

"I've always talked about waiting for marriage, but now it looks like I may wait forever. My friends were right. I wish I'd let myself have a little more fun back in school."

Even Asaph the psalmist experienced envy when, for a time, he regretted his righteous decisions. "For I was envious of the arrogant, as I saw the prosperity of the wicked. For there are no pains in their death; and their body is fat. They are not in trouble as other men; nor are they plagued like mankind. . . . Behold, these are the wicked; and always at ease, they have increased in wealth. Surely in vain I have kept my heart pure, and washed my hands in innocence; for I have been stricken all day long, and chastened every morning" (Ps. 73:3–5, 12–14). In response to this kind of impulse, Proverbs states, "Do not envy a man of violence, and do not choose any of his ways" (Prov. 3:31). Further, "Do not let your heart envy sinners, but live in the fear of the LORD always" (23:17).

Individuals fall into envy and conceit because of their pride, and groups follow the same pattern. For example, consider once again the response of racial groups to the question of intelligence. In America average IQ scores consistently differ from one race to another. Those whose groups achieve higher averages find it easy to believe the tests are accurate, and they conclude that intelligence is innate. These people believe they have been successful in society because of their greater intelligence, and they believe that less intelligent people, often those of other races, could not be as successful even if they were given the same opportunities. Those whose groups have lower average scores generally argue that the tests are biased, and they believe that intelligence is acquired, not innate. They believe that others have been more successful than they because privileges have not been fairly distributed. Given the same opportunities they would have been just as successful. Both sides demonstrate collective pride, but one turns to conceit, and the other to envy. They then appeal to the prevailing values of the society to justify their sin. The conceited believe they have profited by using their gifts in a system based on freedom and equality. The envious believe they would profit if only they were given a free and equal chance to use their gifts.

Anger

Unsatisfied envy often leads to anger. That combination may have been part of Cain's motivation in attacking his brother, and it apparently contributed to the plot against Jesus. His opponents envied His influence, so they delivered Him over to the Romans (Matt. 27:18). An envious man explains his neighbor's good fortune as the result of luck, choices, or other circumstances that could easily have been his own. But the angry man has gone a step further by concluding that the deck is stacked against him. His misfortune is not the result of chance or his own misguided choices; it is the consequence of someone else's malevolent deeds.

At a group level, envy leads to anger when people see violent revolution as a way to correct injustice. Believing they have been denied equal opportunity in the society, members of the envious group conclude that they have been systematically excluded. The only way they can obtain justice, they reason, is to sieze control of the system.

Some of the clearest examples of collective envy and anger may be found in the writings of liberation theologians like Gustavo Gutiérrez, a Roman Catholic priest in Peru. He argues that the deep poverty in Latin America has resulted from European and North American exploitation. "The underdevelopment of the poor countries, as an overall social fact, appears in its true light; as the historical by-product of the development of other countries. The dynamics of the capitalist economy lead to the establishment of a center and a periphery, simultaneously generating progress and growing wealth for the few and social imbalances, political tensions, and poverty for the many."[17]

Many North Americans, undoubtedly showing some measure of corporate conceit, suggest that Latin American poverty has resulted from corruption and native incompetence. They offer to show poorer nations how to build their own free-market economies, encouraging them to follow the example of more prosperous countries. In response, the liberation theologians have asserted that wealthy countries obtained their wealth by plundering their neighbors. Latin America cannot follow that example because there is no one left to plunder.

The liberationists seem to perceive wealth the way my boys see pie. If I eat more than my share, the boys naturally complain. They have been shorted because of my gluttony. They have less pie because I had more. My natural response, "I get more pie because I'm bigger than you," is never accepted as satisfactory, and the day is coming when I won't be able to use it. As the boys get bigger, they may assume the right to some of *my* pie!

Liberation theologians have essentially accused the wealthy nations of taking too much pie. Many critics have responded that this accusation depends on a faulty view of wealth. Those who have good ideas have the ability to create wealth, meaning that we don't all have to share the same pie. The poorer nations can and should make their own. The liberationists, however, say that the wealthy have already picked all the berries. They will not return them willingly, for power is relinquished only when power is raised against it. From the liberationist perspective, justice will only be obtained by revolution and the redistribution of wealth. Gutiérrez expressed the problem this way: "Attempts to bring about changes within the existing order have proven futile. This analysis of the situation is at the level of scientific rationality. Only a radical break from the status quo, that is, a profound transformation of the private property system, access to power of the exploited class, and a social revolution that would break this dependence would allow for the change to a new society, a socialist society—or at least allow that such a society might be possible."[18] In the liberationist program, collective envy has turned to anger, and violent deeds are justified as acts of compassion. On the other side, the wealthy who are caught up in collective conceit may just as easily maintain their interests by force, justifying such actions as attempts to preserve individual rights and principles in a free society. Neither side is without sin, but both sides believe themselves to be righteous.

A society's anger and violence is not always directed toward an external enemy, for it sometimes turns against an internal scapegoat. In this case the anger is not usually provoked as much by envy as by fear. The community that seeks a scapegoat is often under unusual pressure—perhaps a natural disaster or some other crisis—and they come to regard an individual or a group of persons as responsible for their distress. The chosen scapegoat is enough a part of the community to represent an internal threat, but he is also different enough that his place in the community may be challenged. When that challenge comes, and the selected individual or group suffers persecution, the community expects a return to those halcyon days before their present distress. It never comes, for the scapegoat was never the cause of their problem, but that lesson is not easily learned, and it will not be long before another victim is selected.[19]

Sloth

We usually think of farmers as an industrious lot. Tending their animals before dawn and working in the fields until dark, they have great loyalty to the land as the source of their livelihood. But not all farmers conform to that stereotype.

"I passed by the field of the sluggard, and by the vineyard of the man lacking sense; and behold, it was completely overgrown with thistles, its surface was covered with nettles, and its stone wall was broken down. When I saw, I reflected upon it; I looked, and received instruction. 'A little sleep, a little slumber, a little folding of the hands to rest,' then your poverty will come as a robber, and your want like an armed man" (Prov. 24:30–34). The farmer described in these verses was guilty of the sin of sloth. In his laziness he had ignored his responsibilities, and the farm had so deteriorated that it was no longer productive. People have been tempted by sloth ever since the Fall, for we would rather have a life of ease than one of hard labor. We would rather live in a world in which the fruit could never be overtaken by nettles and thistles, but that world was lost when Adam and Eve were driven from the Garden of Eden. We must now eat bread by the sweat of our faces (Gen. 3:19).

Like thievery, the sin of sloth violates the legitimate expectations of one's community. The Thessalonians who ate their neighbors' bread while performing no work of their own were placing an unfair burden on their friends (2 Thess. 3:7–12). They were also damaging the church by filling up their free time with gossip and inappropriate behavior, highlighting another problem that often accompanies sloth. By keeping us from having too much idle time, work often protects us from ourselves. Sloth, on the other hand, chooses to do whatever is most pleasant. Given the natural inclinations of fallen people, that is a rather frightening prospect.

The concept of sloth covers much more than one's vocation, however, for even the most industrious workers may be slothful with regard to their other responsibilities. They may neglect their families or their communities because they are so wrapped up in their jobs. They may also demonstrate sloth with regard to the faith. The slave in Jesus' parable who buried his talent in the ground was guilty of sloth (Matt. 25:14–30). But Jesus was concerned about more than the care of one's wealth. He wanted those who had been entrusted with divine resources (most notably, revelation) to handle that treasure appropriately. If they neglected their responsibilities through spiritual apathy or sloth, they would lose what they had been given.

William May called this kind of sloth "the last sign on the road to death."[20] It reveals a hardness of heart, a coldness of the soul, that is utterly unconcerned with the things of God. In this sense it is much more than just laziness or the enjoyment of idle time with friends. In the words of Fairlie, sloth is "a state of dejection that gives rise to torpor of mind and feeling and spirit; to a sluggishness or . . . a poisoning of the will; to despair, faintheartedness, and even desirelessness, a lack of real desire for anything, even for what is good."[21] Dorothy Sayers said it best. "It is the sin that believes in nothing, cares for nothing, seeks to know nothing, interferes with nothing, enjoys nothing, hates nothing, finds purpose in nothing, lives for nothing, and remains alive because there is nothing for which it will die."[22]

Groups or communities, like individuals, can easily succumb to the sin of sloth. When they feel trapped by poverty, illiteracy, lawlessness, and unemployment, some populations conclude that no amount of effort will change their circumstances. They depend on others to meet their needs and they discourage their members from breaking the cycle of despair. They demonstrate apathy and indifference in a collective demonstration of sloth.

At the same time, more prosperous communities may also be slothful in their neglect of the poor. They do not intend to bring harm to their neighbor. They simply fail to notice that they have a neighbor. Suburban-ites may work in the city, but they don't travel through urban neighborhoods, and they call the police if they see suspicious persons on their own streets. Jesus spoke of the poor man Lazarus, who lay outside the rich man's gate (Luke 16:19–21), but today the disadvantaged would be hard pressed to get that close. A modern-day Lazarus would see little more than the blur of a Lexus on the freeway, and the rich man would not see him at all, let alone know his name (16:24).

Contemporary society has shown sloth not only in the apathy of both rich and poor, but in what Kenneth Gergen has described as "the saturated self."[23] In the last several decades transportation and communication tech-nologies have advanced so quickly that many of us have become socially saturated. We have more acquaintances than any people in history, and we have immediate access to more information than anyone ever thought pos-sible. We expected those technologies to bring us closer together, but they have fractured our local communities in several ways. First, they have helped us maintain relationships while moving from town to town, enabling us to be more committed to friends a thousand miles away than to our own neigh-bors. Second, they have multiplied our acquaintances with people all over the world, diminishing our local connections. Third, these technologies have provided such wide exposure to ideas and persons that many find it in-creasingly difficult to be dogmatic about their beliefs. One may be tempted to view these developments positively, for weaker local communities may not generate as much group pride. However, the absence of a common cause often signals the arrival of collective sloth. In group pride, a commu-nity may easily care about the wrong things, but in sloth they care about nothing. When people are so saturated by relationships and information that they become indolent and apathetic, they will probably be more at home in Babel than in the city of God.

Avarice

Jesus said that the foremost commandment demands love for God, and the second, love for one's neighbor (Mark 12:30–31). The Seven Deadly Sins violate those commands by directing love elsewhere or abandoning it altogether. The first three sins—pride, envy, and anger—reveal a love so selfish that it results in violence against one's neighbor. The fourth—sloth—demonstrates the absence of love. Real passions have been lost. The three remaining sins—avarice, gluttony, and lust—reveal what some have described as an excessive love for things or people. However, this love is more of a perverted desire, a once-healthy appreciation turned into an unbounded obsession.

Jesus said, "No one can serve two masters; for either he will hate the one and love the other, or he will hold to one and despise the other. You cannot serve God and mammon" (Matt. 6:24). Those with an inordinate love for riches demonstrate avarice, a desire for possessions that surpasses their love for God. The sin of avarice pursues things rather than God, neglecting the fact that He "richly supplies us with all things to enjoy" (1 Tim. 6:17). It also loves things more than it does people, neglecting the command to "be generous and ready to share" (6:18). It never seems so at the time, but avarice can be deadly. "For the love of money is a root of all sorts of evil, and some by longing for it have wandered away from the faith, and pierced themselves with many a pang" (6:10).

Recognizing the natural tendency of sinful people to love money and maximize their own profits, the Levitical Law directed harvesters to leave behind a portion of their crop for those who had no food of their own (Lev. 19:9–10). That Law helped Ruth and Naomi survive when they returned to Bethlehem at the beginning of the barley harvest, for Ruth was able to glean behind the reapers (Ruth 2:1–16). Had Boaz and the other farmers of Bethlehem attempted to maximize their profits, what would have become of the gleaners?

When a society exercises collective avarice, bent on seeking wealth, it establishes structures that show no mercy toward the poor. If it is to help them, as Israel did, the society must consciously adopt standards that contradict its selfish tendencies.

Unfortunately, because communities and corporations are governed by collective self-interest, they will not generally follow such recommendations unless they are convinced they have something to gain. For example, if support for the poor promises favorable public relations, tax credits, or expanded markets, companies will participate. If nothing is promised in return, it is unrealistic to expect their support. John Steinbeck, in describing the bank in *The Grapes of Wrath*, highlighted the inability of avaricious institutions to show compassion. In the story, representatives from the bank apologize to a man they are about to evict. They do not like what they are doing, but they explain that the bank cannot show mercy. It must obtain its profits.

"We're sorry. It's not us. It's the monster. The bank isn't like a man."

"Yes, but the bank is only made of men."

"No, you're wrong there—quite wrong there. The bank is something else than men. It happens that every man in a bank hates what the bank does, and yet the bank does it. The bank is something more than men, I tell you. It's the monster. Men made it, but they can't control it."[24]

Those words provide a vivid description of structural sin—"Men made it, but they can't control it." We attempt to create organizations or associations that will obey our commands and satisfy our desires—machines that remain under our control. But those machines too easily become monsters. They take on lives of their own and may even turn against their makers. An individual may act alone when he establishes a profit-making company, but when it expands, he is quickly joined by other avaricious people whose personal gain is bound to that of the corporation. As more and more people assume responsibility for its operations, the company becomes increasingly independent of its founder. It develops a life of its own, one that is maintained for the collective good of its participants. At that point, like a nation, the corporation can act only according to self-interest. It has become a monster.

A similar pattern may be seen in our relationship to technology, which provides another example of collective avarice. Hoping to avoid suffering and obtain the things they desire, modern societies have treated technology as the answer to all evils. But the machine has become a monster, threatening the existence of those who made it.

People have long recognized technology as a double-edged sword. It is a tool that has great potential for good but just as many possibilities for evil. Nuclear energy can be used to energize cities or to destroy them, and global computer networks can be used for emergency aid or for industrial espionage. However, technology has become more than just a machine that can be used for good or evil. Its human creators have given it such a prominent place in modern life that they are no longer able to control it.

Instead of trusting God to meet their needs, modern communities have placed their hope in technology's ability to deliver the things they desire. Driven by collective avarice, they have attempted to discover "the good life" independently of the Creator. As David Berger wrote, "The ultimate threat of technology is its ability to replace our faith in and need for God with a never-ending stream of goods, cures, conveniences, and entertaining diversions."[25] By promising power over the uncontrolled and threatening elements of life and assuring us that it will maximize our pleasure, technology essentially repeats the boast of Lamech (Gen. 4:24)— it claims to do God's job better than God. That boast was stated clearly in a recent television drama involving infertility and cloning. The doctor told a woman, "God can't help you now, but I can." Functioning as a false god for modern communities, technology promises blessing while carrying a curse. Neil Postman described it well when he wrote that technology "is a god that speaks to us of power, not limits; speaks to us of ownership, not stewardship; speaks to us only of rights, not responsibilities; speaks to us of self-aggrandizement, not humility."[26] That siren call appeals to our avarice and pride, but we must remain sober and recognize our limitations.

We cannot change the fact that we live in a technological society, and it would be inappropriate to deny all the resources of our day in an attempt to reproduce a bygone era. However, since researchers have a habit of asking ethical questions only after they have made a name for themselves by developing new techniques, and since those techniques increasingly impinge on the sanctity of human life, we must be prepared to draw some lines in the sand. Technology has given us the ability to do some things we should not do, because in our collective avarice we have sought after more than we have been given.

Gluttony

A visit to Hershey, Pennsylvania, will convince any chocolate lover that the kingdom has arrived. The streetlights are shaped like Hershey Kisses, alternating between wrapped and unwrapped, and the famous candy factory sits in the middle of town, filling the neighborhood with a smell like that of fresh-baked brownies. Elsewhere people live out their days near stockyards or chemical plants, and they endure odor as a necessary evil. The good folks of "Chocolate Town, USA" have nothing to endure but temptation. It seems that one could gain weight just by breathing the air, but fresh chocolate is everywhere to be consumed.

When my wife and I visited Hershey a number of years ago, we discovered Hershey bars in the hotel lobby, Hershey Miniatures in our room, and a big display with every variety in the local drugstore. The generous people at the golf course where Julie was playing in a tournament, provided chocolate in the locker room, on the practice range, and on every tee. When they gave us a tour of the factory, we saw huge conching vats mixing the warm chocolate paste, legions of Hershey Kisses marching in parade down the conveyor belt, and several thousand perfectly molded chocolate bars being packaged for shipment. The tour guide obviously understood the temptation, repeatedly reminding us not to scoop up any samples!

Had I been given the freedom to pluck chocolate candies off the conveyor belt, I probably would have overindulged, making the most of the opportunity, and I would have bragged about it to my friends. It is very unlikely that any of them would have said anything about gluttony. Instead, they would have enjoyed the story and looked at me with envy.

Gluttony, it seems, is the most easily excused of the Seven Deadly Sins. It is as if we have been presented with Six Deadly Sins and One Funny One. But there's nothing funny about gluttony.

The Bible often treats an abundance of food as a sign of God's blessing. Just as thorns and thistles reveal His displeasure, full harvests and lavish banquets come as a consequence of God's favor (Num. 14:8; Ps. 81:10, 16; Isa. 25:6; Ezek. 36:29–30). Proverbs 28:25 states that the one who trusts in the Lord "shall be made fat" (KJV). That verse does not appear on refrigerator magnets in a society obsessed with fitness and beauty, but many cultures still regard a few extra pounds as an indication of prosperity, especially when most of the population is poor.

However, plumpness may also be a sign of hardness of heart. Asaph described wicked men in his own day as obese, wealthy, and arrogant. "For there are no pains in their death; and their body is fat. They are not in trouble as other men; nor are they plagued like mankind. Therefore pride is their necklace; the garment of violence covers them. Their eye bulges from fatness; the imaginations of their heart run riot. They mock, and wickedly speak of oppression; they speak from on high. They have set their mouth against the heavens, and their tongue parades through the earth. . . . And they say, 'How does God know? And is there knowledge with the Most High?' Behold, these are the wicked; and always at ease, they have increased in wealth" (Ps. 73:4–9, 11–12).

These people gave no credit to God for their prosperity, regarding themselves as self-made. They maintained their proud position by oppressing the poor, many of whom, like the psalmist, were far more righteous than they. Amos addressed the same kind of people when he wrote, "Therefore, because you impose heavy rent on the poor and exact a tribute of grain from them, though you have built houses of well-hewn stone, yet you will not live in them; you have planted pleasant vineyards, yet you will not drink their wine" (Amos 5:11). He also wrote, "Woe to those who are at ease in Zion, and to those who feel secure in the mountain of Samaria, the distinguished men of the foremost of nations, to whom the house of Israel comes. . . . Those who recline on beds of ivory and sprawl on their couches, and eat lambs from the flock and calves from the midst of the stall, who improvise to the sound of the harp, and like David have composed songs for themselves, who drink wine from sacrificial bowls while they anoint themselves with the finest of oils, yet they have not grieved over the ruin of Joseph" (6:1, 4–7).

These people were not condemned for enjoying good things; they were condemned for enjoying those things independently of God and at great cost to the poor. As Jeremiah wrote, "They are fat, they are sleek, they also excel in deeds of wickedness; they do not plead the cause, the cause of the orphan, that they may prosper, and they do not defend the rights of the poor" (Jer. 5:28).

That is the pattern of the glutton. Oblivious to the role of God's grace, and uncaring about the needs of those around him, the glutton is obsessed with the delights of his table, indulging his ever-increasing desire for food. His appetite has more to do with the extravagance of his heart than the needs of his body, and it easily evolves into sloth. He squanders his health, his money, and his time on the trough, but does not care as long as he remains well fed. It all becomes very tedious, but it cannot continue indefinitely. "Do not be with heavy drinkers of wine, or with gluttonous eaters of meat; for the heavy drinker and the glutton will come to poverty, and drowsiness will clothe a man with rags" (Prov. 23:20–21).

Communities demonstrate gluttony when they gratify their appetites apart from God while ignoring the needs of the poor. It is difficult to deny the corporate gluttony of our world's wealthiest nations. As Ron Sider observed, "Over a billion people lack access to elementary health services, and 1.6 billion people do not even have safe water to drink. The cost of such services is relatively small. The World Health Organization has reported that if we would only increase our annual investments in preventive care by 75 cents per person in the Third World, we could save 5 million persons every year. That would take less than $3 billion. Surely the people of the wealthier nations can help find $3 billion to save the lives of 5 million people. U.S. citizens alone spend $5 billion a year on special diets to lower their caloric intake."[27]

Further, "the rich minority of the world devours an unequal share of the world's available food."[28] Sider continued, "In the years 1987–89, 816 million people in the developed nations consumed almost as much grain (440 million tons) as the 2.812 billion people (551 million tons) in less developed nations. We eat much of our grain (63.2 percent) indirectly via meat. People in the poor countries eat almost all of their grain (81.8 percent) directly. The United Nations reported in 1974 that livestock in the rich countries ate as much grain as did all the people of India and China."[29]

Some may object, saying that one nation's poverty does not constitute another nation's gluttony, but there is little doubt that the wealthy are overindulging. "Whereas people in many poor nations have less than the daily minimal requirements, people in North America and Western Europe have more calories than they need. While lack of food destroys millions in poor lands, too much food devastates millions in affluent countries. According to a 1980 survey by the National Center for Health Statistics, 32 percent of American men and 36 percent of American women between the ages of twenty and seventy-four are overweight."[30]

I don't expect the developed countries to alter their lifestyles simply for the sake of the poor. We know enough about sin to avoid such an optimistic notion. However, we should have higher expectations for the church. Indwelt by the Spirit of God, Christians should break the pattern of self-interest that prevails among unbelievers. The fact that we follow the rest of our culture in justifying our gluttony does not speak well of our condition.

Lust

Lust is more often condemned than gluttony, though we probably commit both sins with equal frequency. If we feed in front of the television, in a public place, or with a vivid imagination, we may even commit both sins at the same time. However, lust is more widely forbidden, and that makes us more aware of our transgression. We display gluttony in public, smiling at one another as we line up at the buffet, but we keep our lust to ourselves. We wear mirrored sunglasses to the beach and, when caught in a lecherous gaze, we avert our eyes, feigning a casual glance. We log onto the Internet, view movies, or contemplate our fantasies in the privacy of our homes. At an individual level, gluttony is an essentially private affair that we don't mind putting on display, but lust is an interpersonal affair that we usually try to keep private.

When considered at a collective level, however, lust is not private at all. It propels advertising and entertainment all over the world, as companies pose attractive models alongside their products and use sex to sell everything from swimming pools to soda pop. When pornography is a multibillion-dollar industry and even "family" entertainment is filled with sexual overtones, there is little doubt that we are living in a lustful society.

Unfortunately the social experience of lust tends to make its private expression more acceptable. Advertisers use models to capture attention. When they no longer succeed, our lack of response demonstrates not maturity but numbness. If it takes something more—or a model wearing something less—to attract our attention, we can expect the market to move in that direction. In the end, as with avarice and gluttony, lust finds itself settling into sloth. An excess of passion, impossible to satisfy with externals because it comes from within, eventually turns cold. Fairlie wrote, "The offense of our age is not that it excites sex, but that it withers it, takes away all dewiness from it, shrivels it to a husk. The reason why Lust often turns to perversions is that the flesh itself has ceased to please it."[31]

Summary

The Seven Deadly Sins were laid out in the medieval era as warnings to those who were living lives of solitude. However, they are just as applicable to modern communities and their members. As individuals we find ourselves battling pride, envy, anger, sloth, avarice, gluttony, and lust, and we see the same sins at work in society. Mohandas Gandhi also identified "seven social sins," and his inventory bears many similarities to our own: "politics without principle, wealth without work, commerce without morality, pleasure without conscience, education without character, science without humanity, and worship without sacrifice."[32]No matter which list we use, we are guilty both as individuals and as communities. Our corporate responsibility does not give us the freedom to blame others for our personal sinfulness, nor does our personal righteousness allow us to avoid identifying with our communities. We contribute to and benefit from the collective self-interest of the city, and we cannot excuse ourselves that easily.

However, we can find our hope in a new community. God will resolve the problem of structural sin with His own city, something He has already begun in the church. As participants in the "new humanity," we are collectively "being renewed to a true knowledge" according to the image of our Creator (Col. 3:10), and we are expected to live differently from those around us.

ii |

Salvation from Sin
and the
Restoration of Life

EVERY SUMMER, vacationing families in minivans con-
verge on America's theme parks. Inside the gates, the crowds discover
cobblestone streets and quaint shops from some bygone era, bright flowers lining the immaculate sidewalks, and horse-drawn carriages easing
their way past baby strollers on the avenue. Talking animals offer hugs to
the children, who squeal with delight and smile for the camera. Coins in
the sparkling fountains express the hope that wishes will come true, and
the park itself makes such thoughts seem realistic. Roller coasters and
bungee jumps offer adrenaline to those who can handle it, and those who
prefer something a little quieter can ride the train, the Model-T cars, or
the bumper boats. Actors stage old Western gunfights in which the good
guys always win, and the park's cheerful employees serve ice cream and
cotton candy in the food court.

The theme park offers a pleasant escape from the daily routine, but only
the smallest of children fail to see that it is nothing more than an illusion.
Behind its facade, the old-fashioned business district is a product of mar-
keting and technology, carefully designed to make a friendly impression
while earning a profit. The young women inside the animal suits are soaked
with sweat and envious of their coworkers who get to dress in shorts and
pick up litter from the sidewalk. Gardeners arrive every morning to pull the

weeds, and the gunfighters always fire blanks. In the real world, however, the good guys may not win and those in free fall are rarely caught by a bungee cord. Outside the theme park, frightening experiences don't always end with a smile, and we may not find a seat on the ride of our choice.

From where we stand, sheltered by the walls of the modern city, Eden is such a remote memory that it seems more like a theme park than a genuine human experience. The very thought of a world without sin sounds too good to be true, and many treat it as a fantasy, a myth suitable only for little children who haven't yet lost their youthful idealism. Those who know better might enjoy mulling over the concept, but like the mothers and fathers who carry their tired kids back out to the parking lot, they know they can't live forever in a theme park. Unhappy as they may be to leave, the family must return to the real world.

In that world, people struggle to cope with the same sorts of problems from one generation to the next. They labor against the elements to provide for their families; they fight among themselves; they experience pain; and they get sick and die. They develop technologies to ease their physical burdens, succeeding in many remarkable ways, but the same basic obstacles remain. A farmer may sit in an air-conditioned tractor, spreading chemicals over genetically engineered plants, but he's still fighting the weeds.

So much of human experience consists of a struggle with sin's consequences that we find it difficult to imagine the world any other way. But it really was different once, and it will be once again. Eden was not a theme park, and the kingdom of heaven is not a pipe dream. Lest we forget their reality, especially after a lengthy discussion of sin, this chapter outlines a broader perspective on human history from creation to redemption.

THE LOSS AND RESTORATION OF THE IDEAL

God created man and woman in His image, investing them with divine glory and ordaining them to rule as His vice-regents. We people thus have unique dignity and value in both the material and the immaterial aspects of our nature. We were designed to live in an intimate relationship with one another and with God, making responsible choices both individually and corporately as we honor Him.

Sin has prevented people from fulfilling that mandate. All human beings continue to exist in God's image, but that image has been tarnished and defaced as the glory of God has been exchanged for idols of every imaginable kind. Denying the existence of a Creator, people have consistently attempted to explain the world apart from God. That effort has encouraged them to reject the dignity and sanctity of human life, leading to irresponsible and barbarous actions by both individuals and groups.

If we have obtained this state of affairs by striving for equality with God, it has not been a very good exchange. The consequences of sin repeatedly leave creation so unraveled that the ideal can be salvaged only by a new creation. However, God has demonstrated His grace throughout history by offering salvation and re-creation in the midst of our depravity.

The Fullness of Life

We usually speak of life and death in terms of physical survival. If someone is alive, then he's not dead. If he's dead, then he's no longer alive. The distinction is simple, understandable, and appropriate. However, we as Christians profess to believe in life after death. That is, even when someone is physically dead, he is alive in the sense that his spirit continues in conscious existence apart from the body, either in Christ's presence or in torment. We also believe unbelievers are spiritually dead (Eph. 2:1), and that means someone can be physically alive but dead in the sense that he is alienated from the Spirit of God. When we say someone can be alive while dead and dead while alive, we obviously believe life consists of more than just physical survival.

As we have seen, the Old Testament view of life reflects the ideal of a peaceful existence in the land of promise, characterized by abundant blessing and fellowship with God. We might call this "Life with a capital L." Those who lack any of those things lack Life. That model was established when God placed the man in the fruitful Garden. Adam experienced physical life through the animating presence of God's breath (Gen. 2:7), and he enjoyed inexhaustible blessing through "every tree that is pleasing to the sight and good for food" (2:9). His fellowship with the Creator had not yet been broken by sin, and he delighted in the land God had set apart for him. No foreign invaders threatened his territory; no animals would attack him; and there was no possibility of famine. I don't know if Adam ever looked around and said, "This is the life!" but he certainly had reason to. He enjoyed Life in its fullness.

The day they ate from the tree of the knowledge of good and evil, Adam and his wife died (2:17). They were still alive in that they survived physically, but they lost fellowship with the Creator because of their sin (3:8), they lost God's fruitful blessing through His curse on the ground (3:17–18), and they lost their land by banishment from the Garden. They would remain alive in the sense that their immaterial souls would survive death, but they were doomed to die physically when God separated them from the tree of life (3:22). They lost all the elements that made Life what it was supposed to be. They died.

Adam and Eve's children were born outside Eden, alienated from God and from one another because of the sin of their parents. Some, most notably Abel and Seth, found mercy in God's sight as they brought sacrifices to Him and called on His name (4:4, 26). They still died physically, but they sought and received the blessing of God (Heb. 11:4). Others, led by Cain and his descendant Lamech, founded a rival civilization on self-interest, technology, and violence (Gen. 4:16–24). They lived out their lives as those who were dead.

Before long, God both judged and preserved the world through the Flood. Most of the earth experienced judgment—the undoing of creation—but Noah and his family were sustained in physical life along with enough animals to renew the created order. God restated humanity's original mandate, ordering these survivors to populate the earth, and He "blessed" them (9:1), but this re-creation did not renew Life in its fullness. God made a limited promise of physical survival—He would never again destroy the earth and its creatures with a flood (9:11). But the covenant made no mention of sustained prosperity or fellowship with God, and it gave no guarantee that Noah and his family would be protected in their land. They would not coexist peaceably with animals (9:2), and their immediate experience demonstrated that they would not live peaceably with one another (9:22–27). They were still alive, and they retained something of the image of God (9:6), but they did not thoroughly experience Life.

God's Promise to Abraham

With Abraham, God took steps toward the restoration of Life. He told him, "Go forth from your country, and from your relatives, and from your father's house, to the land which I will show you; and I will make you a great nation, and I will bless you, and make your name great; and so you shall be a blessing; and I will bless those who bless you, and the one who curses you I will curse. And in you all the families of the earth shall be blessed" (12:1–3).

This promise to Abraham included *physical survival*, for he would endure long enough to father a great nation and God would protect him by cursing his enemies. He would "be buried at a good old age" (15:15). The promise included *blessing*, for Abraham's descendants would come out of captivity with "many possessions" (15:14), and he himself would be "exceedingly fruitful" (17:6) while receiving a "very great" reward (15:1). Abraham's name would be made great; he would be blessed by God; and he and his seed would provide blessing to all the nations of the earth (22:18). The promise also included *fellowship with God*, as Abraham was declared righteous on account of his faith (15:6) and experienced an eternal covenant with the Creator (17:7), so that he was later regarded as the friend of God (2 Chron. 20:7). And the promise included *land*, as God told Abraham that his descendants would possess the territory from "the river of Egypt" to the Euphrates River (Gen. 15:18).

Abraham was promised Life, but he did not get to experience it fully. He "died in faith, without receiving the promises," but "welcomed them from a distance" (Heb. 11:13). He sought a country of his own, a heavenly city prepared by God (11:14), but did not receive it in his lifetime. Ironically, the only land Abraham actually owned was a plot of ground purchased for the burial of his dead (Gen. 23; 25:9–10). Life in its fullness had not yet been restored, but it had been promised, and it was coming.

God initially made the promise to Abraham and his descendants (17:7; 22:18), but that covenant apparently did not include all his children, for the promise was repeated only to his son, Isaac (26:3–4, 24). In the same way, God told Isaac He would give the land to him and to his descendants, but He then repeated the promise only to his son Jacob (28:13–15).

In both cases God narrowed the promise to a single son and his family. However, that narrowing process stopped with Jacob, whom God renamed Israel (35:10). The sons of Israel and their families became the descendants (or "seed") to whom the Abrahamic promise was extended. From that point on God's people expressed their trust in the Lord's commitment to these promises by identifying Him as "the God of Abraham, Isaac, and Jacob" (Exod. 2:24; 3:6; Deut. 29:13; Acts 3:13). He was the God of Israel who had pledged to bring blessing to the world.

Life and the Law

As heirs of the promise of Life, the Israelites were given a covenant through which they might experience it. Moses made their options clear in Deuteronomy 28–30. If they demonstrated their faith in God by "holding fast to Him" and "obeying His voice," the Israelites would experience a peaceful life in the land promised to their fathers. They would experience blessing and prosperity, and they would live in fellowship with God, as they would be His people and He would be their God (29:13). In short, they would enjoy Life. However, that experience was conditioned on Israel's faithful obedience. If they did not trust God enough to obey Him, if they turned to idols in search of greater prosperity, they would die. They would experience the curse instead of blessing, plagues and famine instead of prosperity (28:15–61), and enemy invasion instead of peace. They would have no assurance of physical life, for other nations would overtake them and they would be torn from the land (28:62–68). Even if exile came, God promised that He would still remember His commitment to Abraham, Isaac, and Jacob. Should the Israelites return to the Lord, He would bring them back to the land, where they would enjoy unsurpassed prosperity (30:1–5). They would experience intimate fellowship with God at His initiative, for "the LORD your God will circumcise your heart and the heart of your descendants, to love the LORD your God with all your heart and with all your soul, in order that you may live" (30:6).

The Mosaic Law, like the promise given to Abraham and his descendants, was extended to all the sons of Israel. If they were blessed, they would be blessed together, and if they were punished, they would be punished together. Like all nations or groups, they demonstrated sin both individually and collectively, and they were responsible both to one another and to God. However, one individual, the king, was more directly accountable to the Creator than anyone else, for he mediated the rule of God to the people. God directed Israel's king to write for himself a copy of the Law. "And it shall be with him, and he shall read it all the days of his life, that he may learn to fear the LORD his God, by carefully observing all the words of this law and these statutes, that his heart may not be lifted up above his countrymen and that he may not turn aside from the commandment, to the right or to the left; in order that he and his sons may continue long in his kingdom in the midst of Israel" (17:19–20). As the king obeyed the Law and directed the people accordingly, the nation would continue under God's covenant and experience Life in the land.

The outcome of this arrangement should not have been much of a mystery. Nothing was wrong with the Mosaic Law, which was not too difficult to obey and was readily available to the people (30:11–14). God's commandments were pure and right, with no hint of injustice (Ps. 19:7–10). Indeed, they were "holy and righteous and good" (Rom. 7:12). However, no law can change the human heart, and sinful people will not be made righteous simply by being told what to do (Gal. 2:21). Like a plumbline, which shows that a crooked wall is leaning but which cannot make it straight, the Law made people aware of their sin but could not make them righteous. "Now we know that whatever the Law says, it speaks to those who are under the Law, that every mouth may be closed, and all the world may become accountable to God; because by the works of the Law no flesh will be justified in His sight; for through the Law comes the knowledge of sin" (Rom. 3:19–20).

The covenant Moses summarized in Deuteronomy "was to result in life" (Rom. 7:10) as the people obeyed in faith, but it could not "impart life" to those who were spiritually dead, naturally inclined to disobey (Gal. 3:21). In the hands of sinful people, the Law highlighted sin's presence and increased their accountability to God, so that through the commandment sin became "utterly sinful" (Rom. 7:13). Knowing the condition of their hearts even before they entered the land, God told Moses that His people would eventually pursue other gods and experience His wrath (Deut. 31:16–21).

251

This rebellion would occur in spite of the faithful leadership of a king like David, who trusted in the mercy of God (Ps. 51:1) and was a man after God's own heart (Acts 13:22). God promised David that his kingdom would be established forever, giving him a unique role in fulfilling Israel's hope of Life (2 Sam. 7:12–16). Through the reign of the righteous king the nation would enjoy prosperity, the poor would be treated with compassion, the oppressed would be delivered, and God would be praised throughout the land (Ps. 72:1–16). God had promised Abraham that his name would be made great and that the nations would be blessed through him (Gen. 12:2–3). Now that promise would be fulfilled through the righteous king, of whom it was said, "May his name endure forever; may his name increase as long as the sun shines; and let men bless themselves by him; let all nations call him blessed" (Ps. 72:17; Jer. 33:15–26). The Life promised to Abraham and his seed would be experienced under the leadership of David's righteous Descendant.

But it soon became apparent that the promise would have to be fulfilled sometime in the future. Though David and many faithful individuals with him trusted in God and diligently applied themselves to the Law, most of his successors and their subjects abandoned the covenant, fell into idolatry, and openly demonstrated their sinful disposition. As a result, they lost their land, their prosperity, and their fellowship with God when they were taken into exile. Rather than filling the earth through the reign of a righteous king (Ps. 72:19), God's glory departed from the temple and from Jerusalem (Ezek. 10:3–4, 18–19; 11:22–23), and the people were cut off from their intimate worship of Him (Ps. 137). Hosea summarized the experience succinctly. "When Ephraim spoke, there was trembling. He exalted himself in Israel, but through Baal he did wrong and died" (Hos. 13:1–2).

The New Covenant Promise of Life

God remained faithful to His promises to Abraham and David, promises that were not ultimately conditioned on Israel's obedience. Through a "new covenant" announced by the prophets, He reaffirmed His promise of Life for Abraham's descendants (Jer. 31:31–34). He promised to bring them back to the land, where they would enjoy prosperity and protection from their enemies. He would forgive their sins and restore them to a right relationship with Himself, and He would sustain them in that relationship forever. The agent of this restoration would be the Holy Spirit, God's animating breath, who brings life to all creation. The Spirit's presence would change the hearts of the people, and their rebellious inclinations would be removed.

God outlined the strategy in Ezekiel 36:24–30.

> For I will take you from the nations, gather you from all the lands, and bring you into your own land. Then I will sprinkle clean water on you, and you will be clean; I will cleanse you from all your filthiness and from all your idols. Moreover, I will give you a new heart and put a new spirit within you; and I will remove the heart of stone from your flesh and give you a heart of flesh. And I will put My Spirit within you and cause you to walk in My statutes, and you will be careful to observe My ordinances. And you will live in the land that I gave to your forefathers; so you will be My people, and I will be your God. Moreover, I will save you from all your uncleanness; and I will call for the grain and multiply it, and I will not bring a famine on you. And I will multiply the fruit of the tree and the produce of the field, that you may not receive again the disgrace of famine among the nations.

Further, David's throne would be restored through the One who would be called "Wonderful Counselor, Mighty God, Eternal Father, Prince of Peace" (Isa. 9:6). "There will be no end to the increase of His government or of peace, on the throne of David and over his kingdom, to establish it and to uphold it with justice and righteousness from then on and forevermore" (9:7; see also Jer. 23:5; 30:9). When the nation returned to its fruitful land, David's Descendant would reign as the righteous King (Ezek. 34:23–31; 37:24–25) and the people would live in prosperity and peace forever.

The features of the New Covenant were not wholly new or different. For the most part, the covenant simply renewed God's promises to Abraham and David. However, the New Covenant did promise a new means by which those promises would be fulfilled—they would be satisfied by God's own initiative. His people would put away their idols, but only after He washed them clean from their sin. They would walk in accord with His statutes, but only after He changed their hearts. They would experience Life, but only after He raised them from the dead (Ezek. 37:1–14). David's reign would be restored, but it would have to be established by "the zeal of the LORD of hosts" (Isa. 9:7). Coming as an expression of God's covenant faithfulness, these actions would not have a merely temporary effect. They would be everlasting. The Spirit, whose presence would restore the people to Life, was also pledged as a sign of that permanence. "'And I will not hide My face from them any longer, for I shall have poured out My Spirit on the house of Israel,' declares the Lord GOD" (Ezek. 39:29). "'And as for Me, this is My covenant with them,' says the LORD: 'My Spirit which is upon you, and My words which I have put in your mouth, shall not depart from your mouth, nor from the mouth of your offspring, nor from the mouth of your offspring's offspring,' says the LORD, 'from now and forever'" (Isa. 59:21).

This expectation of Life, together with the hope that it would be applied to Israel's offspring forever, evoked the language and content of the Abrahamic Covenant. The promised blessing would come to the seed of Abraham by the Spirit. Isaiah wrote, "I will pour out My Spirit on your offspring, and My blessing on your descendants; and they will spring up among the grass like poplars by streams of water" (Isa. 44:3–4). The prophet also wrote, "The Spirit [will be] poured out upon us from on high, and the wilderness [will become] a fertile field and the fertile field [will be] considered as a forest. Then justice will dwell in the wilderness, and righteousness will abide in the fertile field. And the work of righteousness will be peace, and the service of righteousness, quietness and confidence forever. Then my people will live in a peaceful habitation, and in secure dwellings and in undisturbed resting places" (32:15–18).

Before the Old Testament era came to a close, several groups of Jews did return to their land, but they never experienced the prosperity and the enduring peace God had promised, and they did not see the glory of a renewed Davidic kingdom. They were not yet restored to Life in its fullness. God had given Abraham the promise of Life—not just survival—and the patriarch died in hope. God gave the nation His Law, through which Life might have been chosen, but the people pursued other gods and expericnccd death. God renewed the promise of Life through the prophets, committing Himself to changing hearts by the Spirit while restoring justice and prosperity through a righteous King. However, like Abraham and Moses, the prophets and their contemporaries never got to see that hope fulfilled. For the promises to come to fruition, something else had to happen, and that brings us to Jesus.

JESUS AND THE FULFILLMENT OF ISRAEL'S HOPE

The Arrival of the Son

The prophets left Israel with the hope of restored Life in a restored kingdom. God had promised to forgive their sins, change their hearts, and provide them with a peaceful and fruitful Life in the land forever. The essential message of the New Testament is that all these things come only through Jesus Christ— Son of David, Son of Abraham, Son of Man, and Son of God.

Resonating with the hope that had sustained God's people for centuries, each of the four Gospels introduced Jesus as the One who fulfills the promises given to the patriarchs and the prophets. Matthew opened his book with a genealogy that was divided into three portions: fourteen generations from Abraham to David, fourteen from David to the Exile, and fourteen from the Exile to Jesus Christ (Matt. 1:1–17).[1] By highlighting four pivotal events—the promise to Abraham, the promise to David, the nation's judgment in captivity, and the coming of Jesus—Matthew demonstrated that the stage had been set for the arrival of Christ, the expected Messiah (1:1). The fullness of Life and the eternal reign of a righteous King had been promised but not yet experienced. Now the long-awaited One had arrived, and those hopes were about to be fulfilled.

Herod was called king because he was the political ruler at the time, but Jesus was "born King of the Jews" (2:1–2). He was the Son of David, born in David's city as a ruler who would shepherd the people of Israel, just as the prophets foretold (2:6). His arrival caused John the Baptist to say that the kingdom of heaven was at hand (3:2), and Jesus demonstrated that reality by bringing significant (if not universal) deliverance to the poor and oppressed. Several times in Matthew's Gospel, those in need of healing cried out, "Have mercy on us, Son of David," and each time He removed their affliction, just as they hoped the Messiah would do (9:27; 15:22; 20:30–31). On another occasion, when Jesus' power was revealed, the crowds wondered, "This man cannot be the Son of David, can He?" (12:23). Some of the Pharisees were angered by such talk, just as they were when the people cried out, "Hosanna to the Son of David" (21:9, 15). But Jesus said to them, "If I cast out demons by the Spirit of God, then the kingdom of God has come upon you" (12:28; see also Luke 11:14–23). The righteous King had arrived and the messianic age had dawned.[2]

A similar presentation may be found in Luke's Gospel, where the angel's annunciation to Mary includes the statement, "He will be great, and will be called the Son of the Most High; and the Lord God will give Him the throne of His father David; and He will reign over the house of Jacob forever; and His kingdom will have no end" (1:32–33). God had "raised up a horn of salvation for us in the house of David His Servant" (1:69), just as He had promised (2 Sam. 7:12; Pss. 89:3–4, 18; 132:11–17). Jesus Himself claimed to fulfill the messianic expectation when He read from the scroll of Isaiah, "The Spirit of the LORD is upon Me because He anointed Me to preach the gospel to the poor. He has sent Me to proclaim release to the captives, and recovery of sight to the blind, to set free those who are downtrodden, to proclaim the favorable year of the LORD" (Luke 4:18–19; see Isa. 61:1–2a). After He sat down, Jesus said, "Today this Scripture has been fulfilled in your hearing" (Luke 4:21).

He came as the Son of David, the preeminent King, but Jesus was also recognized as the Son of God. The two titles are not incompatible, and Jewish tradition had applied them both to the expected Messiah.[3] In the Old Testament, God had called Israel His "son" because of His unique relationship with the nation (Hos. 11:1), and He called Israel's king His "son" because he represented the people (2 Sam. 7:14; Ps. 89:26–27). Representing the king's enthronement, God said, "Thou art My Son, today I have begotten Thee" (Ps. 2:7). Grasping this royal connection, it is understandable that the evangelists would not hesitate to speak of Jesus as God's Son, but they applied the title to Him in a greatly heightened sense. He is the Son of God because He possesses deity and He reigns with truly divine authority.

Matthew implied that Jesus was the Son of God by describing His virginal conception, in which Mary was "found to be with child by the Holy Spirit" (Matt. 1:18, 20). However, the title was first applied to Him at His baptism, when the Father said, "This is My beloved Son, in whom I am well-pleased" (3:17). That statement, together with the Spirit's descent on Jesus on the same occasion (3:16), alluded to Isaiah 42:1: "Behold My Servant, whom I uphold; My chosen one in whom My soul delights. I have put My Spirit upon Him; He will bring forth justice to the nations." The Isaiah passage introduces an additional and unexpected theme to our understanding of Jesus. He is the righteous King who has come to reign in justice through the Spirit, but He is also the Suffering Servant, who came to bear the sins of the people (53:11–12). Those ideas seemed incompatible to someone like Peter, who was quick to acknowledge Jesus' divine Sonship but unable to reconcile that idea with Jesus' own words about the cross (Matt. 16:16, 21–22).

The Jewish leaders had a similar struggle. They could not believe Jesus was the Son of God when He was so obviously a man whose common background they understood. "Is not this the carpenter's son? Is not His mother called Mary, and His brothers, James and Joseph and Simon and Judas? And His sisters, are they not all with us?" (13:55–56). How could such a person be the Messiah? Peter did not understand how the Son of God could meet an inglorious end, and the scribes did not understand how the Son of God could have such inglorious beginnings. In both cases their perspective was limited to what they could see. The scribes knew nothing of the glory Jesus possessed before Bethlehem, and Peter could not foresee the glory He would receive after Calvary.

The demons knew He was the Son of God (8:29), even when the religious people refused to believe it (26:63–66). After the Father had affirmed Jesus' Sonship in the baptismal pronouncement, Satan taunted Him, essentially saying, "If You are the Son of God, then prove it" (4:3, 6). As our Savior hung on the cross, the scribes and elders reissued the challenge— "If You are the Son of God, come down from the cross" (27:40). Obviously they did not realize that divine Sonship could never be demonstrated by disobedience. The true Son is always faithful to His Father, and Jesus continually submitted to His will (26:39, 42), permitting the Father to vindicate

His authority in His own time (27:51–54). Jesus looked ahead to that vindication when the high priest pressed Him for an explanation: "I adjure You by the living God, that You tell us whether You are the Christ, the Son of God." Jesus answered, "You have said it yourself; nevertheless I tell you, hereafter you shall see the Son of Man sitting at the right hand of Power, and coming on the clouds of heaven" (26:63–64). Caiaphas tore his robes and cried "Blasphemy!" but Jesus' point was clear. Alluding to Psalm 110:1 and Daniel 7:13, Jesus said He is the One who would have an "everlasting dominion" over all humanity (Dan. 7:14). When His opponents see Him on that day, Jesus implied, they will understand who He is. They may be judging Him now, but ultimately He will be judging them (Matt. 16:27). He is not just a king, a "son" of God; He is the King of kings, God the Son.

John also knew that his readers must understand this crucial point, and he wrote his Gospel so they would recognize that "Jesus is the Christ, the Son of God" (John 20:31). More than any other Gospel writer, John emphasized the divine nature of Jesus, identifying Him as the preexistent Creator God (1:1–3) and the eternal "I AM" (8:58). John frequently described Jesus as the Son of God, stressing that He has no peer. He is the "only begotten God" (1:18), the "unique Son" (3:16), the one who "was calling God His own Father, making Himself equal with God" (5:18). At the same time, John never questioned Jesus' humanity.[4] He is the Word made flesh (1:14), whose humanity was obvious enough that His opponents said, "You, being a man, make Yourself out to be God" (10:33). Again, that is the paradox with which Jesus' contemporaries struggled. He is the Son of David, but also the Suffering Servant. He is the Son of God, but also the son of a carpenter.

Luke provided some insight into the tension. Like Matthew, he recorded the Father's declaration of Jesus' sonship at the baptism—"Thou art My beloved Son, in Thee I am well pleased" (Luke 3:22). This statement is just as rich with messianic implications as the one in Matthew. But Luke added another twist by immediately proceeding to a genealogy. Jesus is recognized as the Son of God (3:22), but he was thought to be the son of Joseph, the son of Eli, the son of Matthat, the son of Levi, the son of Melchi, and so forth (3:23–38). The genealogy winds its way all the way back to "Enosh, the son of Seth, the son of Adam, *the son of God*" (3:38, italics added). Jesus has His place in that genealogy for He is truly human, but He also brought it full circle. Adam, the son of God, was the head of the human race. Jesus, the Son of God, is the last Adam, the head of a new humanity (Rom. 5:14; 1 Cor. 15:45).

The Gospel writers described Him as the Son of David and the Son of God, but Jesus most frequently identified Himself as the Son of Man. The phrase was used in many Aramaic texts as an idiomatic way of saying "I," but Jesus appropriated it to Himself as a personal title.[5] It likely speaks of both His humanity and His messianic authority (reflecting Dan. 7:13). "Son of Man" seems a much more humble title than "Son of God," but Jesus often used it when speaking of His power and exaltation. "The Son of Man has authority on earth to forgive sins" (Mark 2:10). "The Son of Man is Lord even of the Sabbath" (2:28). The Son of Man will be rejected and killed, but He will be resurrected (8:31; 9:9, 12, 31). The Son of Man will come "in the glory of His Father with the holy angels" (8:38). He is one of us, but also far greater.

Jesus' titles denote both humanity and deity, and they anticipate both suffering and glory. After centuries of anticipation, those combinations came as something of a surprise. Jesus' opponents found it difficult to embrace the fact that He came as both God and man, and His followers struggled with the idea that He came both to reign and to die. However, only in this seeming contradiction could God fulfill the promises He made to Abraham and David.

The Seed of Abraham

God promised Life to Abraham and his seed, and He said that through them all the nations would be blessed. He narrowed the focus of that promise to Israel and his sons, and then told David that he would have a special role in its fulfillment. Through the righteous King of Israel, blessing would come to all the nations, the needy would be delivered, and the people would live in prosperity. Abraham's offspring had an opportunity to choose Life by means of the Mosaic Law, but it only made their sinful inclination more obvious. It became apparent that His promises could be fulfilled only by His own initiative, and God promised to accomplish those things through the coming of the Spirit in the New Covenant. Israel's sins would be forgiven and they would be restored to Life in the land under the leadership of the righteous Son of David.

Those are the promises Jesus came to fulfill. He entered our world as the Son of God, following the initiative of the Father; as the Son of David, the righteous King through whom the blessing would come; and as the Son of Abraham, the true heir of the promise (Matt. 1:1). Luke emphasized the connection to Abraham and his covenant when he recorded the words of Mary in the Magnificat: "He has given help to Israel His servant, in remembrance of His mercy, as He spoke to our fathers, to Abraham and his offspring forever" (Luke 1:54–55). Zacharias said virtually the same thing a few verses later. "Blessed be the Lord God of Israel, for He has visited us and accomplished redemption for His people . . . to show mercy toward our fathers, and to remember His holy covenant, the oath which He swore to Abraham our father, to grant us that we, being delivered from the hand of our enemies, might serve Him without fear, in holiness and righteousness all our days" (1:68, 72–75).

Paul connected Jesus' coming to the Abrahamic promise even more explicitly when he wrote, "Now the promises were spoken to Abraham and to his seed. He does not say, 'And to seeds,' as referring to many, but rather to one, 'And to your seed,' that is, Christ" (Gal. 3:16). Since God had promised that Abraham's seed would be as numerous as the stars of heaven (Gen. 15:5), Paul's statement seems rather odd. The word *seed* is singular, but it usually functions as a collective plural, referring to a great many people. How could Paul say that it refers to only one?

We have already seen that God narrowed the focus of the promise to only one of Abraham's sons, Isaac, and to only one of Isaac's sons, Jacob. He narrowed it further to the righteous King, who would mediate God's blessings to the nations (Ps. 72:17). Paul believed that the promise had now focused on Jesus Christ as Abraham's consummate Descendant, his singular Seed. It is only through Him that the promises may be experienced. As a result, anyone who belonged to Christ would be "Abraham's seed, heirs according to promise" (Gal. 3:29). Likewise, anyone who did not belong to Christ would be excluded. As the true seed of Abraham, Jesus mediates the promise of Life.

From Paul's perspective it was plain to see how the nations would be blessed through the seed of Abraham. Since the gospel of Christ was offered to Gentiles as well as to Jews, ethnicity no longer constitutes a barrier of any kind (3:8, 28). Everyone has access to the promise of Life, provided he or she believes in Jesus. In that sense many who were "far off," "excluded from the commonwealth of Israel and strangers to the covenants of promise," have now "been brought near by the blood of Christ" (Eph. 2:12–13). At the same time, some who considered themselves heirs may in fact be strangers and aliens. Just as Ishmael was Abraham's son, but not an heir of the promise, other children of Abraham have no claim to his covenant apart from faith in Christ (Rom. 4:10–16; 9:6–8).[6]

When the prophets described the New Covenant, they said that God would forgive sins, change the hearts of the people, and restore them to Life through His animating Spirit. He would bring them back to their land and bless them with peace and prosperity forever under a Davidic king, fulfilling His promises to Abraham and David. The New Testament teaches that those promises have been channeled through Christ, who is uniquely qualified to bring God's blessing because of who He is and what He has done.

The Incarnation and the Cross of Christ

Jesus Christ—Son of God, Son of David, Son of Man, and Son of Abraham—came into the world He had created in order to deliver us from sin and give us eternal Life. He came to fulfill God's promises to the patriarchs. But if we are to understand His work, we must remember four essential doctrines: the love of God, the holiness of God, the sinfulness of humanity, and the Incarnation.

At this point we need not say much about the sinfulness of humanity. We have seen in the last several chapters that people are by nature spiritually dead because of the sin of Adam, compounding their guilt through choices made both individually and corporately as an expression of their depravity. We are thoroughly guilty and utterly unable to save ourselves.

However, in the course of our discussion we may have forgotten God's love for the world. John Calvin appropriately saw the free love of God in

Jesus Christ as the starting point for the doctrine of the Atonement.[7] In his commentary on John 3:16, he described God's love as "the first cause and as it were source of our salvation." Similarly, in his commentary on Hebrews 2:9, Calvin wrote "the ground of our redemption is that immense love of God towards us by which it happened that He did not even spare His own Son."[8] God acted in love when He sent His Son to die for our sins. "For God so *loved* the world that He gave His only begotten Son, that whoever believes in Him should not perish, but have eternal life" (John 3:16). "In this is love, not that we loved God, but that He *loved* us and sent His Son to be the propitiation for our sins" (1 John 4:10). "But God demonstrates His own *love* toward us, in that while we were yet sinners, Christ died for us" (Rom. 5:8).

A popular spiritualist wrote recently, "People judge us; God doesn't. When we listen to God, it's very clear to us that we're more than good enough already."[9] But that is simply not true. God is not just a God of love. He is also a holy God whose wrath makes simple forgiveness impossible. "God is a righteous judge, and a God who has indignation every day" (Ps. 7:11).

We should not have any difficulty visualizing righteous judgment, because we use the same concept in our own courtrooms. The last time I was on jury duty, the judge wanted to make sure we would punish the guilty and absolve the innocent, so he asked each of us questions to determine how impartial we might be. "Do you know the defendant, his attorney, or the prosecuting attorney?" "Have you ever been arrested for this kind of crime?" As always, those who wanted to go home had only to convince the judge that they were biased in one way or another, and they would be excused. One of the men in our jury pool said he wanted to wear a T-shirt that read, "Hang 'em all and let God sort 'em out!" Obviously an attitude like that would make him an unjust jurist, but it did acknowledge one important truth—God is a just judge!

If God simply acquitted the guilty, He would be unfair, unjust, or to use another biblical term, "unrighteous." He has told us He is not that kind of judge (Exod. 23:7). He "will by no means leave the guilty unpunished" (34:7). God never ceases to be loving, but He also never ceases to be holy, and His holiness demands payment for sin.

Still, throughout the Old Testament God forgave the sins of those who showed faith in Him (Heb. 11:2). Their faith was often demonstrated through the obedient presentation of sacrifices, which turned aside God's wrath (for example, Lev. 5:1–10), but no animal could ever provide an adequate substitute for a man or a woman. Our sin is far too severe to be dealt with so lightly. "For it is impossible for the blood of bulls and goats to take away sins" (Heb. 10:4). God forgave their sins, but His wrath was never really satisfied.

When Jesus Christ died on the cross, He "made propitiation for the sins of the people" (2:17). That means that once and for all, God satisfied His own wrath. If He had not done that, He would be unjust in extending forgiveness to sinful people. Offering forgiveness without demanding satisfaction would be an unrighteous act, and it would contradict God's own nature. However, by making a public display of His demand for justice, the Cross demonstrated God's righteousness (Rom. 3:25). Further, by satisfying His wrath, the Cross enabled God to forgive freely all those who trust in Him. He is able to declare them righteous because the penalty has been paid. In Paul's words the Cross makes God both "just and justifier of the one who has faith in Jesus" (3:26). He is just, for He has demanded justice. He is Justifier, because He declares us righteous on the basis of faith. "In the cross of Christ God's justice and love are *simultaneously* revealed."[10]

But why did the holy love of God compel Him to pay the penalty Himself? Could not infinite wisdom have devised an easier way? Consider some of the options. Our own obedience to the Law could never have saved us. Our depravity prevents us from doing what we should, but even if we were morally able to obey, simply satisfying our present and future obligation could never erase our past guilt. Doing what is expected of us today cannot atone for our failure to do what was expected yesterday. If sin is to be punished, not merely overlooked, legal obedience will never deliver us from its burden. John R. W. Stott summarized the problem well in these words: "All inadequate doctrines of the atonement are due to inadequate doctrines of God and man. If we bring God down to our level and raise ourselves to his, then of course we see no need for a radical salvation, let alone for a radical atonement to secure it. When, on the other hand, we have glimpsed the blinding glory of the holiness of God, and have been so convicted of our sin by the Holy Spirit that we tremble before God and acknowledge what we are, namely 'hell-deserving sinners,' then and only then does the necessity of the cross appear so obvious that we are astonished we never saw it before."[11]

No animal or angelic sacrifice could satisfy God's wrath against our sin, for that would be beyond their capacity. As Arthur Pink wrote, "Sin is an evil of *infinite* magnitude . . . committed against an *infinite* Person, unto whom every creature is under *infinite* obligations of rendering unceasing and joyful obedience."[12] Further, the penalty is only ours to pay—nonhumans cannot take our place.

However, the sacrifice of a human scapegoat could never be sufficient either. All persons born since Adam have been guilty of original sin and have not been in any position to represent the rest of us. Jesus, who was without sin and who, as the last Adam, ushered in a new humanity, is the only exception.

That is why the Atonement would not have been possible apart from the Incarnation.[13] The penalty for humanity's sin should be paid only by a man, and only by a man who was both sinless and able to represent everyone. However, the penalty could be paid only by God Himself, because the obligation was infinite. If only God *could* satisfy the penalty, but only a man *should* do it, then only the God-Man truly *can*. "Since the children have flesh and blood, he too shared in their humanity so that by his death he might destroy him who holds the power of death—that is, the devil—and free those who all their lives were held in slavery by their fear of death" (Heb. 2:14–15, NIV). Anselm (1033–1109), one of the church's great theologians, wrote,

> For the one who is divine will not do it, because He will not be under obligation to do it; and the one who is human will not do it, because he will not be able to do it. Hence, in order that a God-man will do this, it is necessary that one and the same [individual] be fully divine and fully human, so as to make this satisfaction. For only one who is truly divine can make satisfaction, and only one who is truly human ought to make it. Therefore, since it is necessary to find a God-man who retains the integrity of

both natures, it is no less necessary that these two integral natures conjoin in one person . . . for otherwise it is impossible that one and the same [individual] be fully divine and fully human.[14]

We can identify another reason for the Incarnation and the Cross. God had promised to carry out the promises of the New Covenant by His own initiative. As a result, only He could bring salvation to us. As Leon Morris wrote, "Unless Jesus was fully God, our salvation did not originate from God. Rather it would have been wrung from Him."[15] In Jesus' death, God both originated and accomplished our salvation.

In short, without the Incarnation, the Atonement would not have been possible. Without the sinfulness of humanity, it would not have been necessary. Without the holiness of God, it would not have been required. Without the love of God, it would never have taken place.

The Exaltation of Jesus and the Gift of the Spirit

Because He forever paid the penalty of sin through His death, Jesus had to be resurrected. He could not stay dead, for in that case the penalty would have remained in force and He would have been under its dominion for all eternity. But "it was impossible for Him to be held in its power" (Acts 2:24), and "death no longer is master over Him" (Rom. 6:9). He broke the stranglehold of sin and death for all time, making His supremacy obvious to all in the resurrection (Col. 2:15; Acts 17:31). Having been raised from the dead, He was given all authority in heaven and on earth (Matt. 28:18) and "the name which is above every name" (Phil. 2:9). He has been seated at the right hand of God, "far above all rule and authority and power and dominion," with "all things in subjection under His feet" (Eph. 1:20–22).

From that exalted position, Jesus has poured out the Holy Spirit. Peter said on the Day of Pentecost, "This Jesus God raised up again, to which we are all witnesses. Therefore, having been exalted to the right hand of God, and having received from the Father the promise of the Holy Spirit, He has poured forth this which you both see and hear" (Acts 2:32–33). By sending the Spirit, Jesus accomplished an essential feature of the New

Covenant, but that could never have happened without His death and resurrection.

Again, God had promised Life to Abraham and his descendants, and He renewed that commitment in the New Covenant, pledging to forgive sins, change the hearts of the people, and restore them to Life by His Spirit. He promised to bring His people back to their land, where they would live in peace under the reign of the righteous King. As Son of Abraham, Son of David, Son of God, and Son of Man, Jesus died to pay the penalty for our sins and make possible the coming of the Spirit. He had been introduced by John the Baptist as the One who would usher in the promised Holy Spirit (Matt. 3:11; Mark 1:8; Luke 3:16; John 1:33), but apparently not even John understood that the cross would have to come first. The dead cannot be raised unless the cause of death is revoked. In our case that cause was sin. Adam's sin brought spiritual death to all people, and in that state we committed our own sins and compounded our guilt. If God had simply given us Life when we deserved only death, He would have been unjust and unholy. However, since His wrath was forever satisfied by the cross, sin's penalty was overcome and Life may now be given freely. God remains righteous while declaring us righteous because of the blood of Christ.

When Jesus promised both Life (John 3:16, 36; 4:14; 10:10) and the Spirit (7:37–39), He was promising essentially the same gift. Since Life comes through the presence of the Spirit, one cannot have Life without the Spirit or the Spirit without Life. Those who are "born again," receiving new Life, are "born of the Spirit" (3:3–5), and those who receive the Spirit will live (14:16–19). The prophets, of course, had said the same thing. When the Holy Spirit would come, God's people would be restored to the Life promised to Abraham and his descendants. Alluding to the expectation that Abraham's blessing would come through the outpouring of the Spirit (Isa. 44:3), Jesus identified Himself as the One through whom the Spirit would be given. "If any man is thirsty, let him come to Me and drink. He who believes in Me, as the Scripture said, 'From his innermost being shall flow rivers of living water'" (John 7:37–38). John added, "But this He spoke of the Spirit, whom those who believed in Him were to receive; for the Spirit was not yet given, because Jesus was not yet glorified" (7:39).

Why was the Spirit not given until Jesus was glorified? Because Jesus' glorification was the inevitable result of a death that destroyed the power of sin, and the Spirit of Life could not be given while the penalty of death remained in effect. Jesus told His disciples that, when He returned to the Father, He would ask Him to send the Spirit (14:12–17). Jesus' departure would undoubtedly make His followers sad, but He told them it was actually to their benefit. Unless He left, He could not send the Spirit (16:7). That is, unless He went to a death that would satisfy sin's penalty so thoroughly that He had to be raised from the dead and restored to glory, He could not send the Spirit of Life.

If Jesus had remained with His disciples, avoiding the cross, death would never have been conquered. The Spirit could never have been given, the promises never fulfilled, the curse never overturned, and the Edenic ideal never restored. We would have remained in our sins forever, trapped in spiritual death, and the image of God could never be renewed. Humans would never again bear the glory of God and rule as His vice-regents. But instead, "Christ redeemed us from the curse of the Law, having become a curse for us . . . in order that in Christ Jesus the blessing of Abraham might come to the Gentiles, so that we might receive the promise of the Spirit through faith" (Gal. 3:13–14).

When Jesus was exalted as a result of His atoning death (Phil. 2:9–11), the Father "put all things in subjection under His feet" (Eph. 1:22). That allusion to Psalm 8:6 provides at least two more connections between Jesus' glorification and the fulfillment of New Covenant promises. First, it means that God has again placed all things under the feet of a glorified Man, restoring the pattern of the original creation. In the Fall, humanity surrendered a large measure of authority to the usurper, Satan, following the direction of this one who is "the ruler of this world" and its "god" (John 16:11; 2 Cor. 4:4; see Eph. 2:2). As a result, we no longer see all things subjected to us (Heb. 2:8). Jesus, by experiencing death and glorification as a man, became the leader of a new, re-created humanity. By delivering us from death, He has enabled us to share in His glorious reign, restoring the authority God had initially given Adam. " 'Thou hast put all things in subjection under his feet.' For in subjecting all things to [humanity], He left nothing that is not subject to him. But now we do not yet see all things subjected to him. But we do see Him who has been made for a little while lower than the angels, namely, Jesus, because of the suffering of death crowned with glory and honor, that by the grace of God He might taste death for every one. For it was fitting for Him, for whom are all things, and through whom are all things, in bringing many sons to glory, to perfect the author of their salvation through sufferings" (Heb. 2:8–10). Crowned with glory and honor and with all things under His feet, Jesus has reestablished the creation ideal described in Psalm 8. Further, He has successfully paved the way for believers to reign alongside Him (Rom. 8:29–30; 1 Cor. 15:21–28; Rev. 20:4), restoring the human oversight of creation that was distorted by the Fall. In short, we could not be glorified unless Jesus was glorified before us, and He could not be glorified unless He first suffered on the cross.

Second, Jesus has been given authority over all things not only as a glorified Man, but also as the Son of David, the promised righteous King. Born of David's seed and exercising humility in His earthly ministry, He "was appointed Son of God in power" in His resurrection from the dead (Rom. 1:4). In that office He will reign forever in fulfillment of the Davidic Covenant (Acts 2:30–33), rightly distributing the blessings promised to Abraham and renewed through the prophets (3:14–26).

Though Jesus' kingdom has already been inaugurated, His government will not be fully manifested until the future. Paul used Psalm 8 and the subjection of all things to Christ to describe the still-future consummation of His reign (1 Cor. 15:25–27; see also Heb. 10:12–14). This will apparently include the final fulfillment of the New Covenant blessings, which were themselves built on God's promises to Abraham. The Son of David will rule over a regathered Israel in the land (Ezek. 37:24–25). However, Jesus' activity on that day should not be considered a wholly new work, for in a sense His reign has already begun, the New Covenant has been inaugurated (Luke 22:20; 2 Cor. 3:6; Heb. 8:6–10:18), and believers have experienced a "down payment" on the Abrahamic promise of Life through the Spirit (2 Cor. 1:22; 5:5; Eph. 1:14; 4:30).

Abiding in us as the firstfruits of the Life to come (Rom. 8:23), the Holy Spirit serves as a divine deposit on the rest of the promise. His presence means that God has already made good on His commitment, even though we have not yet seen the earthly reign of Christ (Rev. 11:17; 20:4) or the final end of the curse (21:3–4; 22:2–3). Jesus' death has secured the victory, but since the consummation of His kingdom demands the judgment of His enemies, He has paused to show patience and mercy toward them, giving them ample opportunity for repentance (2 Pet. 3:3–13). In the meantime the promised Spirit has arrived, but He has not "unpacked all His bags." In Him we have a foretaste of the life to come, along with the secure promise of Life in its fullness. We are still subject to physical death, but the same Spirit who already indwells us in regeneration will one day give life to our mortal bodies in resurrection (Rom. 8:11; Eph. 2:5–6; Titus 3:5–6). These are two different stages of His single life-giving work. In the same way, the Spirit is now changing our hearts by His presence (Rom. 8:13; Col. 3:12), but that process will not be complete until we are in the presence of our Savior (1 John 3:2).

Even now, since the Spirit's presence challenges the native depravity of our hearts and gives us the moral capacity to obey God, we who have trusted in Christ are being transformed into His likeness (2 Cor. 3:18). We are expected to live differently than others in our society, being "blameless and innocent, children of God above reproach in the midst of a crooked and perverse generation" (Phil. 2:15).

Because believers have the distinctive experience of the Spirit in fulfillment of the prophetic expectation, the church functions as an "outpost" for the kingdom of God. As the salt of the earth and the light of the world (Matt. 5:13–14), the church should not be confused with a theme park. It presents much more than a facade, and its members don't wear costumes to please the public. The church—the new humanity—is designed to give the rest of the world a glimpse of God's plan for people, a taste of Eden in the midst of an immoral society.

FINAL THOUGHTS:
REFLECTIONS ON THE HUMANITY OF JESUS

This survey of biblical history has highlighted the central role of Jesus Christ, the Son of Abraham, Son of David, Son of Man, and Son of God. As our study of humanity comes to a close, there can be no more appropriate conclusion than to turn our thoughts to Him, the "one mediator also be-tween God and men, the man Christ Jesus" (1 Tim. 2:5).

One of our sons was born just a few days before Christmas in 1988. As I held him in my hands—a seven-pound, wiggly baby boy with tender pink skin and long dark eyelashes—I gained a new appreciation for the humility of our Savior. It's difficult to imagine the voice that spoke worlds into existence being reduced to the pathetic cry of an infant, the hand which held the universe in its span clenching newborn fingers into a tiny fist. But the Lord of all became just like my little baby boy—dependent on others for nourishment and protection, vulnerable to the cold, and unable to hold up His own head. Christ entered our realm in the most humble of circumstances, experiencing all the realities of life in a fallen world. As a toddler, my oldest son examined our little crèche and de-clared, "Jesus lay on hay. It's pokey!" John Dwight expressed the same insight with words that have become familiar to many: "The King of kings lay thus in lowly manger, in all our trials born to be our Friend. He knows our need, to our weakness is no stranger. Behold your King, before Him lowly bend."[16] It must have looked odd when grown men bowed down before a baby that night in Bethlehem, but no act of worship was ever more appropriate, even though no king was ever more out of place.

As an adult, Jesus experienced as difficult a life as anyone could imag-ine. He knew poverty, temptation, and persecution, and He grew up in an occupied and oppressed nation. He knew all the pain we could possibly experience, and He died as the innocent victim of a violent mob after being falsely accused by His enemies and abandoned by His friends. "For we do not have a high priest who cannot sympathize with our weaknesses, but one who has been tempted in all things as we are, yet without sin" (Heb. 4:15). Further, His power brought temptations that were unknown to other men. Instead of walking down dusty roads, He could have flown a donkey to His destination, but He didn't, because He came to share our weaknesses. For thirty years, He could have healed everyone for whom He felt compassion, perhaps even Mary's husband Joseph, who seems to have died before Jesus' public ministry began. But He came to fulfill the will of the Father, and all things had to be done at the proper time. He "learned obedience from the things which He suffered" (5:8) and knew submission in the midst of pain. That lesson was applied most clearly when He refused to summon angelic armies to prevent His own execution (Matt 26:53). He came to bear our sin, and He would not be deterred by self-interest, for He knew that suffering had to come before glory.

The birth of Jesus captures our imagination because we cannot fathom the idea of God in the flesh, let alone God in a manger. The life of Jesus provides inspiration as we recognize that He shared our temptations and sufferings, enabling Him to understand our experience. Yet our thoughts of the glorified Christ almost always neglect His ongoing humanity. We tend to think of Jesus as someone who is no longer a man—once God, then the God-Man, and then just God again. But that approach neglects the fact that, in His exaltation, all things have been placed under the feet of a glorified Man. The Incarnation does not simply mean that Jesus was one of us two thousand years ago. It also means He became one of us then and continues to reign as one of us now. Believers will follow Him in resurrection and rule with Him into eternity—not as lesser gods, elect angels, or reincarnated beings, but as transformed men and women, delivered from the curse of death and renewed in the image of God.

Until then we wait, in obedience and faith, as we hope in the One who came humbly in the flesh, shared our sufferings to the point of death, and leads us now as "the firstborn among many brothers" (Rom. 8:29, NIV).

To Him be all glory and praise!

Endnotes

CHAPTER 1—THE BIBLICAL DOCTRINE OF CREATION

1. *Enûma elish* 4.129–40, from *Near Eastern Religious Texts Relating to the Old Testament,* ed. Walter Beyerlin, trans. John Bowden (Philadelphia: Westminster, 1978), 83.

2. Carl Sagan, "A Pale Blue Dot: The Earth from the Frontiers of the Solar System," *Parade,* 9 September 1990, 20–21.

3. Stephen Hawking, *A Brief History of Time: From the Big Bang to Black Holes* (New York: Bantam, 1988). For responses, see William Lane Craig, "'What Place, Then, for a Creator?': Hawking on God and Creation," *British Journal of Philosophy and Science* 41 (1990): 473–91; and idem, "The *kalam* Cosmological Argument and the Hypothesis of a Quiescent Universe," *Faith and Philosophy* 8 (1991): 104–8.

4. Daniel Dennett, *Darwin's Dangerous Idea: Evolution and the Meanings of Life* (New York: Simon and Schuster, 1995), 185.

5. Timothy Ferris, *Coming of Age in the Milky Way* (New York: Doubleday, 1988), 353.

6. Richard Dawkins, *The Blind Watchmaker* (New York: Norton, 1986).

7. The observations which follow have been gleaned from Hugh Ross, "Astronomical Evidences for a Personal, Transcendent God," in *The Creation*

Hypothesis: Scientific Evidence for an Intelligent Designer, ed. J. P. Moreland (Downers Grove, Ill.: InterVarsity, 1994), 160–63; and John Polkinghorne, "Creation and the Structure of the Physical World," in *Readings in Modern Theology: Britain and America,* ed. Robin Gill (Nashville: Abingdon, 1995), 31–33. The metaphor of the "knobs" is Polkinghorne's. See also Fred Heeren, *Show Me God* (Wheeling, Ill.: Searchlight, 1995).

8. Hawking, *A Brief History of Time,* 125. Hawking argues that it is unreasonable to believe that the vast universe has all been created for the sake of life on earth. However, Polkinghorne contends that we should not be daunted by the immensity of the universe, for "if the world were not about that big, we should not be here to be dismayed by it. A smaller universe would have run its course before we had time to appear upon its scene. It takes about eighteen thousand million years to make us the way we are" (Polkinghorne, "Creation and the Structure of the Physical World," 32). For readers who are uncomfortable with that estimate of the universe's age, another response may be helpful. If the cosmos has been created for the benefit of humanity, it does seem to be vastly overcreated. However, if it has been created to glorify the Creator, it could never be big enough.

9. For additional examples see Hugh Ross, *The Creator and the Cosmos* (Colorado Springs: NavPress, 1993).

CHAPTER 2—THE DEBATE OVER HUMAN ORIGINS

1. Nicholas Wolterstorff, "Theology and Science: Listening to Each Other," in *Religion and Science: History, Method, Dialogue,* ed. W. Mark Richardson and Wesley J. Wildman (New York: Routledge, 1996), 98–99. See also idem, *Reason within the Bounds of Religion,* 2d ed. (Grand Rapids: Eerdmans, 1984).

2. See Paul Feinberg, "The Meaning of Inerrancy," in *Inerrancy,* ed. Norman L. Geisler (Grand Rapids: Zondervan, 1980), 267–304.

3. Phillip E. Johnson, *Reason in the Balance: The Case against Naturalism in Science, Law, and Education* (Downers Grove, Ill.: InterVarsity, 1995), 38.

4. *McLean v. Arkansas Board of Education,* 1529 F. Supp. 1255 (W. D. Ark. 1982), cited in Phillip Johnson, *Darwin on Trial* (Downers Grove, Ill.: InterVarsity, 1991), 112.

5. See Amos Funkenstein, *Theology and the Scientific Imagination* (Princeton, N. J.: Princeton University Press, 1986).

6. See Richard J. Blackwell, *Galileo, Bellarmine, and the Bible* (Notre Dame, Ind.: University of Notre Dame Press, 1991); and Pietro Redondi, *Galileo Heretic* (Princeton, N. J.: Princeton University Press, 1987).

7. Alister McGrath, *The Science of Theology* (Grand Rapids: Eerdmans, 1986), 208–9.

8. Holmes Ralson III, "Science, Religion, and the Future," in *Religion and Science: History Method, Dialogue,* 61–81.

9. Charles Thaxton, Walter Bradley, and Roger Olsen, *The Mystery of Life's Origin* (New York: Philosophical Library, 1984), 44.

10. Gordon C. Mills, "Presuppositions of Science as Related to Origins," *Perspectives on Science and Christian Faith* 42 (1990): 158.

11. Michael Behe, *Darwin's Black Box: The Biochemical Challenge to Evolution* (New York: Free, 1996), 169–70.

12. Thaxton, Bradley, and Olsen, *The Mystery of Life's Origin,* 42.

13. Ibid., 164.

14. Behe, *Darwin's Black Box,* 172.

15. Dennett, *Darwin's Dangerous Idea,* 314.

16. See ibid., 315, n. 1.

17. Johnson, *Darwin on Trial,* 104.

18. Stuart Kauffman, *At Home in the Universe: The Search for the Laws of Self-Organization and Complexity* (New York: Oxford University Press, 1995).

19. Dawkins, *The Blind Watchmaker,* 6.

20. Interestingly Gregor Mendel, the father of genetics, was himself a special creationist. He was familiar with Darwin's *Origin of Species* but opposed it. See L. A. Callender, "Gregor Mendel: An Opponent of Descent with Modification," *History of Science* 26 (1988): 41–75; and B. E. Bishop, "Mendel's Opposition to Evolution and to Darwin," *Journal of Heredity* 87 (1996): 205–13.

21. Eldredge wrote regarding creationism, "But that form of explanation, by its very nature, lies outside the bounds of the scientific enterprise" (Niles Eldredge, *Reinventing Darwin: The Great Debate at the High Table of Evolutionary Theory* [New York: Wiley and Sons, 1995], 33).

22. Lane P. Lester and Raymond G. Bohlin, *The Natural Limits to Biological Change* (Dallas: Probe, 1984), 166.

23. Michael Denton, *Evolution: A Theory in Crisis* (Bethesda, Md.: Adler and Adler, 1985), 146.

24. Richard Dawkins, *Climbing Mount Improbable* (New York: Norton, 1996), 138–97.

25. For a more detailed discussion of these examples see Denton, *Evolution: A Theory in Crisis*, 199–232. Also see A. H. Brush, "On the Origin of Feathers," *Journal of Evolutionary Biology* 9 (1996): 131–42.

26. Behe, *Darwin's Black Box*, 22.

27. Ibid., 185–86.

28. Richard Dawkins, *River Out of Eden: A Darwinian View of Life* (New York: HarperCollins, 1995), 133.

29. John H. Sailhamer, *Genesis Unbound: A Provocative New Look at the Creation Account* (Sisters, Ore.: Multnomah, 1996).

30. Ibid., 70–72.

31. Cassuto, *A Commentary on the Book of Genesis, Part I: From Adam to Noah,* trans. Israel Abrahams (Jerusalem: Magnes, 1978), 12–17.

32. Ibid., 251–66. See John C. Whitcomb and Henry M. Morris, *The Genesis Flood: The Biblical Record and Its Scientific Implications* (Grand Rapids: Baker, 1961), 477–78.

33. For a much more detailed discussion of these issues, see Roger Wiens, "Radiometric Dating: A Christian Perspective" (American Scientific Affiliation and Affiliation of Christian Geologists n.d. [available from http://asa.calvin.edu/index.html; Internet]).

34. For more on moon dust, the shrinking sun, and several similar arguments, see Howard J. Van Till, Davis A. Young, and Clarence Menninga, *Science Held Hostage* (Downers Grove, Ill.: InterVarsity, 1988).

35. See Marvin Lubenow, *Bones of Contention: A Creationist Assessment of Human Fossils* (Grand Rapids: Baker, 1992).

36. Denton, *Evolution: A Theory in Crisis,* 357–58.

CHAPTER 3—CREATED IN THE IMAGE OF GOD

1. Matthew 13:43; Acts 9:3; 26:13; Revelation 1:16; 10:1; 21:23; 22:5; Wisdom 7:29; Sirach 50:6.

2. For example, Tanch Pikude 2 and Midrash Tadsche 4. See Jacob Jervell., *Imago Dei: Gen 1, 26f. in der Gnosis und in den paulinischen Briefen* (Göttingen: Vandenhoeck & Ruprecht, 1960), 100–103; and Alan Goshen Gottstein, "The Body as Image of God in Rabbinic Literature," *Harvard Theological Review* 87 (1994): 171–95.

3. Other extrabiblical texts to consult include 4 Ezra 7:97; 8:51; 2 Baruch 15:8; 54:15, 21; 1 Enoch 38:4; 50:1; 58:2, 3; 103:2, 3; 108:11–13 and 2 Enoch 22:8. See Gerhard Kittel, "δόξα," in *Theological Dictionary of the New Testament*, ed. Gerhard Kittel and Gerhard Friedrich (Grand Rapids: Eerdmans, 1964), 2:246–47.

4. Seyoon Kim, *The Origin of Paul's Gospel* (Tübingen: Mohr, 1984), 263.

5. Herman Ridderbos, *Paul: An Outline of His Theology*, trans. John R. de Witt (Grand Rapids: Eerdmans, 1975), 225.

6. The controversial issue in this verse is not whether unbelievers are included, but whether women are included. Since women are described as "the glory of man" in the next verse, some believe Paul meant to exclude them from the image of God. However, the flow of Paul's argument suggests that women are not being deliberately excluded. A. T. Robertson and Alfred Plummer rightly argue that Paul omitted referring to the woman as God's image because his point concerned her relation to the man (*A Critical and Exegetical Commentary on the First Epistle of St. Paul to the Corinthians*, International Critical Commentary [Edinburgh: Clark, 1911], 231). The apostle had been arguing that a head covering was required of women because of the order of submission. The male submits directly to God as His image and glory. The woman (though she is still in the image of God) submits to God through the man and covers her head as a symbol of this submission. On the positive side of the argument, Paul made no distinction between male and female when he spoke of our renewal in the divine image (Gal. 3:28).

   We should also note that some believe Genesis 1 includes only males in the image of God. That this was the common position of the church for centuries is one of the theses of *The Image of God: Gender Models in Judaeo-Christian Tradition*, ed. Kari Elisabeth Børressen (Minneapolis: Fortress, 1995).

   Early Jewish sources did not raise the question but also did not counter a strongly androcentric culture. Evidently it was not until the divine image was emphasized as being nonphysical that Christian theologians began to affirm the possibility that it would also apply to women. As one who rejects that model while still affirming the inclusion of women, I lean more heavily on Genesis 5:1–2, which defines "man" as "male and female" in the context of creation according to God's image. Further, if dominion is a critical function of those who are made in the image of God (as it certainly seems to be), women are thereby included, for dominion in that context requires multiplication (Gen. 1:28). But because of the influence of their culture, it is understandable, though still regrettable, that earlier theologians would overlook these points.

7. On this translation see Ulrich Wilckens, "υστερος κ.τ.λ." in *Theological Dictionary of the New Testament,* (Grand Rapids: Eerdmans, 1972), 8:596.

8. Helga Kuhse, *The Sanctity of Life Doctrine in Medicine: A Critique* (Oxford: Clarendon, 1987), 2–3.

9. Derek Humphry, letter to the editor, *Newsweek,* 16 March 1992. See also Katie Letcher Lyles, "A Gentle Way to Die," *Newsweek,* 2 March 1992, 14.

CHAPTER 4—THE MATERIAL ASPECT OF HUMAN NATURE

1. Walther Eichrodt, *Theology of the Old Testament,* Old Testament Library, trans. John A. Baker (Philadelphia: Westminster, 1967), 2:46–47.

2. This variant is found in the Qumran text.

3. Eichrodt, *Theology of the Old Testament,* 2:49.

4. Marvin Minskey, quoted by David Gelman, "Is the Mind an Illusion?" *Newsweek,* 20 April 1992, 72.

5. Wilder Penfield, *The Mystery of the Mind* (Princeton, N.J.: Princeton University Press, 1975), 77, quoted in Laurence W. Wood, "Recent Brain Research and the Mind-Body Dilemma," *Asbury Theological Journal* 41 (Spring 1986): 72.

6. See the criticisms offered by J. P. Moreland, *Scaling the Secular City*

(Grand Rapids: Baker, 1987), 77–103.

7. Marianne Williamson, *A Return to Love: Reflections on the Principles of A Course in Miracles* (New York: HarperCollins, 1992), 58.

8. Shirley MacLaine, *Out on a Limb* (New York: Bantam, 1983), 268.

9. David Steindl-Rast and Fritjof Capra, *Belonging to the Universe: Explorations on the Frontiers of Science and Spirituality* (New York: HarperCollins, 1991), 117.

10. John W. Cooper, *Body, Soul, and Life Everlasting: Biblical Anthropology and the Monism-Dualism Debate* (Grand Rapids: Eerdmans, 1989), 19.

11. Steindl-Rast and Capra, *Belonging to the Universe*, 88.

12. Cooper, *Body, Soul, and Life Everlasting*, 30–33.

13. John W. Cooper, "The Identity of Resurrected Persons: Fatal Flaw of Monistic Anthropology," *Calvin Theological Journal* 23 (1988): 24–25.

14. Osei-Bonsu noted Philo's *De virtutibus* 76 and several texts from Plato: *Cratylus* 403 B; *Republic* 577 B; *Gorgias* 523 D, 524 D (Joseph Osei-Bonsu, "Does 2 Cor. 5:1–10 Teach the Reception of the Resurrection Body at the Moment of Death?" *Journal for the Study of the New Testament* 28 [1986]: 90, 99).

15. See Peter Brown, *The Body and Society: Men, Women, and Sexual Renunciation in Early Christianity* (New York: Columbia University Press, 1988), 77.

16. Joni Eareckson Tada, "Assisted Suicide: A Good Policy for a Better Society?" *Discernment* 1 (Fall 1992): 2.

17. Karl Barth, *Church Dogmatics*, vol. 3: *The Doctrine of Creation* (Edinburgh: Clark, 1961), part 4, 423–24 [55.2].

CHAPTER 5—THE IMMATERIAL ASPECT OF HUMAN NATURE

1. Wayne Grudem, *Systematic Theology: An Introduction to Biblical Doctrine* (Grand Rapids: Zondervan, 1994), 477.

2. Carl Schultz, "Spirit," in *Evangelical Dictionary of Biblical Theology*, 744.

3. Bruce K. Waltke, "Heart," in *Evangelical Dictionary of Biblical Theology*, 331.

CHAPTER 6—HUMAN NATURE AND HUMAN BEHAVIOR

1. Herbert Spencer, *Social Statics* (New York: Appleton, 1864), 414–15, quoted in Richard Hofstadter, *Social Darwinism in American Thought*, rev. ed. (New York: Braziller, 1959), 41.
2. Degler, *In Search of Human Nature*, 45. Incidentally these laws were upheld in the Supreme Court case of *Buck v. Bell*, which has never been overturned (*Buck v. Bell*, 274 U.S. 200, 47 S.Ct. 584, 71 L.Ed 1000 [1927]).
3. See Robert Marshall and Charles Donovan, *Blessed Are the Barren: The Social Policy of Planned Parenthood* (San Francisco: Ignatius, 1991).
4. See Degler, *In Search of Human Nature*, 202–3.
5. David Gelman, "Born or Bred?" *Newsweek*, 24 February 1992, 52.
6. Charles Murray and Richard Herrnstein, *The Bell Curve: Intelligence and Class Structure in American Life* (New York: Free, 1994).
7. Ibid., 269–315.
8. For a more complete discussion, see Robert A. Pyne, "The Ethical Ring of *The Bell Curve*," *Dialog* 35 (Winter 1996): 51–57.
9. Ted Peters, *Playing God? Genetic Determinism and Human Freedom* (New York: Routledge, 1997), 6–7.
10. See Charles Taylor, *Sources of the Self: The Making of the Modern Identity* (Cambridge, Mass.: Harvard University Press, 1989), 313.

CHAPTER 7–SIN IN THE GARDEN (AND IN OUR BACKYARDS)

1. Ted Peters is one of many to use this term. In this portion of the chapter I retrace some elements of the "seven steps to radical evil" from his book *Sin: Radical Evil in Soul and Society* (Grand Rapids: Eerdmans, 1994).
2. Reinhold Niebuhr, *Beyond Tragedy: Essays on the Christian Interpretation of History* (New York: Scribner's Sons, 1937), 28.
3. Peters, *Sin: Radical Evil in Soul and Society*, 87.

4. Ibid., 13.

5. Reinhold Niebuhr, *Discerning the Signs of the Times: Sermons for To-day and To-morrow* (London: SCM, 1946), 164–65.

6. Frederica Mathewes-Green, "Embarrassment's Perpetual Blush," *Christianity Today,* 14 July 1997, 37 (italics hers).

7. Augustine, *Confessions* 2.4, trans. Henry Chadwick (Oxford: Oxford University Press, 1991).

8. Peters, *Sin: Radical Evil in Soul and Society,* 13–14.

9. Ibid., 162.

10. See Robert A. Pyne and David G. Moore, "Neil Anderson's Approach to the Spiritual Life," *Bibliotheca Sacra* 153 (January–March 1996): 75–86.

11. Alexander Solzhenitsyn, *The Gulag Archipelago* (New York: Harper & Row, 1974), 168, quoted in Peters, *Sin: Radical Evil in Soul and Society,* 174.

12. Reinhold Niebuhr, *The Nature and Destiny of Man: A Christian Interpretation,* vol. 1: *Human Nature* (Englewood Cliffs, N. J.: Prentice-Hall, 1964), 200.

13. Peters, *Sin: Radical Evil in Soul and Society,* 16.

14. Cornelius Plantinga, Jr., *Not the Way It's Supposed to Be: A Breviary of Sin* (Grand Rapids: Eerdmans, 1995), 70.

15. Barry M. Goldwater, *With No Apologies* (New York: Morrow, 1979), 4–5.

16. Raymond C. Ortlund Jr., "Male-Female Equality and Male Headship: Genesis 1–3," in *Recovering Biblical Manhood and Womanhood: A Response to Evangelical Feminism,* ed. Wayne Grudem and John Piper (Wheaton, Ill.: Crossway, 1991), 108–9.

17. Mary Stewart Van Leeuwen, *Gender and Grace: Love, Work, and Parenting in a Changing World* (Downers Grove, Ill.: InterVarsity, 1990), 44.

18. The word *abide* here depends on the Septuagint, the ancient Greek translation of the Hebrew Scriptures. It represents a slight change in one letter of the Masoretic (Hebrew) text, which is difficult to translate in its present form.

CHAPTER 8—THE EFFECT OF SIN ON HUMAN NATURE

1. Incidentally the skeptic's question, "Who was Cain's wife?", can be answered quite simply from these verses. Marriage to a near relative had not yet been forbidden, and she was apparently one of his sisters.

2. Cranfield wrote, 'οὐκ ἐλλογεῖται'must be understood in a relative sense: only in comparison with what takes place when the law is present can it be said that, in the law's absence, sin 'οὐκ ἐλλογεῖται'. Those who lived without the law were certainly not 'innocent sinners'—they were to blame for what they were and what they did. But in comparison with the state of affairs which has obtained since the advent of the law sin may be said to have been, in the law's absence, 'not registered,' since it was not the fully apparent, sharply defined thing, which it became in its presence" (*The Epistle to the Romans*, 1:282).

3. See G. C. Berkouwer, *Studies in Dogmatics: Sin*, trans. P. C. Holtrop (Grand Rapids: Eerdmans, 1971), 436–37.

4. John Murray, *The Imputation of Adam's Sin* (Phillipsburg, N. J.: Presbyterian and Reformed, 1959), 24.

5. S. Lewis Johnson, Jr., "Romans 5:12—An Exercise in Exegesis and Theology," in *New Dimensions in New Testament Study*, ed. Richard N. Longenecker and Merrill C. Tenney (Grand Rapids: Zondervan, 1974), 316.

6. Smith, *With Willful Intent: A Theology of Sin*, 366.

7. Berkouwer, *Studies in Dogmatics: Sin*, 435 (italics his).

8. Pelagius, *Letter to Demetrius* 8, in *Theological Anthropology*, ed. and trans. J. Patout Burns, Sources of Early Christian Thought (Philadelphia: Fortress, 1981), 49.

9. Ibid., 16, in *Theological Anthropology*, 52–53.

10. Augustine, *On the Grace of Christ* 5.6, in *Theological Anthropology*, 64.

11. Augustine, *Confessions* 10.40, trans. Henry Chadwick (Oxford: Oxford University Press, 1991).

12. Augustine, *On the Grace of Christ* 8.9, in *Theological Anthropology*, 67.

13. Augustine, *On Rebuke and Grace* 38, in *Theological Anthropology*, 107.

14. Augustine, *On the Grace of Christ*, 8.9, in *Theological Anthropology*, 67.

15. Ibid., 14.15, in *Theological Anthropology*, 72–73.

16. Augustine, *On Rebuke and Grace* 34, *Theological Anthropology,* 104.

17. J. Patout Burns, introduction to *Theological Anthropology,* 14.

18. George Vandervelde, *Original Sin: Two Major Trends in Contemporary Roman Catholic Reinterpretation* (Washington, D.C.: University Press of America, 1981), 41.

19. See Pyne, "Dependence and Duty," 149–51.

20. Arthur W. Pink, *Gleanings from the Scriptures: Man's Total Depravity* (Chicago: Moody, 1969), 133 (italics his).

21. Martin Luther, *The Bondage of the Will,* trans. J. I. Packer and O. R. Johnston (New York: Revell, 1957), 99.

22. John Taylor, "The Doctrine of Original Sin according to Scripture, Reason, and Experience," in *Changing Conceptions of Original Sin,* ed. H. Shelton Smith (New York: Garland, 1987), 18 (italics his).

23. Luther, *The Bondage of the Will,* 102.

24. C. Samuel Storms, *Tragedy in Eden: Original Sin in the Theology of Jonathan Edwards* (Lanham, Md.: University Press of America, 1985), 170–71.

25. Ibid., 172 (italics his).

26. Calvin, *Institutes of the Christian Religion,* 2.5.14.

27. Luther, *The Bondage of the Will,* 102.

28. Ibid., 202.

29. Some would prefer to describe this as regeneration, but for a defense of this terminology, see Robert A. Pyne, "The Role of the Holy Spirit in Conversion," *Bibliotheca Sacra* 150 (April–June 1993): 203–18.

30. See E. P. Sanders, *Paul and Palestinian Judaism: A Comparison of Patterns of Religion* (London: SCM, 1977).

31. Giacomino di Verona, quoted in Jean Delumeau, *Sin and Fear: The Emergence of a Western Guilt Culture,* trans. Eric Nicholson (New York: St. Martin's 1990), 17.

32. Ibid., 308.

33. Berkouwer, *Studies in Dogmatics: Sin,* 116 (italics his).

34. Reinhold Niebuhr, "The Ethic of Jesus and the Social Problem," in *Love and Justice: Selections from the Shorter Writings of Reinhold Niebuhr,* ed. D. B. Robertson (Louisville: Westminster/Knox, 1957), 33.

CHAPTER 9—EVIL AND THE ESSENCE OF SIN

1. Fyodor Dostoevsky, *The Brothers Karamazov,* trans. Constance Garnett, rev. Ralph E. Matlaw, in *The Problem of Evil: Selected Readings,* ed. Michael L. Peterson (Notre Dame, Ind.: University of Notre Dame Press, 1992), 59.

2. David Hume, *Dialogues concerning Natural Religion,* ed. Henry D. Aiken, Hafner Library of Classics (New York: Macmillan, 1948), 66.

3. In the conversation that follows, I will focus more on evil acts (sin, or moral evil) than on natural disasters (natural evil). For a more complete discussion of the various kinds of evil and arguments concerning them, see John S. Feinberg, *The Many Faces of Evil: Theological Systems and the Problem of Evil* (Grand Rapids: Zondervan, 1994).

4. D. A. Carson, *How Long, O Lord? Reflections on Suffering and Evil* (Grand Rapids: Baker, 1990), 181.

5. Ibid., 172 (italics his).

6. Anne Rice, *Memnoch the Devil: The Vampire Chronicles* (New York: Knopf, 1995).

7. Alister E. McGrath, *The Mystery of the Cross* (Grand Rapids: Zondervan, 1988), 159 (italics his).

8. Berkouwer, *Studies in Dogmatics: Sin,* 18–19 (italics his).

9. Ibid., 26.

10. Nicholas Wolterstorff, *Lament for a Son* (Grand Rapids: Eerdmans, 1987), 63.

11. Plantinga, *Not the Way It's Supposed to Be: A Breviary of Sin,* 9–10 (italics his).

12. Richard C. Trench, *Synonyms of the New Testament,* 9th ed. (London, 1880; reprint, Grand Rapids: Eerdmans, 1983), 239.

13. K. Koch, "חָטָא," in *Theological Dictionary of the Old Testament,* 4:311.

14. Daniel Doriani, "Sin," in *Evangelical Dictionary of Biblical Theology,* 739.

15. Berkouwer, *Studies in Dogmatics: Sin,* 238.

16. *Catechism of the Catholic Church* (Vatican City: Libreria Editrice Vaticana, 1994), 1857.

17. Ibid., 1858.

18. Ibid., 1860.
19. Ibid., 1862.

CHAPTER 10—LIFE IN AN IMMORAL SOCIETY

1. See James Montgomery Boice, *Two Cities, Two Loves: Christian Responsibility in a Crumbling Culture* (Downers Grove, Ill.: InterVarsity, 1996), 78.
2. I say "apparently" here because commentators debate whether Nimrod is to be seen as the subject of verse 11.
3. Larry Terlizzese, "Living in Nature and the City" (student paper, 403 Anthropology, Dallas Theological Seminary, fall 1997).
4. Henry Fairlie, *The Seven Deadly Sins Today* (Notre Dame, Ind.: University of Notre Dame Press, 1978), 25.
5. Others have taken a similar approach. See Stanford M. Lyman, *The Seven Deadly Sins: Society and Evil* (New York: St. Martin's, 1978).
6. Reinhold Niebuhr, "History (God) Has Overtaken Us," in *Love and Justice*, 293.
7. Reinhold Niebuhr, *Moral Man and Immoral Society: A Study in Ethics and Politics* (New York: Scribner's Sons, 1932).
8. Reinhold Niebuhr, "Social Christianity," in *Essays in Applied Christianity*, ed. D. B. Robertson (New York: Meridian, 1959), 103.
9. Niebuhr, *Moral Man and Immoral Society*, 9.
10. Reinhold Niebuhr, "The Ethic of Jesus and the Social Problem," in *Love and Justice*, 33.
11. James Burtchaell, *The Giving and Taking of Life: Essays Ethical* (Notre Dame, Ind.: University of Notre Dame Press, 1989), 219, quoted in Plantinga , *Not the Way It's Supposed to Be*, 58–59.
12. Miroslav Volf, "Exclusion and Embrace: Theological Reflections in the Wake of 'Ethnic Cleansing,'" in *Emerging Voices in Global Christian Theology*, ed. William A. Dyrness (Grand Rapids: Zondervan, 1994), 34.
13. See Eric L. McKitrick, ed., *Slavery Defended: The Views of the Old South* (Englewood Cliffs, N.J.: Prentice-Hall, 1963).
14. Daisy L. Machado, "Kingdom Building in the Borderlands: The

Church and Manifest Destiny," in *Hispanic/Latino Theology: Challenge and Promise,* ed. Ada Marîa Isasi-Diaz and Fernando F. Segovia (Minneapolis: Fortress, 1996), 71.

15. See Robert A. Pyne, "The New Man and Immoral Society," *Bibliotheca Sacra* 154 (July–September 1997): 259–74.

16. Fairlie, *The Seven Deadly Sins Today,* 43.

17. Gustavo Gutiérrez, *A Theology of Liberation: History, Politics and Salvation,* trans. and ed. Caridad Inda and John Eagleson (Maryknoll, N.Y.: Orbis, 1973), 84.

18. Ibid., 26–27.

19. See René Girard, *The Scapegoat,* trans. Yvonne Freccero (Baltimore: Johns Hopkins University Press, 1986).

20. William F. May, *A Catalogue of Sins: A Contemporary Examination of Christian Conscience* (New York: Holt, Rinehart, and Winston, 1967), 202.

21. Fairlie, *The Seven Deadly Sins Today,* 113.

22. Dorothy Sayers, *Creed or Chaos?* (New Hork: Harcourt, Brace, 1949), 81.

23. Kenneth J. Gergen, *The Saturated Self: Dilemmas of Identity in Contemporary Life* (New York: HarperCollins, 1991).

24. John Steinbeck, *The Grapes of Wrath* (New York: Viking, 1939), quoted in Walter Wink, *Engaging the Powers: Discernment and Resistance in a World of Domination* (Minneapolis: Fortress, 1992), 50.

25. David O. Berger, "The Theology of Technology and Vice Versa," *Concordia Journal* 19 (October 1993): 336.

26. Neil Postman, "Science and the Story That We Need," *First Things* 69 (January 1997): 31.

27. Ronald J. Sider, *Rich Christians in an Age of Hunger,* 3d. ed. (Dallas: Word, 1990), 10–11.

28. Ibid., 23.

29. Ibid.

30. Ibid., 25.

31. Fairlie, *The Seven Deadly Sins Today,* 177.

32. Mohandas Ghandi, quoted in Jim Wallis, *The Soul of Politics: A Practical and Prophetic Vision for Change* (Maryknoll, N.Y.: Orbis, 1994), xv.

CHAPTER 11—SALVATION FROM SIN AND THE RESTORATION OF LIFE

1. For helpful comments on Matthew's numbering and its theological motivation, see D. A. Carson, "Matthew," in *The Expositor's Bible Commentary,* (Grand Rapids: Zondervan, 1984), 8:68–69.

2. Ibid., 289.

3. D. R. Bauer, "Son of God," in *Dictionary of Jesus and the Gospels,* ed. Joel B. Green, Scot McKnight, and I. Howard Marshall (Downers Grove, Ill.: InterVarsity, 1992), 770; and James R. Brady, *Jesus Christ: Divine Man or Son of God?* (Lanham, Md.: University Press of America, 1992).

4. See Marianne Meye Thompson, *The Humanity of Jesus in the Fourth Gospel* (Philadelphia: Fortress, 1988).

5. I. H. Marshall, "Son of Man," in *Dictionary of Jesus and the Gospels,* 780.

6. See Pyne, "The Seed, the Spirit, and the Blessing of Abraham," 211–22.

7. Robert A. Peterson, *Calvin's Doctrine of the Atonement* (Phillipsburg, N.J.: Presbyterian and Reformed, 1983), 1.

8. John Calvin, quoted in ibid., 2.

9. Marianne Williamson, *A Woman's Worth* (New York: Ballantine, 1994), 94.

10. G. C. Berkouwer, *Studies in Dogmatics: The Work of Christ,* trans. Cornelius Lambregtse (Grand Rapids: Eerdmans, 1965), 277 (italics his).

11. John R. W. Stott, *The Cross of Christ* (Downers Grove, Ill.: InterVarsity, 1986), 109.

12. Arthur W. Pink, *The Satisfaction of Christ* (Grand Rapids: Zondervan, 1955), 56 (italics his).

13. This argument was used as early as Athanasius (around 296–373), but Anselm is known for its clearest statement. See H. D. McDonald, *The Atonement of the Death of Christ: In Faith, Revelation, and History* (Grand Rapids: Baker, 1985), 130–34.

14. Anselm, *Cur Deus Homo* 2.7, in *Anselm of Canterbury,* ed. and trans. Jasper Hopkins and Herbert Richardson (New York: Mellen, 1976), 3:103–4.

15. Leon Morris, *The Cross in the New Testament* (Grand Rapids: Eerdmans, 1965), 372.

16. John S. Dwight, "O Holy Night," in *The Hymnal for Worship and Celebration* (Waco, Tex.: Word Music, 1986), 148.

Bibliography

Augustine. *The City of God.* Translated by Marcus Dods. New York: Random House, 1950.

_____. *On Free Choice of the Will.* Translated by Thomas Williams. Indianapolis: Hackett Publishing Co., 1993.

Berkouwer, G. C. *Studies in Dogmatics: Man: The Image of God.* Translated by Dirk W. Jellema. Grand Rapids: Wm. B. Eerdmans Publishing Co., 1962.

_____. *Studies in Dogmatics: Sin.* Translated by P. C. Holtrop. Grand Rapids: Wm. B. Eerdmans Publishing Co., 1971.

Burns, J. Patout, ed. and trans. *Theological Anthropology.* Sources of Early Christian Thought. Philadelphia: Fortress Press, 1981.

Bynum, Caroline Walker. *The Resurrection of the Body in Western Christianity, 200–1336.* New York: Columbia University Press, 1995.

Cooper, John W. *Body, Soul, and Life Everlasting: Biblical Anthropology and the Monism-Dualism Debate.* Grand Rapids: Wm. B. Eerdmans Publishing Co., 1989.

Gundry, Robert H. *SŌMA in Biblical Theology, with Emphasis on Pauline Anthropology.* Cambridge: Cambridge University Press, 1976.

Hughes, Philip E. *The True Image: The Origin and Destiny of Man in Christ.* Grand Rapids: Wm. B. Eerdmans Publishing Co., 1989.

Luther, Martin. *The Bondage of the Will.* Translated by J. I. Packer and O. R. Johnston. New York: Fleming H. Revell Co., 1957.

Murray, John. *The Imputation of Adam's Sin.* Phillipsburg, N.J.: Presbyterian and Reformed Publishing Co., 1959.

Niebuhr, Reinhold. *Moral Man and Immoral Society: A Study in Ethics and Politics.* New York: Charles Scribner's Sons, 1932.

_____. *The Nature and Destiny of Man: A Christian Interpretation.* Vol. 1: *Human Nature.* New York: Charles Scribner's Sons, 1941.

_____. *The Nature and Destiny of Man: A Christian Interpretation.* Vol. 2: *Human Destiny.* New York: Charles Scribner's Sons, 1943.

Owen, John. *The Works of John Owen,* vol. 6. Edited by William H. Goold. Carlisle, Pa.: Banner of Truth Trust, 1967.

Peters, Ted. *Sin: Radical Evil in Soul and Society.* Grand Rapids: Wm. B. Eerdmans Publishing Co., 1994.

Pink, Arthur W. *Gleanings from the Scriptures: Man's Total Depravity.* Chicago: Moody Press, 1969.

Plantinga, Cornelius Jr. *Not the Way It's Supposed to Be: A Breviary of Sin.* Grand Rapids: Wm. B. Eerdmans Publishing Co., 1995.

Wolff, Hans Walter. *Anthropology of the Old Testament.* Translated by Margaret Kohl. Philadelphia: Fortress Press, 1974.

Scripture Index

2 Peter
2:7 222
3:9/10 196

1 John
1:8/10 149
1:8–9 188
2:4 189
3:2 269
3:2–3 86

3:16 110
4:10 262

Revelation
2:23 115, 117
6:9 103, 111
6:9–11 83
11:17 269
12:9 142, 154
16:19 218

18:14 103
18:21 218
20–21 220
20:4 66, 103, 268, 269
20:10 83
20:13 80, 99
21:3–4 269
21:4 157
22:2 160
22:2–3 269
22:3 157

Subject Index